I hope this book validates in
your heart the Value of all
committed partnerships.

Jim Bawden

VALIDATING COMMITTED PARTNERSHIPS:
A Still More Excellent Way

A new relational paradigm supported by the
high way of God's love and justice

JIM BOWDEN

Order this book online at www.trafford.com
or email orders@trafford.com

Most Trafford titles are also available at major online book retailers.

Printed in the United States of America.

ISBN: 978-1-4669-7148-6 (sc)
ISBN: 978-1-4669-7150-9 (hc)
ISBN: 978-1-4669-7149-3 (e)

Library of Congress Control Number: 2012922968

Trafford rev. 02/12/2013

 www.trafford.com

North America & international
toll-free: 1 888 232 4444 (USA & Canada)
phone: 250 383 6864 ♦ fax: 812 355 4082

CONTENTS

APPRECIATION AND DEDICATION

In deep appreciation I dedicate this book to the following:

To Jere, my wife of fifty-four years who has supported me in my ministry of forty-one years in time of joy and sorrow, of success and failure, of fantasy and reality, and in time of relaxation and long hours of diligent stressful work. Like an angel on high she has spent hours and hours listening to my conclusions in biblical research on the topics covered in this book. She shared her perceptions which expanded my views. Finally, she allowed me to interrupt her schedule and shared her knowledge when I was uncertain about grammatical structure during the proofing stage of the manuscript.

To the compassionate and open minded members of Covenant Presbyterian Church Athens, Georgia where I served as pastor for nearly thirty-five years. They not only instilled within me the courage to reflect upon this practical aspect of my ministry, but two adult classes used two chapters of the manuscript as a resource for study and then gave me helpful objective feedback. They have also been a wonderful example in continuing the ministry of Jesus Christ embracing His spirit of the open door and receptive heart.

To two professors (now deceased) who inspired me greatly during my theological studies at Columbia Seminary in Decatur, GA: Dr.

Neely McCarter and Dr. Shirley Gutherie. When I began researching and writing the manuscript twenty years ago, Shirley read the first five chapters which focus upon the biblical perspective and responded with much helpful advice. I am greatly indebted to them.

PREFACE

William Barclay wrote in his commentary on Romans: "Christianity is the religion of the open hand, the open heart, and open door."[1] These words aptly describe Jesus Christ who was responsive to all who came in contact with him. Jesus' life and teachings ring with hope as he introduces the people of Palestine to a seeking God whose heart has room to embrace all people and their differences.

I believe the Christ of two thousand years ago continues to manifest God's intention today through the life and mission of the church, corporately and individually. The risen Christ says to his followers: "You will receive power when the Holy Spirit has come upon you; and you will be my witnesses in Jerusalem, in all Judea, and Samaria, and to the ends of the earth" (Acts 1:8). The church exists, first and primarily, to exhibit the presence of the risen Christ. Said in another way, God calls the church, gathered and scattered, to continue Christ's mission in the world: in our homes, in our workplace, in our communities, in our congregations, and in the marketplace. Emil Brunner observed, "The church exists by mission as a fire exists by burning." The church as a body of Christ followers is called to be "the open hand, the open heart, and the open door"; it is called to practice the hospitality of God.

To respond authentically to that call, the church will have a diversity of members like the different members of our physical bodies. Without

diversity the church lacks authenticity. As the body of Christ the church
will cherish its diversity. The physical body also gives a clue to the
church's unity. As the members of the physical body follow directions
from its head, all the members work together for the wellbeing of the
whole body. So it is for the church. As its different members follow the
lead of its head, Jesus Christ, they will use their God-given gifts for the
wellbeing of the whole body. As expressed in the study paper "Is Christ
Divided?", communication among the members of the church body is
important: "love for persons with diverse theological convictions means
actively seeking to know and understand each other's experiences and
expressions of faith . . . and to create an inclusive community where
all experiences and expressions of faith in the one Jesus Christ are
welcomed." [2] That ideal picture coincides with Christ's ministry. Sadly,
the ideal seldom matches reality.

For the past thirty years mainstream Protestant congregations have
been urged to study issues concerning human sexuality as well as the
biblical history of marriage. Committees have been appointed and
have written study books and position papers. There is little evidence
that much study has been done. The greatest portion of dialogue and
discussion on the subject has occurred prior to a vote on particular
issues related to human sexuality. At that time, persons are divided into
opposing sides. Each hopes to overpower the other verbally and achieve
victory. Win/lose situations rarely encourage fruitful discussion marked
by listening and understanding.

The content of this book does not suggest voting on anything.
Now is the time for study, discussion, and reflection; now is the time
to examine many perspectives compatible with the spirit of Christ and
the biblical witness describing lifestyles for single and married adult
women and men. I will suggest a paradigm that I believe will strengthen
relationships among those who for different reasons have not chosen
marriage as a relational institution. I realize this book comes at a time
when many Christians are retreating into fundamentalist churches and
sects. Many declare they know definitively the biblical truth on the

subject of human sexuality. I believe they are protecting marriage roles that are more secular than biblical.

They are urging homosexual persons through advertisements in major newspapers to repent of their sin and be healed of homosexuality as if it were a disease. This is the Christian voice that many Americans are hearing. I feel it is a voice driven by fear, which puts people in a survival mode. Seldom do we enjoy the gift of life from a survival perspective. Our vision turns inward upon ourselves; our spirituality becomes self-centered till finally we hug ourselves to death. Now is the time to look outward and discover ways the Christian faith can enrich life, not only for ourselves but also for others for whom Christ gave his life; that includes every human being in the world.

If the servant role of the church is going be given new life and revitalized, I believe it will be initiated by the person in the pew. John M. Buchanan writes: "the time of the congregation has come . . . the local church, the congregation, is where energy is located. And it is where the hope of the future will be found."[3] I write this book in a way that it can be used in congregational adult study groups. In the end it will be those sitting in the pew who must determine if we can rediscover the *still more excellent way.* For the most part, ministers who are caught in the middle seem paralyzed to speak and suggest options that ring true for this huge group of committed moderates. Out of a deep love for the church of Jesus Christ and faith in God whose spirit continually works for reconciliation and healing, I am willing to take the risk. What I suggest is not new; it has been tried and tested through the years. Its roots are the bedrock of the ministry of Jesus and Paul; therefore, I suggest *a still more excellent way,* a way of love and justice.

At the beginning of this book, an ethical situation will be created that reflects a reality in many congregations. The seven biblical passages that refer to same-gender sexual activity will be studied to determine if they address the ethical situation with absolute clarity and definitive guidance. This ethical situation will then serve as the backdrop of the entire book as it seeks a biblical response that considers the best interest of the situational characters while at the same time maintaining biblical integrity. In order to give the *still more excellent way* enough substance to be satisfying to moderate/mainstream people, this book attempts to show that in the mind of Christ, in the experience of the early church, and in the central message of Paul in his letter to the Romans the concept of grace strongly supports the *more excellent way*.

The book is also rooted in common biblical and ethical ground upon which all of us stand: *humans are created to live in fulfilling relationships*. I will examine what scripture says about marriage and how it has been practiced in the history of the church and Western civilization and how the church arrived at a biblical position on divorce. When content has been devoted to these topics, I think that it will be evident that we have reached a time in the church and in our culture to examine an option to marriage that also reflects the high ethical standards of Christ and scripture. This option will complement and strengthen marriage and families of the future, and will validate the committed relationship of same-gender persons. Marriage of male and female and the union of same-gender couples will retain their specific uniqueness; however, at the same time they will share the title of *partnership* with the same sacred relational value and safeguarded by the same or similar legal standards.

The content of this book reflects my commitment:

> *First,* to Jesus Christ, who is lord over life and death, this world, and the world to come; the source of spiritual sustenance and guidance for those who respond by following him; the basic norm to interpret the scriptures; and the word who is God who became a human being.
>
> *Second,* to the witness of scripture as God's written word for matters of faith, life, and salvation.
>
> *Third,* to the essentials of the historic Reformed confessions and catechisms of the church.

Fourth, to the high standards of Christian morality that affirm the sacred quality of human life experienced in loving, faithful, compassionate, forgiving, and just relationships.

Fifth, to the good news of God's grace given as a gift to wed us eternally to God and to provide the means of exhibiting the presence of the risen Christ in the way we live without diminishing the purpose of the commandments of God.

Jim Bowden

God of grace and God of glory, on Thy people pour Thy power;
Crown Thine ancient church's story; Bring its bud to glorious flower
Grant us wisdom, grant us courage, for the facing
of this hour, for the facing of this hour.
Set our feet on lofty places; Gird our lives that they may be
Armored with all Christlike graces pledged to set all captives free
Grant us wisdom, grant us courage, that we fail not them nor Thee!
That we fail not them nor Thee!
Harry Emerson Fosdick
"God of Grace, God of Glory"

Endnotes: Preface

[1] William Barclay, *The Letter to the Romans* (Edinburgh: The Saint Andrew Press, 1960.), p. 180

[2] Is Christ Divided? (PCUSA), 1988. pp. 22 & 44

[3] John Buchanan, *Being Church, Being Community* (Louisville: Westminster-John Knox Press, 1966), p. 109

INTRODUCTION

Caught in the middle, that is how I often felt serving as a Presbyterian pastor for forty-one years in a denomination of much diversity and living as a citizen of a country with more diversity. Generally, people enjoy being with people of like mind, tastes, lifestyle, and interests. That's normal and usually the basis of friendships, but this should not be the norm to be a citizen of the United States and a member of a Christian church where people of faith are expected to demonstrate God's grace of acceptance and love.

During my service as a pastor, the institutions of marriage and family have experienced considerable change. Since 1980, nearly one out of two marriages ends in divorce. Children become innocent victims of this family strife and separation. At the present time, about ten million heterosexual male/female adults in this country live together outside marriage. What was rare or nearly nonexistent when I began ministry has now become commonplace. Prior to retirement, about half of the couples I counseled in premarriage sessions already lived together.

For more than thirty years American society and religious institutions have experienced deep division because of divergent views on human sexuality. For the most part, all sides feel their view is morally correct. In our country an amendment to the Constitution has been considered to limit marriage to one male and one female. On July 6, 2012, the General

Assembly of the Presbyterian Church, USA failed to concur with the recommendation of its Civil Union and Marriage Issues Committee to change the definition of marriage from "a civil contract between a woman and a man" to "a civil contract between two persons."

In religious institutions laws have been created to assure that same gender partners cannot be ordained to church office, thus limiting their full membership in the church. The creation of laws has not reduced the tension. Some are actively encouraging their congregations to leave their denominations. This is occurring in the major mainstream denominations such as Presbyterian USA, Episcopal, United Methodist, Lutheran ECLU, and United Church of Christ. Reported by the Pew Research Center in the October 2012 issue of *Presbyterians Today,* support is growing among Presbyterians to legalize same-sex marriage but the percentage of church members who are opposed is still above 50 percent (51 percent) with only 34 percent in favor.[1]

This division among people of faith reflects the same deep divide in American society. One editorial in the *New York Times* on November 6, 2004, had the caption, *Two Nations Under God.* The division has been fueled by the loud rigid voice of the religious right who call themselves people of values. Of course, all people have their set of values. In the same year, eleven states voted by a wide margin to ban same-gender marriages. In some of these states same-gender marriages were already illegal; nonetheless, proponents wanted this issue on the ballot anyway. *That's called pouring salt into the wound.* A few states have legalized same-gender marriage. The Supreme Court has been summoned to respond to this issue that has divided our nation and communities of faith.

I believe we have reached the time when leadership in church and society needs to be more intentional with direction that is substantive and palatable to the large moderate membership of mainline denominations and our culture. This book proposes a new relational paradigm supported by the high way of God's love and justice. This paradigm includes blessing or validating marriages between a female and male and unions of same-gender females and males. I believe we have reached an unhealthy stalemate in trying to squeeze same gender unions into the ancient institution of marriage. In the church community there are radically different views concerning the married relationship between male and female. The time has come to consider another option. Each union needs to maintain its uniqueness. Historically, marriage has been the union of a female with a male. As we know from the content of the Old Testament there were times when a marriage included one male and numerous females. Nonetheless, the union was always between different genders. At the present time the male bears the title *husband* and the female carries the name *wife*. Traditionally, they are united intimately and sexually to produce children. This does not mean that couples of the same gender cannot have and in some cases produce children, but it is altogether different.

The union of two same-gender persons likewise needs to maintain its uniqueness rather than simply be blended into the picture created by the term *marriage*. Unlike the tradition in marriage, the two people in a same-gender union usually share authority equally. They are partners. One is not owned or subject to the other as still declared by many in present-day marriages although that ancient practice is gradually being replaced by mutuality. Same-gender couples are free to help identify the gifts of each other and together define their roles in the relationship whereas in many marriages roles are often imposed upon the male and female by the unwritten norms of culture or religious groups. The content of the book gives additional attention to the uniqueness of same-gender unions in contrast to marriages.

At the same time, since both are unions marked by a commitment of love and responsibility for one another, they need to remain connected sharing the same sacred relational value and safeguarded by the same or similar legal standards. For this reason, I propose a new relational paradigm centered upon the term *partnership,* which will be the common title shared by those who are married and those who are of the same gender. For the married male and female, their title will be a *marital partnership,* and for two people of the same gender their committed relational title will be a *same-gender partnership.*

The term *partnership* describes a special relationship bound by public commitment. For that reason, the manuscript is entitled *Validating Committed Partnerships.* This is not a play on words, for the words we choose to use can be powerful, sometimes creating unity, but sometimes causing anger and division. Using the term *marriage* for a committed relationship between two people of the same gender has created a major roadblock in guiding the religious community and culture to validate and support two people of the same gender who genuinely love one another and want to live in a committed relationship.

For a committed partnership among two people to be fully valued it requires validation and support from family, friends, and faith community. It also needs to be sealed by love, a public commitment and legal safeguards. When the relationship becomes a validated committed partnership, the two people need further support through full inclusion into the life of the church and society. This relationship of two people in a marital or same gender *partnership* bound by love and validated publicly remains "a still more excellent way."

At the present time in the religious community, accepting and validating a committed relationship between two people of the same gender remains a major issue with deep division. I believe most people, religious or not, do not want to exclude categorically anyone from being full members of the church or full citizens of this country. As God reaches out to us by coming in Christ to welcome us into relationship, we who are thankful recipients of grace eagerly seek ways compatible with scripture to welcome fellow children of God into service through Christ's church. In the past century, the way was found for women and remarried divorcees to be full members of church and society.

In this book, I propose a new relational paradigm centered upon the term *partnership,* which will be the common title shared by those who are married and those who are of the same gender, enabling both to enjoy full inclusion into the life of the church and society. At the same time, I feel this more excellent way maintains biblical integrity. It is also hoped that the relational paradigm will help resolve division in church and society concerning the issue of human sexuality. At the same time, I believe this relational paradigm will support and enrich the institution of marriage and family life.

For same-gender partners tension still exists in the church concerning what constitutes an authentic call from God to serve in all arenas of life. About 1997, Presbyterian, Lutheran, and Methodist denominations created church laws to prohibit those in same-gender partnerships from being ordained to office. In the past two years the Lutheran and Presbyterians denominations deleted those laws from their governance manuals. The United Church of Christ leaves this decision to each congregation. In 2003 the Episcopal Church elected a bishop who has a same-gender partner. The reactions have been strong, both positive and negative.

On both sides there are good people advocating high values and standards of morality. One side advocates being true to self in using God's gifts for service upholding the high commandment of God's love as the way to bridge the gap caused by diversity. The opposing side responds with its perception of biblical truth and the standards of church tradition as it seeks to maintain purity in church and society. Both sides are concerned about the health of the family in our society.

I feel that marriage needs to be reexamined by the church since it has been primarily a secular institution blessed by the church, and since it has been the only legal institution for men and women who desire to live together. In response to the cultural changes in relational desires outside marriage among both heterosexual and homosexual persons, the church has a unique opportunity to influence our culture in strengthening both marriage and family.

Reactionary and hasty measures are seldom successful; often they do not reflect the spirit of scripture. I agree with Jack Rogers, who believes at this time church denominations "are not prepared to make a wise decision on this issue."[2] Yet they have created rules before thorough biblical study could be made within local church congregations. Much of the research was done in the seventies and early eighties providing some data that was either incorrect or incomplete.

Until recently it was assumed that being homosexual was a preference and choice, and could be changed at will. Many people still embrace this assumption; however, following studies among homosexual persons, we realize they do not choose their sexual orientation any more than others choose to be heterosexual. If sexual orientation can be changed, it is usually sublimation of same-gender attraction with intense discipline to maintain celibacy accompanied by emotional trauma.

In 1948 the publication of Alfred Kinsey's report on human sexual behavior contained a significant finding about male sexuality: sexual orientation exists on a continuum with 5-10 percent of the population identifying themselves as exclusively homosexual and as many as 25 percent identifying themselves as "incidentally homosexual." Since 1948 the percentages have been reduced, but the descriptions have not been changed. Then in 1951 came the first comprehensive study by an acknowledged homosexual person. It was not until 1973 that the American Psychiatric Association removed homosexuality from the category of a pathological illness or disease.[3]

In one of the few verses of the New Testament referring to same-gender sexual activity, the word *homosexual* is inserted incorrectly and inappropriately: "Do not be deceived; neither the immoral, nor idolaters, nor adulterers, nor *homosexuals* . . . will inherit the kingdom of God." (1 Corinthians 6:9b-10). This term was introduced in the first modern translation of the Bible, *The Revised Standard (1952)*. The term *homosexual* was used because people knew very little about homosexuality in 1952. *The New Revised Standard Version* and the *New International Version* translate the Greek term *malakoi* as a *male prostitute*, which more closely reflects its meaning in context, but much damage has already been done in shaping the minds of people about biblical teaching on this subject. Today, we know there is an enormous difference in being homosexual and in being a male prostitute. How would all heterosexual persons feel if the word *heterosexual* were confused with prostitution? The term *homosexual* is not found in the original language in the Bible. It was first coined and used in the nineteenth century.

So much bias exists about homosexuality that church and society need adequate time for research and study before rules and laws are created, especially those that judge, condemn, create barriers, and marginalize. I think the church will eventually regret decisions of this nature, which already impair our effectiveness as reflectors of the grace of God. In the biblical and historical study I have done on the subject of human sexuality, the scripture does not clearly address either, being a homosexual person or living in same-gender committed partnerships or cohabiting before civil marriage. It condemns same-gender sexual activity in the context of prostitution in the same way it condemns heterosexual prostitution. Likewise, the sexual orientation of those involved in same-gender prostitution is not mentioned in scripture.

Upon learning the historical context, the two Old Testament and three New Testament references about same-gender sexual activity likely involved heterosexual rather than homosexual persons. No one knows for sure, and the person in the pew needs to hear this from biblical scholars since the person in the pew has heard so many definitive statements about the "abomination of homosexuality." At the present time, rather than belonging to the mainstream, most homosexual persons are marginalized, walking a shaky tightrope with no option but to choose an alternative lifestyle if they desire to live in a committed relationship with another adult. Most Protestant denominations will not bestow God's blessing on their partnership, so they remain *people without a promise.*

In this book, I am using the term *single* as a way to distinguish from those who are married. I realize that some feel that *single* denotes social status and is "the negation of the legal term *married* . . . defining people by what they do not have rather than who they are as individuals."[2] Brian Childs and John Patton in their book, *Christian Marriage and*

Family: Care For Our Generations, therefore use the term *individuals* to refer to those who do not have partners in marriage.

For this book, the use of the term *individual* would create confusion because it can apply to persons who are married as well as those who are not married. It is my intention to show that marriage does create a unique relational status with purpose, but is not the only relationship that is fulfilling and enables human beings to enjoy wholeness. For this reason I place male and female committed relationships and same-gender committed relationship beneath the same umbrella labeled *partnership*. At the same time, I consider partners in a committed relationship are no longer single.

The content of the book emerges from forty-one years of pastoral experience in the practice of ministry. It is written for laypeople as well as clergy who have not explored in their congregations what scripture says and does not say about marriage, human sexuality, homosexuality, being single, and developing human wholeness through relationships. It is designed for individual study or group study with the aid of lesson plans.

It is my observation that ministers and vocal laypeople have spoken for congregations rather than leading them in honest explorations of these topics, especially as they impact human sexuality. I believe fear of the loss of financial support from the congregation is a strong reason. Richard F. Lovelace writes: "Like the indulgence issue in the time of Luther, the problem of homosexuality touches the nerve of many crucial spiritual and theological questions. It also grips the attention of the laity and threatens the economic base of clergy and administrators."[4] When the church allows the profit incentive to determine its ethical agenda, it mirrors segments of our culture rather being like salt, enriching the quality of human life for all.

People like myself, caught in the middle, feel that something critical is missing in this tension. Also, I do not think the church has seriously sought the help of scripture and the mind of Christ in dealing with the complexity of being single in our culture—a segment of our population that is growing at a fast pace because young adults are waiting longer to get married, some are lifetime singles, and every divorce automatically creates two single people, and many with children. As the population of older adults soars in the second millennium, the death of a spouse creates a single older adult who knows from experience the value of living in relationships. Even though I refer to *singleness* in our culture in one chapter, an entire book with in-depth study needs to give attention to this station of life.

If we are concerned about the stability of the family as the primary base for healthy human development, the time has come for the church to explore what scripture does and does not say about marriage. We may be surprised, and we may be placing expectations on marriage today that are unrealistic and do not resemble the purpose of marriage in the days of Abraham, Moses, David, Jesus, and Paul.

Also, I think there has been too much focus upon sexuality in church discussions about single adults, which seems to be consistent with the trend of our society or culture, and too little focus on the need and value of relationships marked by justice, love, mercy, faithfulness, kindness, and grace. If we would put minimal emphasis upon sexual activity and maximum emphasis upon our common needs as human beings and examine this issue from the perspective of scripture's highest ethical standards, I think we will discover *a still more excellent way* that will eliminate this either/or standoff. It may also enable a large group of God's people who have been marginalized to respond to God's call and have it validated, freeing them to use all God's gifts to enrich God's world. They will also have an opportunity to become, *people with a promise.* In this case everyone wins.

Also, it may be noticed that I have used the terms *same gender* rather than the popular terms *same sex* in referring to two or more males or females. In our culture, where so much attention is given to sexual behavior and the physical body, to use the terms *same sex* for *same gender* creates additional bias when the emphasis should be on committed relationships rather sexual relationships. I have never heard anyone refer to a male and female committed relationship with the terms *opposite sex.* Since my pastoral experience has been within the Christian community, I will use the term *church* most often, but the term could refer to all religious communities.

At the present time in the religious community and our society, we have reached an impasse in trying to be responsive to a more open mainstream homosexual community. Religious communities have a unique opportunity to provide leadership for our culture. By being proactive rather than reactive, the positive influence of the religious community can lead our culture toward strengthening marriage and the family. If the religious community says and does nothing, I believe the standard will be set by the secular community. To remain silent is not being responsive to those in pain who have been marginalized by a fearful society, nor is it healthy for our society as a whole.

The philosopher Plato feels that life's goal is to seek the *golden mean,* the perfect balance, which is the means between the two extremes. It is seldom a comfortable position because it gets hit by the storm blowing from both directions. Perhaps, in this case, the *golden mean* will be the means by which to quell the storm and bring peace, healing, and wholeness to the church and to our society, and also bring a promise to a group of people who live without a promise. Such is my hope and prayer.

Jim Bowden

Endnotes: Introduction

[1] Jack Marcum, "Go Figure: Same Sex Marriage," *Presbyterians Today,* October, 2012, p. 7

[2] Jack Rogers, "Ecclesiastical McCarthyism?" *The Presbyterian Outlook,* March 18-25, 1996, p. 8.

[3] John Patton and Brian Childs, *Christian Marriage and Family: Caring For Our Generations* (Nashville: Abingdon Press, 1988), p. 48.

[4] Richard Lovelace, *Homosexuality and the Church* (Old Tappan, NJ: Fleming H. Revell, 1986), p. 11.

CHAPTER ONE

A Biblical Response:
Literal or Contextual

Seeking Definitive Biblical Guidance for
a Contemporary Ethical Situation

Open my eyes, that I may see glimpses of truth Thou hast for me;
Place in my hands the wonderful key that shall unclasp and set me free.
Silently now I wait for Thee, ready, my God, Thy will to see;
Open my eyes, illumine me, Spirit divine!
Clara H. Scott

In religious communities, people of faith possess a broad spectrum of attitudes and beliefs toward fellow human beings who are homosexual. Some feel the God of their faith encourages disapproval of all homosexuals as expressed in a recent letter to Ann Landers: *My nephew is getting married and has asked our nine-year-old daughter to be in the wedding party. I know the bride-to-be has several gay friends, and we learned that the wedding will be held in a known gay church instead of in our family church . . . My husband and I are deeply religious and do not approve of gays.* In some way, this couple has learned that being homosexual is sinful.

Others believe that the church should be open and accepting of homosexuals, but they believe the Bible clearly condemns same-gender sexual activity as sinful. It makes no difference if the two people are living in a committed and loving relationship or not. Nearly all Christian denominations embrace this belief; therefore, they exclude this group from full membership in the church by declaring through ecclesiastical law this group is not qualified to serve as officers and ministers. Many who embrace this view sincerely believe the Bible clearly and without question condemns all forms of homosexual practice as sinful.

Using the Word to Respond to Ethical Situations

I feel that an ecclesiastical law that categorically excludes groups of people from full membership in Christ's body needs to be definitively supported by scripture, without a shadow of a doubt. I also feel that the burden of proof rests with those who support such rules. In my lifetime most Christian denominations in the southeastern portion of the United States struggled with excluding three other groups from full membership in the church based on support from scripture. First, prior to desegregation, African-Americans were excluded from worship much less membership in exclusively white congregations. During that time, I often heard: *nowhere in the Bible are we commanded by God to integrate the races.* Their view of interpretation rested on the foundation: *if the Bible does not clearly made demands, then humans are free to do as they please.*

Second, at the same time, many denominations were examining their rule that women could not be full members of the church. Third and earlier, those divorced and remarried were not granted full membership. In both cases, it was said over and over again, *the Bible clearly teaches that divorcees who remarry and women are not qualified to serve as officers and ministers.* Concerning all three issues, when the church sought the guidance of the Holy Spirit and the authority of the fullness of scripture, corrections and difficult changes were made. Concerning those divorced and remarried, the decision was not an endorsement of divorce, but an affirmation of trust in governing bodies to make wise decisions concerning those who are qualified rather than automatically disqualifying groups of people.

Norms for Biblical Interpretation

Does scripture declare every situation of intimacy among homosexual persons to be sinful? Prior to creating an ethical situation facing many congregations, I will share my basic standards for biblical interpretation. First, I am guided by the Westminster Confession of Faith where it says, *the infallible rule of interpretation of Scripture, is the Scripture itself.* I understand this to mean when every text (verse or verses) is seen alongside the remainder of Scripture, its truth will become clearer. Also, in the same chapter are these words: *All things in Scripture are not alike plain in themselves, nor alike clear unto all; yet those things which are necessary to be known, believed, and observed, for salvation, are so clearly propounded*[1] . . . Belief on any side of the homosexual issue is not necessary for salvation. The remaining guideposts for interpretation come from a study adopted by the 123rd General Assembly of the Presbyterian Church in the United States.[2]

Second, I seek to understand the text in light of the centrality of Jesus Christ, God's word made flesh. Third, I examine the text alongside the highest law given to us by God, *the law of love.* Fourth, to the best of my ability I attempt to see the text within its cultural, social, and psychological setting. People of faith described in scripture were influenced by their culture in much the same way Christians today are influenced by culture. Fifth, I seek to interpret the text with the help of how it was understood in the tradition of the church. Finally, I believe the primary purpose of scripture provides what is necessary for faith and ethical living. In conclusion, before I seek guidance from scripture for an ethical situation, it is important to determine the message of a particular text by using these six norms for interpretation. This is what I mean by the term, *contextual* which amplifies the importance of the text.

In contrast, another popular form of biblical interpretation can be identified by the term *textual or literal.* Those who embrace this approach in understanding scripture believe every word and verse stand alone as God's authoritative word or message. For the most part, little attention and guidance are given to the context.

A Stereotypical View

The most controversial human sexuality issue facing the church in the new millennium is homosexuality. Unlike heterosexuality, a large number of people view homosexuality through stereotypical lenses. First, many feel it is a chosen sexual orientation. When they think about it, they realize they did not choose their own sexual orientation. Second, they blend homosexual orientation with sexual behavior, assuming homosexual persons are sexually driven and sexually active. They do not make the same assumptions about heterosexual persons. Third, they identify same-gender couples with the sex act, seldom realizing the major interest or need is a committed and meaningful relationship. Perhaps those who embrace this stereotypical picture regard for themselves the sex act more important than the relationship.

Fourth, they do not differentiate between the circumstances and context of homosexual intimacy. When the Bible refers to same-gender sexuality, many feel the Bible condemns homosexuality in general; yet when the Bible refers to sex between heterosexuals, they do not conclude that all heterosexual behavior is being condemned. In this case, they are able to see that the Bible is referring to a specific sexual circumstance like prostitution or adultery. This stereotypical picture of homosexuals and homosexuality compels many to conclude the Bible clearly and unambiguously condemns homosexuality as sinful; at the same time they do not reach the same conclusion about heterosexuality. To provide clarity I have created an *ethical situation.* I will then examine the biblical passages that refer to same-gender sexual activity to see if they address the *ethical situation* and provide a clear sense of direction.

An Ethical Situation

The following situation exists in many churches, but it often remains hidden because of fear. *Two people of the same gender have been housemates for many years. They have also been active in their church for the same number of years teaching in church school, serving as youth advisors, active on committees, ushers and greeters in worship, and participants in the program of their church. They are well liked by all, enjoying the friendship of many. They have lived invisible lives because they are homosexual, not by choice any more than most people choose their sexual orientation. They have enjoyed a committed monogamous caring relationship, but they remain invisible out of fear: fear of losing their jobs, fear of being hurt by those who are violently homophobic, fear of being marginalized by their community and church family, no longer welcomed to be youth advisors or church school teachers, no longer qualified to be an officer, or to continue to use their God-given gifts.*

Does scripture interpreted alongside the norms mentioned earlier clearly support excluding these persons from being full members of the body of Christ, his church, if they reveal who they have been for these many years? In the next chapter, I will examine the Old Testament passages that are often cited as clearly declaring homosexuality to be sinful.

Endnotes: Chapter One

1   The Book of Confessions of the Presbyterian Church (USA), *The Westminster Confession of Faith,* (Louisville: The Office of the General Assembly, 2001), p. 127.

2   The Constitution of the Presbyterian Church (USA), *Book of Order,* (Louisville: The Office of the General Assembly, 2001), G-6.0106b.

CHAPTER TWO

Old Testament: Listening to God's Word—What It Says and Does Not Say

In its thirty-nine books the Old Testament refers to same-gender sexual activity only four times. Two of the references are presented in the form of laws or prohibitions. The other two passages describe adversarial assaults by people of the same gender. Each of these Old Testament references will be examined textually and contextually.

Genesis 19:1-11

Three angels visit Abraham and Sarah to announce that God will bless them with a son birthed by Sarah. They tell Abraham, God is sending them to the towns of Sodom and Gomorrah to pronounce God's judgment upon the people. Abraham convinces God not to destroy the towns and those who are innocent if God finds ten righteous people. Two of the three angels go to Sodom; they plan to sleep in the city square, but Lot, Abraham's nephew, extends hospitality to them, and they spend the night in his home. The practice of hospitality to strangers was one of the most important ethical acts for the ancient Hebrews. In this situation comes the first biblical reference to same-gender sexual activity.

The text indicates that all the men of Sodom, young and old, go to Lot's house. They demand that Lot send his two male guests outside so they can have sex with them—that is to say, so they can rape them. In a counter offer, Lot offers to bring his two virgin daughters to them. Lot is zealous about protecting his two male guests by not violating the high ethic of hospitality. Now, consider the message of this event to determine if it provides guidance for the predesigned *ethical situation* of same-gender partners.

First, the passage reveals the wickedness of the people as seen in the men who are sexual abusers (rapists). Second, it also reveals the sacred role of hospitality in ancient Palestinian culture. The men of Sodom are attempting to humiliate Lot by sexually abusing his guests. The importance of hospitality is magnified when Lot is willing to give the men his two virgin daughters; he is willing to sacrifice his own flesh and blood at the expense of protecting two strangers who are guests in his home. In this time and place in history, *hospitality* is considered a supreme ethic. Third, this passage reveals the origin of the word *sodomite,* men who sexually abuse (rape) other men.

This passage does not specifically address homosexuality. *Merriam-Webster* defines *homosexuality* "as the quality or state of being homosexual which means two people who are sexually attracted to each other," in the same way that heterosexuals are sexually attracted to those of the opposite gender. The act of sex is more than sexual attraction. Since all the men of Sodom wanted sex with the male angels it is unlikely their sexual orientation was homosexual. Very likely they were heterosexuals seeking a thrill by sexually abusing those of the same gender. Abuse in this way would be extremely humiliating for a Hebrew male. A similar experience is described in Judges 19:1-39, but this time the male (a Levite) being sought by the men (sexual abusers) puts his female concubine outside. They sexually abuse her until she dies; initially they wanted the male priest, but were satisfied with a female.

In both cases, the men of the city wanted to rape another male. Neither of these texts provide guidance for our ethical situation where two people of the same gender are living in a committed, loving, and faithful monogamous relationship. Obviously, these are stories of sexual abuse. The Bible contains similar incidences between males and females. An example is the story of the rape of Jacob's daughter, Dinah by Hamor, a Hivite (Genesis 34:1-31). Surely most agree that it would be a poor interpretation to conclude the story of Dinah and Hamor is condemning all heterosexual attraction and sexual intimacy. The same truth applies to the story of the angels in Sodom.

Leviticus 18:22; 20:13

I link the two passages in Leviticus because their focus is the same: the eighteenth chapter lists forbidden sexual practices and the twentieth chapter describes the punishment for these forbidden practices. Leviticus 18:22 reads: "You shall not lie with a male as with a woman; it is an abomination." Leviticus 20:13 reads: "If a man lies with a male as with a woman, both of them have committed an abomination; they shall be put to death."

What do these passages say? When read textually, both passages declare same-gender sexual activity among males to be unclean or disgusting, an abomination. When seen in their contextual setting, these two verses are likely addressing a particular situation when same-gender sexual activity is an abomination. The main theme of Leviticus is the importance of worshiping God and only God, who is holy. The book also shows how the Hebrews are to maintain holiness in their relationship with the "holy God." *Holy* in this setting means sacred and separate from all other aspects of that which God has created. God, through Moses, is preparing the liberated Hebrews for the sacred life when they reenter the "Promised Land" and must live alongside people whose religious practice is polytheistic.

The context becomes more pointed in the first four verses of Leviticus 18. God communicates through Moses, warning the Hebrews not to follow the practices of their previous master, Egypt, nor the people with whom they will eventually live, the Canaanites. More than once God reminds Moses to tell the Hebrews, "I am the Lord, your God." In the verse prior to verse 22, the Hebrews are warned again: "You shall not give any of your offspring to sacrifice them to Molech, and so profane the name of your God." The warnings prior to verse 22 clearly focus upon the practice of idolatry. The first five verses and the last five verses of chapter 20 likewise warn against the practice of idolatry by worshiping the Canaanite gods. So when 18:22 and 20:13 declare it to be unclean for a male to lie with a male, it is first and primarily concerned with the practice of idolatry.

The worship of the Canaanite fire god Molech was closely connected with the worship of the Canaanite goddess Asherah, which involved fertility religious rituals where there was male sexual activity with both male and female prostitutes. As early as the Sinai experience, the Israelites are told to tear down altars and symbols of the goddess Asherah (Exodus 34:13). A heightened concern about being involved in the fertility rituals of the Canaanite goddess Asherah occurs in the addresses of Moses when the forty-year journey in the wilderness comes to an end and the Israelites are ready to cross the Jordan and occupy the Promised Land. The Ten Commandments are given along with continual warnings against the practice of idolatry. When Moses warns about idolatry, he often refers to the worship of Asherah (Deuteronomy 7:6; 12:3; 16:21). Moses also says, "None of the daughters of Israel shall be a temple prostitute; none of the sons of Israel shall be a temple prostitute" (Deuteronomy 23:17).

Moses lived and died long before Solomon built the Hebrew temple in Jerusalem, so this text refers to the Canaanite temples or houses of prostitution that were central to the worship of the goddess Asherah.

Sure enough, the Israelites were continually involved in the practice of idolatry through their involvement in temple prostitution, the only specific reference in the Old Testament where it was common practice for males to be involved sexually with males. These Canaanite temples were a major problem for the Hebrews through biblical history until King Josiah finally destroyed them about 622 BC, which is only about thirty-five years before the Jewish nation is totally conquered and the Hebrews are taken to Babylon as slaves (2 Kings 23:1-20).

So when Leviticus 18:22 and 20:13 are seen in the biblical context and since specific warnings about the practice of idolatry are mentioned in Leviticus 18 and 20, is Moses primarily concerned about sexual ethics or is he primarily concerned about the practice of idolatry through participation in the Canaanite temples of prostitution? It makes more sense to me to conclude that Moses is primarily concerned about the practice of idolatry. In Leviticus 20:13 Moses says the punishment for a man to lie with a man is death. Capital punishment was the common sentence for practicing idolatry (Exodus 21:20; Deuteronomy 13; Leviticus 20:1-5), but capital punishment was not always the sentence for all sexual sins. In Leviticus 20 a variety of sexual relationships are mentioned. In some situations of adultery the punishment is death: with the wife of an Israelite, with one of his father's wives, with his daughter-in-law, with his wife's mother. In other situations adultery is not punished by death: a man committing adultery with his aunt or with his brother's wife. If the laws in Leviticus 18 and 20 were designed for sexual ethics, they lack consistency. An unmarried Hebrew male involved in temple prostitution is not committing adultery, according to Mosaic understanding of adultery.

Why then is death his punishment when he is not committing adultery and when capital punishment is not always the punishment for adultery? Committing adultery is a violation of the seventh commandment, whereas sexual activity between an unmarried male and a male prostitute is not a violation of one of the Ten Commandments according to the letter of the law. Why is the punishment for this man so severe? Obviously, Leviticus 18:22 and 20:13 are addressing something far more important than a sexual indiscretion. They are likely supporting the major concern and theme of Leviticus and Deuteronomy, the practice of idolatry and not giving full devotion to the one God. The death penalty is often exercised when idolatry is practiced.

Another consideration pertains to the purpose of the Holiness Code of Israel; it was designed to maintain religious purity and personal cleanliness. Were these many rules designed to bear authority for the period of time when the Hebrews were to resettle Palestine or were they designed to be eternal rules whose truth and guidance exist above all cultures and all times and places? If taken textually or literally, all the many laws should remain relevant, significant, and authoritative today as they were prior to resettling the land of Canaan about 1250 BC. If the textualist or literalist has integrity, then all the laws of the Pentateuch are to be obeyed and the prescribed punishment carried out. The textualist would then prohibit crossbreeding domestic animals, planting two kinds of seeds in the same field, and wearing clothes made of two kinds of material (Leviticus 19:19). The literalist would support putting to death a child who hits or curses his father or mother (Exodus 21:15, 17). The list goes on and on. To maintain biblical integrity, the literalist takes every text or verse at face value. If Leviticus 20:13 is authoritative for all situations and for all times, so should Exodus 21:17 and Leviticus 19:19 *(above)* and so forth.

On the other hand, the contextual approach seeks to understand the specific text as part of the whole teaching of scripture and Jesus Christ. Were the rules found in the Pentateuch concerning purity and cleanliness given to discourage the liberated Hebrews from adopting the customs of the Canaanites with whom they would be living? The biblical text itself appears to support this option. Toward the end of the twentieth chapter of Leviticus this command is given by God through Moses: "You shall not follow the practices of the nation (Canaan) that I am driving out before you. Because they did all these things, I abhorred them" (Leviticus 20:23).

Over 1,200 years later, both Jesus and Paul question the validity of these purity and cleanliness laws as the means for remaining faithful to God. For example, Jesus did not eat appropriate food or follow the Jewish rituals of purity and cleanliness (Mark 7). This upset the Pharisees and the teachers of the law. On the other hand, Jesus quotes Leviticus 19:18, "love your neighbor as you love yourself," as part of the great or most important commandment of God. Paul, likewise, no longer supported these purity practices (Romans 14, 1 Corinthians 8). Jesus and Paul both emphasize the importance of faithful and fulfilling relationships.

In conclusion, I believe the passages in Leviticus 18 and 20 concerning same-gender sexual activity are referring to the fertility rituals of the Canaanite religion. To participate in these cults of prostitution, therefore, unites the participant with the Canaanite goddess Asherah. For the Hebrews this is the practice of idolatry and a violation of the first two commandments. At this time in history, the Hebrews strongly emphasized the worship of the one God as Lord.

I do not believe these passages were purposely given as guidance for sexual ethics; they are not addressing same-gender sexual practice in general but specifically as a pagan religious act in the Canaanite temples of prostitution. Likewise, there is no evidence that participants are homosexual. As a result, the two verses give no guidance for our *ethical situation* where two people of the same gender have lived for many years in a committed, loving, and responsible relationship. These passages neither condone nor condemn the relationship; they simply do not address the relationship.

Endnotes: Chapter Two

[1] *Presbyterian Understanding and Use of the Holy Scripture,* a Study Adopted by the 123rd General Assembly of the Presbyterian Church (USA), *(Louisville: The Office of the General Assembly, 1992), pp. 14-25.*

CHAPTER THREE

New Testament: Listening to God's Word—What It Says and Does Not Say

In the New Testament, Jesus does not make any references to same-gender sexual activity. He does refer to marriage and divorce and quotes the second chapter of Genesis, *a man shall leave his father and mother and cleave unto his wife.* He is assuming that marriage involves male and female. Paul, other the other hand, does refer to same gender sexual activity in his letters to the church in Corinth and Rome and also to Timothy. Like the reference in Leviticus, each of these references will be studied textually and contextually.

1 Corinthians 6:9

"Do not be deceived! Fornicators, nor idolaters, adulterers, **μαλακοὶ οὔτε ἀρσενοκοῖται**, *(male prostitutes nor sodomites)* thieves, the greedy, drunkards, revilers, robbers—none of these will inherit the kingdom of God" (1 Corinthians 6:9b-10 NRSV). The NIV translation has *male prostitutes nor homosexual abusers*: **μαλακοὶ οὔτε ἀρσενοκοῖταιζ**

When read literally, this text condemns sexual activity of a male prostitute and a male rapist (sodomite) who abuse homosexuals or male prostitutes. Some textualists go one step further and conclude this condemnation of same-gender sexual activity clearly indicates that scripture condemns every situation where a male has a sexual experience with another male. At this point the literalist is reading into the text a personal opinion.

Also, in this same verse there are two references to heterosexual activity. Fornicators and adulterers are condemned. Traditionally those two forms of sexual activity have been associated with heterosexuals; today they could apply to homosexuals as well, but in their context they are addressing heterosexuals. We know that these two words do not apply to all situations of heterosexual activity. *Fornicators* are those who are obsessed with sex; their lives revolve around sexual activity with many different people. The Greek word is *porneia*, from which comes the word *pornography*, which is a depiction of erotic activity in pictures or writing.[1] *Adulterers* are those who are married and desire to possess sexually the spouse of another person or those who act on the desire and commit the sexual act with the spouse of another person.

Both *fornication* and *adultery* are specific situations of sexual activity and attitudes among males and females. Will the textualist broaden these two situations and declare the Bible clearly condemns all heterosexual activity in the same way the textualist interpreted the reference to a specific kind of same-gender sexual experience? To be consistent, the textualist must treat both expressions of sexual activity in the same way.

The contextual approach to understanding Paul's reference validates the choice of words used by the editors of the NRSV and NIV Bibles. In this letter to the church in Corinth, Paul is responding to concerns expressed in an earlier letter. Some in the Corinthian church felt that activity of fellow members was bordering on the practice of idolatry:

eating meat offered to idols and being involved with prostitutes, which was a pagan cultic practice in the temple of Aphrodite, the Greek goddess of love. This was similar to the problem the Hebrews faced with the Canaanites 1,200 years earlier. The Greek temple housed both male and female prostitutes. Since the context is prostitution, it is likely the text in 6.9 is referring to males who use the services of these prostitutes. Since Paul refers to idolatry in the context (5:11), that concern could be in the background as well.

In ancient and first century Greek culture, older men often served young boys as mentors and sometimes abused them sexually.[2] Many scholars believe the term *malakoi* refers to the passive male and the term *arsenakoitai* refers to the active male who like the men of Sodom desired to rape the two male guests of Lot. Although the text refers to same-gender sexual activity, there is no indication that either of the two males is homosexual as we know homosexuality to be in this age. Since the prostitute was likely a slave, he may have been heterosexual. The same is even truer of the abuser. For this reason, it is inappropriate to use the word homosexual to describe either of these two persons.

When seen contextually, what is Paul's message to the church in Corinth? He suggests that all live as God's people who have been purified and put right with God through Jesus Christ. Our whole being is a member of Christ's body. Our bodies do not belong to ourselves but to God; we are trustees of our bodies, so as stewards we are to use our bodies for the glory of God. We degrade the body of Christ when we unite our body with a prostitute's. Since this list describes people who abuse others, Paul reminds us to avoid those patterns of living that thrive on abusing others.[3] Since the context shows Paul addressing abusive sexual behavior by a male with a male prostitute, we are given no guidance for our *ethical situation* where two people of the same gender have lived for many years in a committed, loving, and responsible relationship. This passage, like Leviticus, neither condones nor condemns the relationship in the *ethical situation*.

1 Timothy 1:9

This text reads: "This means, understanding that the law is laid down not for the innocent but for the lawless and disobedient, for the godless and sinful, for the unholy and profane, for those who kill their father or mother, for murderers, fornicators, *sodomites* (ἀρσενοκοίταις), slave traders, liars, perjurers, and whatever else is contrary to sound teaching . . ." (1Timothy 1:9-10 NRSV). The NIV translation has *for perverts* (ἀρσενοκοίταις).

When read textually, this passage declares lawless a male who rapes other males. Sodomy (act of male rape) is considered a perversion or deviation from God's good purpose for sexuality. Once again, some expand this literal interpretation to include all same-gender sexual activity because they believe all same-gender sexual activity is a perversion of God's good intention for sexuality. At this point the textualist goes beyond what the text is saying because of personal belief. This passage, like the Corinthians passage, includes *fornicators* in the list. To be consistent the textualist must conclude that all sexual experiences between male and female are also contrary to God's will. Of course, there are many passages in the Bible that refute that conclusion, whereas there are no passages in the Bible that refute the expansion of sodomy to include all same-gender sexual activity. Nonetheless, this example illustrates the superficiality of the expanded literal view of this text. I think it is best to let the text say what it says and refrain from adding personal biases. This passage, of course, should be evaluated in light of other passages and teachings in the scripture. What then is the contextual meaning of the passage?

Paul writes his young apprentice, Timothy, who is the appointed leader of the church or churches in Ephesus. Ephesus, like Corinth, has a popular temple of prostitution that has strong religious connotations because of the connection with the goddess of love, who exists in a pantheon of gods and goddesses. As in Corinth and the land of Canaan, to participate in this cultic sexual activity is to be involved in the practice of idolatry. Paul's immediate concern is to encourage Timothy to curb the false teaching of some of the leaders in the church. Apparently, their teachings center upon the law (obeying an endless list of rules to earn God's grace and salvation) rather than centering upon God's grace and mercy. In the latter part of chapter one, Paul refers to himself as being a recipient of God's mercy and grace even though he was formerly a blasphemer and persecutor (1:12-16).

Paul feels strongly the focus should be upon the grace and mercy of God as revealed by Christ rather than a return to the law as the major norm for salvation and living. The strong feeling is communicated in the ninth verse which says, "the law is laid down not for the innocent but for the lawless and disobedient . . ." This begins the list of extreme abusive and sinful acts for which the law is necessary, primarily for the protection of fellow human beings. Paul did not devise the list in order to teach ethics; he created the list of depraved behavior patterns to emphasize grace and mercy should be the spiritual base in the church in Ephesus. The law has a place for those who are extremely wicked with no spiritual or religious intentions. A sodomite (a male who rapes other males) fits very well alongside murderers, kidnappers, and those who use sexual activity as an end in itself. There is no clear indication that Paul is referring to a person whose sexual orientation is homosexual or heterosexual.

Once again, does this specific description of same-gender sexual activity have any relevance for the *ethical situation* where two people of the same gender have been housemates for over twenty years and have enjoyed an intimate, faithful, caring, and just relationship? They are homosexual persons but did not choose that sexual orientation; nonetheless, their relationship helps them fulfill their humanity. I fail to see any connection between Paul's illustration of complete lawlessness, godlessness, and depravity with a monogamous and responsible relationship of two people of the same gender, who while not of their making, are deeply attracted to each other at the same depth that heterosexuals can be attracted to each other. This passage neither condemns nor condones the *ethical situation*.

Romans 1:26-27 (NRSV)

"For this reason God gave them up to degrading passions. Their women exchanged natural intercourse for unnatural, and in the same way also the men, giving up natural intercourse with women, were consumed with passion for one another. Men committed shameless acts with men and received in their own persons the due penalty for their error."

When read textually, this passage condemns same-gender sexual activity of males and possibly females. The men are overcome with sexual desire for each other; they participate with each other in sexual or shameful acts rather than with women. Women, likewise, participate in sexual activity out of the ordinary for women. Some textualists believe the text implies that sexual activity occurs between females. As a result, some textualists believe this passage condemns all forms of same-gender sexual activity, thus all situations rather than specific situations of same-gender sexual activity are contrary to God's created purpose.

What then does this passage say when seen in its context? First, this text needs to be seen in the larger context, for it lies within an important block of material located between the first part of Romans 1 and the remainder of the letter beginning with Romans 3:21. In chapter 1:1-17, Paul prepares the reader for the good news of God's love and grace in Jesus Christ. Those who live by faith will enjoy salvation both here and now and beyond this life.

The tenor of the letter changes with verse 1:18 through 3:20. The focus is upon the human condition of sinfulness, which leads to ungodly living without the gospel. In this section Paul shows that all people are affected by sinfulness; therefore, all are dependent upon the grace of God revealed by Christ. All people on the earth are placed into two groups. The first are the Gentiles, which include all human beings except Hebrews or Jews. The reference to same-gender sexual activity is made in this section concerning the wickedness of the Gentiles. Paul concludes that "all people who have sinned apart from the law, will also perish apart from the law" (2:12).

Then, in the largest portion of this section (2:1-3:20), Paul reminds the moralistic Jews that they have no reason to boast because they have the law. He reminds them that no person is able to obey the law completely, so those who live by the law will be judged by the law and likewise perish (2:13). The point Paul attempts to make in this entire section is that all human beings have sinned and lack the spiritual capacity to save themselves. In the end, everyone is dependent upon the grace, mercy, and love of God.

Second, these two verses (1:26-27) need to be seen in the context of this section dealing with the sinful condition of the Gentiles. Very much like the Corinthian and Timothy passages, Paul illustrates the sinful nature of the Gentiles by creating a list of various forms of wicked behavior. Prior to the list, Paul states the root cause of the Gentile problem. In spite of knowing God, the Gentiles exchanged devotion to the creator God with devotion to what God has created: images made with human hands resembling animals and birds.

Paul has heard that Roman Gentiles worship idols very similar to what he experienced in Asia Minor and Greece. He writes: *"therefore God gave them up in the lusts of their hearts to impurity, to the degrading of their bodies among themselves, because they exchanged the truth about God for a lie and worshiped and served the creature rather than the Creator"* (1:24-25). This sounds very much like the concern expressed in the purity or holiness laws of Leviticus 18-20. The preamble to the list of sinful and wicked forms of behavior is the practice of idolatry. The practice of idolatry is Paul's major concern. He documents his conclusion with a list describing various kinds of wicked behavior. Once again, the list does not represent an attempt by Paul to develop the foundation of Christian ethics. The ethical section of this letter begins intentionally with the twelfth chapter. Ethics for Paul does not stand alone as a set of rules. Christian living begins and occurs as a person remains connected to Jesus Christ, the solution to human sinfulness.

Third, these two verses (1:26-27) describing a passion for sexual activity need to be seen alongside the other forms of shameful behavior.

Paul's list includes at least nineteen other forms of wicked behavior such as covetousness, malice, envy, gossip, deceit, God haters, heartless, ruthless, and finally the audacity to applaud others who practice this kind of living. Periodically, the text includes the phrase "they were *filled* with malice or *full* of envy." So Paul describes those who are dominated or controlled by these wicked patterns of living. Today, we may use the word *addicted*. Surely Paul is not describing every Gentile or even one Gentile whose nature is fully corrupted with this menu of darkness. His list simply describes a pattern of ungodly ingredients that generally characterizes life among many Gentiles in Rome, a prototype of sinful behavior.

What are some common characteristics of this list? All in the list are contrary to God's intention for relational living; most patterns of living in the list usually wound other humans physically, spiritually, or emotionally. All in the list will destroy the possibility of living in loving, caring, and just relationships. All characteristics promote self-centeredness and are void of grace. Most could lead to violence and war. All are facets of a wicked and sinful heart. Remember that verses 26 and 27 are included in this list.

Fourth, what is the historical context for these sexual references made by Paul? He had not yet visited Rome but very likely received a description from friends like Priscilla and Aquila or felt that secular life in Rome was much like what he saw in Corinth, Athens, and Ephesus. Since Paul was not writing to address particular situations experienced by the Christ followers in Rome, a general background of Roman culture, religion, and lifestyle may help us understand Paul's statement about sexual practice.

For the first time, women are also mentioned by Paul. They are exchanging "natural intercourse for unnatural." Since women are mentioned, it may be helpful to summarize the role of women in the Roman culture in this era of history. Women were considered the property of men and were used primarily for procreation. Husbands were seldom socially involved with their wives publicly or privately.

Wives had their own living quarters separated from their husbands. Seldom did deep feelings of love accompany sexual activity among husband and wife. Servants escorted wives to the marketplace so they would not be seen alone. Likewise, unmarried females seldom attended gymnasia (public school) and did not go into the public arena without a chaperon. Marriages were arranged. Fidelity in marriage was important for Roman females in order to protect legitimacy of children. Likely, the females described by Paul in this passage are temple prostitutes.

Paul McKendrick writes: "to a Roman, religion was a contractual relation between him and his gods; he scratched their backs and expected them to scratch his."[4] Roman religious life was noted for its ability to borrow creatively from practices throughout the empire. They celebrated festivals that preserved primitive fertility rites similar to ancient Canaan. Much of their religious practice was imported from Greece. They embraced ancestor worship along with worship of the emperor. State religion was used to support the monarch. Roman religion was without theological dogma or ethical code. At most, it was a superficial facade masking a spiritual void. When Paul wrote his letter to the Romans, the philosophy of Epicureanism creatively borrowed from the Greeks was highly influential. It resonated with the affluence of many in the city of Rome who wanted *to eat, drink, and be merry*, but who also wanted to enjoy peace of mind. Rome was also known for its public baths, brothels, and the freedom of males, married or not, to participate in public prostitution. Much illicit sexual activity occurred in groups commonly referred to as *orgies* sometimes held in honor of a Roman deity.

Both female and male prostitutes were used in brothels to accommodate men, who most often were of high rank in military, government, and business. Men of high rank in Roman society who were involved in same-gender sexual activity usually had a wife and a mistress or concubine; therefore, there is no way to determine if their sexual orientation was homosexual as we know it today. A good example is Nero, who lived about the same time of Paul's residence in Rome.

Nero divorced and murdered his wife Octavia and married his mistress Poppaca Sabina. At the same time he enjoyed participating in orgies that included same-gender sexual activity.[5]

So when this passage (1:26-27) is seen in its biblical and cultural context, what is the message Paul desires to communicate? First and primarily Paul shows what happens to the human heart when people worship idols, the created rather than the creator God. When the creator God is not the core of human life, people become vulnerable to obsessions that feed their self-centeredness, creating patterns of behavior that are relationally destructive. In this light, Paul is not attempting to present a treatise on sexual ethics from a Christian perspective. He simply attributes such behavior to their practice of idolatry. To concentrate on the sexual illustration or any of the other nineteen examples is to miss the point Paul is making.

Second, Paul shows how devotion to the created (material and physical) feeds upon itself until the human is totally consumed. "God gave them up to *degrading passions* . . . the men, giving up natural intercourse with women, were *consumed with passion* for one another." Paul describes the power of idolatry, the gods we make with human hands. He shows how that which we have created can turn and control us. That is the point Paul makes with the other nineteen examples. In this sexual illustration, I feel that Paul describes both the men and women dominated by sexual desire and activity. Sexual satisfaction has become an end to itself rather than being the means of expressing love and commitment to one another.

These people are likely satisfying their insatiable lustful desires at the expense of those servicing them. The men being abused are likely young male slaves captured in Roman conquests. If this activity is occurring in a brothel orgy, female prostitutes may be involved with each other, but since it is a group experience that could cause Paul to feel it is out of the ordinary—"they are exchanging natural intercourse for unnatural." It sounds like a group experience since Paul uses the plural, *women* and *men*. How could Paul know enough to be describing the specifics of the orgy? He is not an eyewitness, and very likely those who told him about life in Rome were not eyewitnesses either.

The word unnatural (*para physin*) means *out of the ordinary or unusual*. The Greek word *physin* does not mean *according to the laws of nature or the created design and purpose* as some have assumed. It simply means what is *usual and ordinary*. People who are consumed by the material and physical do some very unusual things. How often do we hear on the news or read in the newspaper about people who are extremely wealthy cheating on their income tax, embezzling, or simply draining the company's assets till they have to declare bankruptcy? Even though they have more money than they can spend, they have an insatiable hunger and thirst for more. From my perspective that kind of behavior is unusual. It makes no sense; it is out of the ordinary. That is what the term *unnatural* means.[6]

Third, I believe those Paul describes to be consumed with sexual passion for each other could be heterosexual by orientation, not what we know today as homosexuals. At least in Paul's mind they were heterosexual. There are two reasons I reach this conclusion. To begin with, Paul is describing sinful activity that has gone to the extreme—"filled with every kind of wickedness," "consumed with passion." Nothing could be more extreme in Paul's mind than a male who normally is sexually attracted to females involved in passionate acts with fellow males. That is definitely unnatural or out of the ordinary.

Another reason those involved may have been heterosexual in orientation is based on what is not included in the list of twenty examples of sinful behavior. Paul does not explicitly mention adultery, fornication, and prostitution, traditional sinful sexual activity between males and females; that is to say, between heterosexuals. This is strange since Rome had a worldwide reputation for being one of the major cities of sexual debauchery. On two other occasions, when Paul creates a list of evil behavior (1 Timothy 1:9 and 1 Corinthians 6:9), he uses two words that clearly describe same-gender sexual activity *(male prostitutes and sodomites*), but he also lists sinful heterosexual activity (*fornication and adultery*). In the Romans list none of these words are present.

In many of Paul's letters he refers to inappropriate sexual behavior among males and females. In fact, he always makes reference to sinful sexual activity between males and females when he refers to sexual behavior. I think it is strange that a clear reference to inappropriate heterosexual behavior is missing in Paul's longest list of sins, unless it is assumed in this illustration where "God gave them up to degrading passions." Very likely Paul assumes the readers in Rome would know, without a shadow of a doubt, that he is referring to males sexually attracted to females and females sexually attracted to males caught up in an orgy that begins with heterosexual activity but concludes with some male sexual activity with young male slaves (pederasty). What the females do is uncertain.

In conclusion, in this entire section (1:18-32), Paul gives a general description of the moral collapse of a culture that has the reputation of worshiping and serving the creature rather than the Creator. Such a culture without the worship of God takes on the character of what Paul describes in the list. When he wrote this letter, he had not yet been to Rome to see for himself. At best his information is second-or third-hand. The sexual activity has to be described in pictures of generality. Paul could not be as precise as he was in his letters to the church in Corinth and to Timothy, who lived in Ephesus. Paul had closer contact with activities in the temple of Aphrodite in Corinth and the temple of Artemis in Ephesus.[7] He stayed longer in those two cities than all the other cities and towns put together. Some of the converts to his message of Christ likely knew from experience the activities that occurred in these temples.

We now return to the contemporary *ethical situation* where two homosexual persons have been housemates and partners for over twenty years and have enjoyed an intimate, faithful, caring, and just relationship. Does this passage in Romans provide spiritual guidance for the church in connection with these members of the same gender who are intimate partners? First, Paul does not intend for his list to be a guide for sexual ethics, but simply a description of what happens when humans practice idolatry or worship the material rather than the Creator. Second, the two homosexual partners who are church members do not practice idolatry; they worship the Creator God as revealed by Jesus Christ. They are deeply devoted to many facets of Christian ministry in the life of the Body of Christ. Third, Paul's list describes people who are consumed by their lustful passions for sex as an end to itself. Once again, these same-gender partners are united because they value most highly their relationship that enables them to enjoy a wholeness that they could not experience if they were required to live alone. Fourth, because of the historical context, Paul is very likely describing licentious sexual activity by a group of people where there is an absence of love, commitment, and relationship. In contrast, to this scene of debauchery, the partners in the *ethical situation* are committed to each other and live in a faithful and loving monogamous relationship supporting each other economically, emotionally, and spiritually. I feel this passage in Romans does not address the *ethical situation*; therefore, it neither condemns nor condones it.

Endnotes: Chapter Three

[1]   Paul Kendrick, *The Roman Mind at Work* (Princeton: D. Van Nostrand Company, 1958), pp. 54-57.

[2]   Ibid., p. 59.

[3]   Ibid., p. 60.

[4]   Daniel A. Helminiak, *What the Bible Really Says About Homosexuality* (San Francisco: Alamo Square Press, 1995), pp. 61-84.

[5]   William Barclay, *The Daily Bible Study: The Letter to the Romans* (Philadelphia: the Westminster Press, 1975), pp. 20-25.

[6]   John Knox, *The Interpreter's Bible: Romans* (Nashville: Abingdon, 1978), pp. 401-402.

[7]   William Barclay, *The Daily Bible Study: The Letter to the Corinthians* (Philadelphia: The Westminster Press, 1975), pp. 96-100.

CHAPTER FOUR

Biblical Reflection:
Responding to God's Word: What to
Say and Not Say

This *ethical situation* examined alongside these biblical passages often cited as "clear, unambiguous, and unequivocal" in their prohibitions of homosexual practice represents many similar situations in our society and in the church. These are persons who did not choose to be homosexual any more than I chose to be heterosexual. In the same way that my relationship with my spouse helps me fulfill God's gift of humanity, their faithful, loving, and monogamous relationship helps them fulfill their humanity. I fail to see any connection between Paul's illustration of complete lawlessness and depravity with this monogamous and responsible relationship of two people of the same gender, who through none of their making, are deeply attracted to each other at the same depth that heterosexuals can be attracted to each other.

If faithful and loving monogamous relationships between two people of the same gender are clearly and unambiguously sinful in the eyes of God, these six passages from scripture do not support that conclusion.

Biblical scholars need to look elsewhere. It is true that all six passages or texts declare specific situations of same-gender sexual activity to be sinful. Without exception, none of the texts were written and included in the canon for the purpose of providing guidance for sexual ethics. Without exception, none make any reference about the nature of the relationship; none are clear about the specifics of the sexual activity. With the exception of the *Sodom* and the *Judges* passages, all likely focus on participating in pagan cultic practices of prostitution, which means the participants who are Hebrew males are practicing idolatry. There is no evidence that those involved are homosexual by orientation.

In dealing with the sexual activity described in the six texts, there is such a lack of clarity that interpreters must interject their own views if they declare scripture clearly, unambiguously, and equivocally condemns the practice of homosexuality. Scripture has numerous examples of illicit and adulterous situations that are heterosexual practices. As a result, no one to my knowledge has gone on record condemning all practices of heterosexuality to be sinful. St. Augustine comes close to embracing this position. I realize scripture validates the practice of male/female sexuality for procreation in the context of a committed relationship even in polygamous situations and among concubines. The absence of biblical validation of same-gender intimate relationships does not automatically condemn such relationships. There are many ethical situations we face today that are not addressed in scripture, such as birth control, abortion, artificial insemination, putting people on life support, which sometimes extends the process of dying, and genetic research, which has led to cloning.

There have been two opposing schools of thought in dealing with ethical issues that are not explicitly addressed in scripture. If there is no direct law of prohibition, then you are free to do it. The other school of thought is the contrast; if there is no direct law of prohibition, then do not do it. Neither of these avenues of ethical guidance reflects very much spiritual depth. When the church is faced with an ethical situation, such as same-gender partnerships, then it is critically important to seek the guidance of scripture, the written word through which God has spoken and continues to speak, with the guidance of the Holy Spirit. It is also important to seek guidance from God's word who became human, Jesus Christ. Although Jesus does not make any direct references concerning homosexuality and same-gender partnerships, he still plays a significant role in helping the church resolve this issue.

It is also important for persons to decide how they are going to interpret scripture. All who rely upon scripture for ethical guidance are interpreters by choosing the norms to assist with interpretation. Some interpreters approach scripture textually where every text is taken literally with every word and verse equally sharing the authority of God's voice for faith and practice and perhaps for every other arena of life. Some interpreters approach scripture contextually. They begin with the text and determine its specific meaning. Then it is examined alongside the verses surrounding it, the book in which it is found, the scripture as a whole, and the teachings and lifestyle of Jesus Christ. It is also examined within its cultural, historical, and geographical context. Finally, it is evaluated in light of its interpretation by the church throughout history. This is done to understand the veracity of the text, not to water down or dispose of the truth. Sometimes the textual approach to scripture will reach a conclusion that differs from those who use the contextual approach. Those using different approaches and arriving at different conclusions can be equally devoted to the authority of God and God's written word. Neither approach guarantees freedom from error in understanding God's message for this difficult ethical situation.

I realize critics of the contextual approach feel contextualists search and search simply to validate their preconceived position about the practice of homosexuality. I think it is important that both the textual and the contextual approach to biblical interpretation be careful to avoid manipulating scripture so that the text validates personal beliefs and practices. At the same time, I believe the words of scripture were written by divinely inspired humans. These messages are addressing both cultural and spiritual issues people of faith face. The different books of the Bible reflect the personality and the literary style of their authors. The contemporary interpreter of scripture attempts to live in the shoes of the persons of scripture, see the world and life from their perspective, and get to know their neighbors and their enemies.

The challenge to the contextualist is to make every effort possible to see all of scripture in its historical, cultural, literary, and social context. The temptation is to interpret passages textually or literally when they agree with a preconceived ethical position and to use the contextual approach when there is no strong feeling about the ethical conclusion or when the contextual approach will support a preconceived position. For example, in his first letter to the Corinthians, Paul has a long exhortation insisting that a woman who prays or prophesies with her head unveiled disgraces her head, her husband, and God (1 Corinthians 11: 5). Today, it is rare to see a woman in corporate worship with a covering over her head.

The challenge for the textualist is to accept with equal value every verse, chapter, and book of scripture from beginning to end and then attempt to live by what has been literally accepted. Today if the female textualist were faithful to her approach to biblical interpretation, she would wear a covering over her head every time she participates in public and corporate worship.

The same norm applies to the contextualist approach to biblical interpretation. If someone is a contextualist, then it is important to examine all passages in their context. The contextual approach to Paul's command in Corinthians sees that it was intended to address a particular situation in Corinth for that time in history. No respectable woman in Corinth and most eastern villages and cities would be seen in public without her veil, which reaches down to her feet. More so, Corinth had a well-known reputation for its immoral sexual practices connected with the temple of Aphrodite, the Greek goddess of love. The temple prostitutes, when in public, did not wear a veil; therefore, it was necessary for female Christians to maintain modesty by wearing their veil so that the practices of the early Christian church would not be connected with such immoral sexual practices. Paul's message of Christian freedom sometimes put these new believers in tension with cultural practices. Often the social and cultural context opens the window for understanding more fully Paul's intention. Such is the case when Paul includes references to same-gender sexual activity in some of his lists that describe people who are consumed with evil and wickedness. To fail to see these references in their social and cultural context could lead to conclusions that the Bible condemns all situations of homosexual behavior.

At this point, what then are some conclusions for Christians and the church in regard to homosexuality? First, I think the church needs to acknowledge scripture does not address all issues of homosexuality; in fact, scripture says very little if anything about homosexuality. Second, the church needs to declare what it believes scripture does say about specific situations of same-gender sexual activity. Third, the church needs to declare specifically and clearly what scripture does not say about same-gender sexual activity.

I believe the references in scripture about same-gender sexual activity do not provide ethical guidance for people who live in faithful, loving, and responsible same-gender monogamous relationships. Since I feel scripture is not absolutely clear about same-gender sexual activity, the church has a couple of options in developing a response to the *ethical situation* described at the beginning of this chapter. It can seek a rationale cloaked in scripture that sets forth rules to prohibit full membership into the body of Christ on the subjective basis that this couple is spiritually impure. With this option the church is turning to law as a way to address what its members perceive to be sinful. In doing so, the church reflects the way our secular society deals with what it perceives to be wrong. More so, the church reflects an ethical pattern that Jesus challenged during his three-year ministry.

Laws are important and necessary for our society, but I believe the church has another option that is more consistent with the heart of our faith. The church can search the heart of scripture to see if there is a biblical basis for the same-gender partners in our *ethical situation* to be full members of the church, the body of Christ with the church's public validation of their committed *partnership*. After all, we are people of grace; it is the heart and cornerstone of the Reformed church.

As our gracious God reaches out to us by coming in Christ to welcome us into relationship, we who are grateful recipients of grace eagerly seek ways compatible to scripture to welcome fellow children of God fully into the body of Christ. We who have been saved by the grace of God through faith in Jesus remain influenced by the spirit of God's grace so that our lives reflect grace. Said in another way, we are people who have been radically dependent on God's grace; therefore, we have an opportunity to live by God's grace as we continue to seek a biblical and Christlike response to this important *ethical situation* that faces the church in our time. God's grace may open the door to a *more excellent way*. The next chapter will examine through biblical study the tension between *law* and *grace*.

CHAPTER FIVE

Maintaining a Perspective: Law through Grace

Building a Biblical Foundation to Give Support for a More Excellent Way

How firm a foundation, ye saints of the Lord,
Is laid for your faith in God's excellent word!
What more can be said than to you God hath said
To you who for refuge to Jesus have fled?

Ed. John Rippon

The grace of God can be more threatening than any other facet of God's nature. There are many reasons for this. To accept God's grace for salvation means we are admitting we lack spiritual strength to save ourselves. At the same time we are expressing dependence upon God instead of taking pride in being self-sufficient. Rather than saying, "I did it," all that we can say is, "thank you." Finally, upon realizing that we are accepted by God in spite of our self-centered condition, we have to deal with God's expectation to accept others as God accepts us.

Our hearts will compel us to search scripture to find ways to be more inclusive rather than using verses in scripture to justify exclusivity. From this point grace often goes no further. Saved by grace, yes! Live by grace, no! The transition from being accepted freely by God to accepting others without strings attached means that we need to return to our sources of faith and practice.

This chapter provides the biblical foundation for creating a new relational paradigm. Although God's grace can be threatening, it serves as one of the foundation pillars of Christ's ministry and the New Testament church. Grace is a good place to begin in addressing our ethical situation because it provides common ground where basic agreement is nearly universal among those who embrace the Christian faith. Also, if we are authentic people of grace, we will search scripture to see if there are biblical grounds to accept into full church membership the two people *(the ethical situation, chapter one)* of the same gender who live in a committed monogamous partnership, rather than searching scripture to find rules to exclude them from full membership.

First, I will review Jesus' perspective and demonstration of faith and life through the eyes of one of his disciples, Matthew. Second comes a transition from Jesus to the church and its witness to Jesus, the Word through the Acts of the Apostles. Third, I will examine one document of the written word by Paul to the church in Rome. Finally, I will assess the place of grace and law in the church today. In each of these, it will be evident that grace comes first as a way to live in relationship with God, others, and ourselves.

Jesus Christ: God's Word of Grace in Human Form

What was the climate of the Hebrew religious community at the time of God's advent in Jesus Christ? The center of Jewish life revolved around the ceremonies and rituals of the temple located in the city of Jerusalem. It was here that lavish Hebrew festivals were celebrated and the leadership and power of the priests and religious parties were felt.

The scribes and Pharisees crafted the commandments of the Old Testament to apply to every circumstance in life hoping to simplify them but in reality making them more complicated.[1] What God gave out of grace to the Hebrew people on Mt. Sinai, the religious leaders turned into legalistic burdens. They exercised considerable power over the people as interpreters, custodians, and practitioners of innumerable religious laws and rules. They imposed upon the people the norm of absolute perfection if the people desired citizenship in God's kingdom or family; that is to say, God accepts and loves those who earn acceptance through obedience to the law. William Barclay writes: "the great principles of the law were broken up into thousands and thousands of little rules and regulations . . . It took more than fifty volumes to hold the mass of regulations which resulted."[2] Rather than renewing and liberating human beings, the first century Jewish religion became oppressive.

Only the well-to-do religious elite experienced dignity and worth in this culture. Perfect adherence to these laws pushed many out of the mainstream of life to the margin. In this large group were children, women, the poor and diseased, the uneducated, Gentile and foreigner, and those who earned a living from the land and sea. The rules became the gatekeeper preventing people from enjoying the benefits of life in community. Laws became the controlling agent for the religious elite, the Scribes, Sadducees, and Pharisees. The religious climate created an air of exclusivism, self-righteousness, and judgment. To the average citizen of Israel, God was perceived as a harsh judge whose justice was satisfied through punishment and condemnation.

It was into this climate of spiritual fatigue that God's advent in Jesus Christ occurs. John writes: "and the Word became flesh and lived among us, and we have seen his glory, the glory as of a father's only son, full of *grace* and *truth*" (John 1:14). So, the wholeness of Christ, his words and deeds, communicate both the grace and truth of God. John does not say *law and truth* but *grace and truth*. William Barclay writes: "with His unique wisdom Jesus never laid down laws and rules and regulations; that is why His teaching is timeless and never gets out of date; He always lays down a very great and very important principle."[3]

The fullness of God's grace is seen through the eyes of Matthew who was a tax collector, an outsider, a member of the community of undesirables. From the onset of Jesus' ministry, the perspective of God changes from one who desires to be gated by the law to the seeker who prefers to be on the street, in the hills, and by the sea with the people in their common labor. Matthew's inclusion of the visit by the Magi, foreigners from the East, sets the tone of the hospitable nature of God revealed by the coming Messiah. Following the visit by the Magi, the infant Christ is taken to Egypt, another example that God in Christ has no geographical boundaries. Then the baptism and temptation of Jesus prior to ministry further validates God's effort to identify with the people rather than being set apart. Jesus' first acts of ministry occur in close contact with the people revealing their worth and value in the eyes of God. In word, he proclaims the "good news" of mercy in God's kingdom; in act, he demonstrates the "good news" by accepting and healing people of sickness and disease. These people represent a cross section of those living in Palestine in the first century.

He then emphasizes the importance of human community by calling disciples to join him in ministry. Once again through Christ we are exposed to the hospitality of God who welcomes as his disciples people from many walks of life. Some who accompany Jesus are even women (Matthew 4:18-22; Luke 8:1-8).

From this point Matthew includes Jesus' *Sermon on the Mount*, a glimpse of God's intention for human life in God's kingdom here on earth. The sermon begins with the *beatitudes*, which means the ultimate condition of happiness or blessedness. Markus Barth believes these eight statements encompass Jesus' formal welcome as citizens of God's kingdom that provides the basis for the condition of happiness. This state of wellbeing then helps the faithful maintain wholeness in time of *mourning and peacemaking, when poor in spirit and persecuted for the sake of righteousness*, and so forth. Once again, through the spirit of welcome in the beatitudes, Jesus once again reveals the hospitable nature of God, the giver of the law.[4]

The sermon of Jesus follows the beatitudes. At its beginning he sets the record straight concerning his relationship with the moral law: "do not think that I have come to abolish the law or the prophets; I have come not to abolish but to fulfill" (Matthew 5:17). Throughout his sermon, Jesus refers to laws in first books of the Bible and expands their meaning by revealing their spiritual purpose for existing. The Pharisees sacrificed the *spirit of the law* by over emphasizing the *letter of the law*. In his sermon Jesus reveals that God's ultimate goal for humans is to live in relationships marked by love, justice, mercy, grace, and faithfulness with guidance of the Ten Commandments. Jesus' ethical ideal far exceeds the ethical expectations of those who adhere only to the letter of the law.

On the surface it then seems that Jesus has made the law more burdensome. Who could possibly be faithful to the law and earn God's acceptance and salvation under these new conditions? No one can accomplish this goal, even the scribes and Pharisees, but now according to the good news in the *beatitudes*, in Christ sinful human beings are already citizens of God's kingdom, an example of God's grace. Our full citizenship is settled once and for all. At no time does Jesus teach that God creates a hierarchical rank of citizens. Privileges and responsibilities, although different, exist in the same realm of mutual servanthood. In the body of his sermon, Jesus is describing the quality of lifestyle God has designed for citizens in the kingdom, realizing that he is talking to citizens who remain sinful. In his sermon, Jesus time and again refers to the importance of the thoughts and attitudes of the human heart as well as human behavior. Because of God's grace, human beings are set free to grow toward wholeness as humans who live in a community sharing love for one another and for God. Read Matthew 5-7. Identify specific examples where grace carries the follower of Christ beyond the expectations of the letter of the law.

Following the word of grace spoken on the mountain, Jesus then authenticates it by the way he lives. Because he was a tax collector,

Matthew knew the anguish of being marginalized by the religious establishment, so his gospel was written primarily for the ears of Hebrews. He wants them to be exposed to the Christ who sets all people free from the law as the means for being made right with God.

Matthew reports the many times Jesus approaches and touches and heals those who are declared unclean because of a dreadful disease or sickness. In ministering to the wholeness of some, Jesus declares them forgiven even though there is no textual evidence of a confession, thus revealing that God's grace is proactive, setting people free to live quality ethical lives. Jesus even receives the enemy into his presence when a Roman officer seeks Jesus' healing help for his sick servant. Jesus reveals the heart of God when criticized by the Pharisees for eating with tax collectors, sinners, and outcasts: "those who are well have no need of a physician, but those who are sick. Go and learn what this means, I desire mercy or kindness, not sacrifice. For I have come to call not the righteous but sinners" (Matthew 9:12-13).

In demonstrating God's grace, Jesus breaks the purity laws of the orthodox Hebrew religion. Matthew experiences the grace of God firsthand because this episode occurs in his home. Read Matthew 8-9 and see the grace of God fleshed out as Jesus responds to the needs of a cross section of Palestinian society.

In the Old Testament the commandments were given out of God's grace and concern for the Hebrews. Jesus attempts to maintain that perspective. There are specific times when Jesus challenges the supreme position of the law in the Hebrew religious structure. He and his disciples pick and eat grains of wheat on the Sabbath; in the synagogue he heals a man's paralyzed hand on the Sabbath. He attempts to put the law in its proper perspective by saying: "the Sabbath was made for humans; humans were not made for the Sabbath" (Mark 2:27).

In Matthew's gospel Jesus says: "I desire mercy or kindness, and not sacrifice" (Matthew 12:7). In both cases Jesus suggests that care for the wellbeing of others takes precedent over the letter of the law; that is to say, the law is not an end in itself but the means to a much higher end. Jesus' violation of the Sabbath law appears to be an intentional test case through which he extends the graciousness of God to those with particular needs; therefore, emphasizing that the spirit of the law stands above the letter of the law.[5] Read Matthew 11:25-13:24, noting how often compassion comes first.

Matthew also includes in his gospel those times when Jesus ignores the mores of the Jewish culture by responding to the needs of women and conversing with them in the public arena, by accepting powerless young children and then referring to them as models of faith for adults, by welcoming young and old in his midst, and by supporting those with little faith as well as affirming those of great faith. And finally when Jesus does recommend a commandment for humankind, he says: "love the Lord your God with all your heart, and with all your soul, and with all your mind. This is the greatest and first commandment. And a second is like it: you shall love your neighbor as yourself. On these two commandments hang all the law and the prophets" (Matthew 22:37-40). Law comes through grace and love as clearly stated by Jesus in what we call *the Great Commandment*.

Often Jesus confronts the scribes and Pharisees, challenging the elevated position they have given the letter of the law and how it leads individuals to becoming self-righteous, judgmental, hypocritical, and spiritually blind. They have lost sight of God's grace from which the law emerges. He encourages people to look within and nurture their hearts with the spirit of kindness, mercy, justice, honesty, humility, trust, and generosity. These words convey the extent that God values people and their potential; the fruits of God's spirit (human and spiritual values) are critically important in developing meaningful relationships among human beings. More will be said about them in contrast to law in the next chapter on relationships. Read Matthew 23 and once again allow the biblical text to speak for itself.

In the end, by putting the value and worth of all humans above Jewish tradition and law, Jesus brings the wrath of the religious leaders upon himself. Following the healing of the man with the paralyzed hand, Matthew writes: "But the Pharisees went out and conspired against him, how to destroy him" (Matthew 12:14). In spite of the threat of death, Jesus does not back down. He deliberately challenges the elevated position of the law with acts of love and grace. As William Barclay writes: "Jesus' love for humanity far surpasses his respect for ritual law."[6] Jesus' demonstration of the grace of God threatens the base of power claimed by the religious leaders. As custodians of law, they were the gatekeepers of God's kingdom with control over the people possessing the power of choosing those who will be insiders and those who will be outsiders.[7] Bruce Bawer writes: "the real Jesus—the Jesus who was incontrovertibly human, even as he was connected to God in a remarkable way that utterly transformed the lives of the people who knew him—was not about asserting power, judging, or destroying; he was about love."[8]

In representing God's grace and mercy, Jesus extends an invitation to everyone to be citizens of God's kingdom. This prompts the religious leaders to devise a plan to kill him. In spite of the threat of death, Jesus does not give in. As a result, Jesus dies on the cross, but his death is not the end of the story. On Easter Sunday the stone that seals the tomb where the crucified Christ lay is rolled away. He lives! God validates Jesus' ministry with new life. Christ introduces a new law or covenant etched upon the hearts of human beings, and that new law is called grace and love from which all other rules and laws are birthed.

The Church: Witness to God's Word of Grace
The Acts of the Apostles

During his ministry Jesus lived in community with those who followed him. He equipped them to continue his ministry following his death, resurrection, and ascension. Gathered with his followers, the risen Christ says, "you will receive power when the Holy Spirit comes upon you; and you will be my witnesses in Jerusalem, in all Judea and Samaria, and to the ends of the earth" (Acts 1:8). On the Jewish festival day of Pentecost, the Holy Spirit's presence becomes known to this small group of no more than 125 followers of Christ. With the physical presence of Christ no longer with them, they are spiritually empowered to be witnesses of the risen Christ through word and deed.

It is assumed that most Christ followers at this time were Jewish. Will they fall back on their tradition of salvation through obedience to the law, or will the guidance of the Holy Spirit enlighten them to the teachings of Christ and his way of love and grace? According to Luke's account in the *Acts of the Apostles*, the early Church as individuals and as a community experiences considerable tension between the poles of law and grace. They have been reared as the people of the law, but now they have been commissioned by God's spirit to bear witness to the Christ who put grace first.

A test of their faithfulness to Christ comes early in the life of the early church with the arrest of their leaders Peter and John, and later the arrest of all the apostles. In spite of this danger, they stand firm by declaring: "we must obey God rather than any human authority" (Acts 5:29). Following the public execution of Stephen, the Jewish leaders, led by the zeal of a Pharisee named Saul, severely persecuted the church in Jerusalem. Many of the devoted leaders of the church flee to other areas of Palestine. At this time, read Acts 1-8.

A second test now occurs. Will the early church, comprised primarily of Jews, practice the grace and hospitality of Christ by reaching out to people of other races, nationalities, faiths, and lifestyles? The answer soon comes. Philip, a deacon of the church in Jerusalem travels to Samaria and proclaims the good news of the risen Christ gladly receiving into the church these Jews who have lost racial and religious purity by marrying foreign inhabitants. Samaritans are bitterly despised by orthodox Jews, so the inclusion of Samaritans is an early sign of faithfulness to the way of Christ under the guidance of the Holy Spirit. Philip also befriends a man from Ethiopia who is a eunuch. As they journey together Philip bears witness to the good news of Christ revealing the church of the open door to someone of another race without distinct gender. Also, according to Old Testament law eunuchs are not to be included into the covenant community (Deuteronomy 23:1).[10]

The unspoken leader of the early church is Peter, one of Jesus' closest disciples. Will he make a transition from purity laws to grace as the means of being made right with God as well as the basis of fellowship among believers whose practices and lifestyle do not conform to orthodox Judaism? It does not come easily for Peter, but over a period of time the transition to grace is made. His first step occurs when sought by Cornelius, who is not only a captain in the Roman army (the enemy) but is also a Gentile. For orthodox Jews, purity law forbids entering the home of a Gentile because God's favor does not include Gentiles. Peter's first lesson occurs in the midst of hunger while on the roof patio of a friend's home. He has a vision of many creatures considered unclean by Hebrew law. He refrains from eating, but quickly learns that what God declares to be clean should not be considered unclean. At this point he realizes that some of the Hebrew laws are petty alongside a relationship with God.

Following this episode, Cornelius' emissaries arrive, wanting Peter to return with them. Laying aside some of the petty purity laws is one thing, but fraternizing with a Gentile in his home and having a meal together is more than petty (see Acts 10). With the encouragement of the spirit of God, Peter bears witness to the grace revealed by Christ. Very likely, he also remembers a Roman Centurion Jesus helped and then referred to as an example of great faith. Peter realizes "that God shows no partiality" (Acts 10:34). So as an instrument of God's grace Peter welcomes Cornelius into the Christian faith and the church. From that time, Peter is instrumental in proclaiming the good news of the risen Christ to Gentiles; he baptizes many and welcomes them into the Christian faith. Peter, rather than Paul, actually takes the first step in demonstrating God's grace and hospitality by reaching out to Gentiles. Read Acts 9-11:18. He sees law from the perspective of grace.

A significant boost to the expansion of the Christian faith occurs when Saul, a devoted persecutor of Christians, is touched by the light of Christ while *en route* to Damascus. He converts to the Christian faith. Saul becomes Paul who uses phenomenal energy and faith to take the message of the risen Christ beyond the borders of Palestine to Asia Minor, Macedonia, Greece, and finally Rome. Paul is a Pharisee, a member of the party of Hebrews who separates themselves from others to become zealous students and practitioners of God's law. He is also a member of the Sanhedrin or Jewish Council, which tries legal cases among Jewish citizens.

Following his conversion to the way of Christ, Paul feels caught in the middle. With a reputation for being a fiery and fervent persecutor of the church, these Christ followers fear and do not trust Paul. With a history of being a zealot for Jewish traditional law and leader among Hebrews, fellow leaders of Judaism hate Paul and regard him a traitor to their religious cause at a critical time in Hebrew history. Paul is also a Roman citizen from the city of Tarsus with the experience of travel. These factors along with God's spiritual guidance compel Paul to take the message of the risen Christ beyond the borders of Palestine.

On this first journey to Asia Minor, Paul faces Jewish opponents who track him and create discontent among the people. In spite of opposition, both Jews and Gentiles embrace the faith and are received into the church. Paul quickly gains the reputation of being the apostle who takes the message of God's grace to the Gentiles. Since Gentiles are responding in high numbers, leadership in the Christian movement must resolve the question: what is the primary means for salvation? Church leaders in the Jerusalem area declare that Gentile believers must be circumcised as law requires before they can experience salvation and become members of the body of Christ. At this point in the early Church, the question of law or grace as the means of being made right with God has not been formally resolved.

Paul speaking in behalf of Gentiles becomes the advocate of God's grace as a means of salvation with law coming through God's grace. He and his opponents meet with the apostles and elders in Jerusalem. The issue in this instance has nothing to do with preaching to Gentiles. Paul's opponents have no problem with Paul's mission to the Gentiles.

But as William Willimon writes, "without circumcision, how could a Gentile possibly participate in the blessings promised to the covenant people; in short, how could they be saved? The concern is not over racial exclusion but covenant inclusion."[11]

With the support of Peter and James, church leaders meet as a council in Jerusalem. They reach a consensus. Paul is satisfied because they decide that circumcision is not a requirement for salvation and inclusion into the church. Jewish Christians who remain proponents of law are satisfied because a letter written to the Gentile converts from this council says they are expected to "abstain from what has been sacrificed to idols, from blood and from what is strangled, and from fornication" (Acts 15:28-29). At this time read Acts 11:1-18.

The decision at the council in Jerusalem represents a monumental move away from the Jewish belief in law as a means of God's acceptance and salvation. At the same time, the decision means that Gentiles may be welcomed into the new church, but not without limits. The lifestyle of Gentiles remains suspect. At this point, no ecclesiastical decision has been made in behalf of living by grace as emphasized so strongly in the teaching and ministry of Christ.[12] That comes later with the help of Paul as the church moves out of its infant stage and matures. In the meantime, the infant church has passed two major tests in continuing the ministry of Christ. First, it has courageously faced opposition without backing down or giving in. Second, it has become the church of the open door, which means it has gone beyond being a Jewish sect and has become a global body of Christ followers whose unity will now have to emerge from diversity rather than uniformity.

The Church: God's Word of Grace Written
Paul's Letter to the Romans

Read: Romans 1-3:20

Being made right with God and living in a right relationship with humankind as a gift from God—that is the prevailing theme of Paul's letter to the Romans. It's ironic that the great biblical spokesperson for the grace of God is the same person who was the zealous spokesperson for the laws of tradition as the means of being made right with God. When on the side of law, he was called Saul, the Pharisee who sat at the feet of Gamaliel, the great and wise teacher of law.

When on the side of the grace and love of God, he is called Paul, the Greek expression for Saul. For many reasons, Paul feels called to carry the good news of the risen Christ beyond the geographical boundaries of Palestine to Asia Minor, Macedonia, and Greece, inhabited primarily by Gentiles. His long-term plan also includes Italy and Spain.

Early in his ministry he collides with Jewish converts who insist that Gentiles have to become Jews before they can be made right with God. The avenue to Judaism was through circumcision. This creates a conflict for Paul. With the law, right relationship is based on perfect obedience; therefore, there is no certainty the relationship is actualized. God's grace, on the other hand, begins with a relationship with God and inclusion into the family of faith very much like a baby being received by loving parents into their family at the moment of birth. With the relationship settled once and for all, Paul realizes followers of Christ are set free to develop their spiritual gifts and grow toward their potential. Rules and laws then assume a supportive role for spiritual growth. They flow from grace.

Paul wrote his letter to the Romans near the end of his journeys to Asia Minor and Greece (Romans 15:23) following the practice of ministry in places like Ephesus, Galatia, and Corinth. The first step in moving away from being a Jewish sect and accepting the primacy of the grace of God occurs at the Council of Jerusalem (Acts 15). At the council, the leadership in the early church decides that Gentile converts do not have to be circumcised. The council affirms salvation by the grace of God through faith in Jesus Christ. This, however, was a compromise because the leadership imposed three other rules upon the Gentiles: eat no food offered to idols, eat no blood, and do not practice sexual immorality or fornication. At the moment Paul seems satisfied with the compromise, but his letters to the Galatians and Romans reveal a change of mind.

Many of Paul's letters are responses to congregations experiencing problems, congregations given birth under his leadership. Although Paul knew many people in the church in Rome, he did not have firsthand experience with the congregation. His letter is a carefully crafted theological treatise supported by his practical experiences in Asia Minor and Greece.[13]

The overriding theme of the letter focuses on how people are made right with God and how people are to live with one another. There are four major divisions to this letter: introduction (1:1-15), our relationship with God or theological (1:16-11:36), our relationship with fellow humans or ethical (12:1-15:21), and conclusion (15:22-16:27). At this time, take a few minutes and read Paul's letter to the Romans.

Introduction—Romans 1:1-15

Paul begins his letter the way we normally conclude our letters, with his signature. At the onset Paul clearly prepares the reader for good news, the news that God has fulfilled the promise proclaimed by the prophets long ago by coming in Jesus Christ. He believes God has called him as apostle to tell all nations, including Rome, they are loved by God and called to be God's people. He extends to them a blessing of peace and grace. He concludes the introduction with words of commendation to the Roman Christians, thanking God for their faith, which has the whole world talking. The tenor of Paul's letter begins with God, good news, Jesus Christ, hospitality, grace, peace, faith, and gratitude. If Paul remains true to his introduction, the major portion of his letter should amplify his positive perspective.[14]

Our Relationship with God: Theology; Romans 1:16-11:36

Paul begins this section with the theme statement that reflects the heart of his theology: "I am not ashamed of the gospel; it is the power of God for salvation to everyone who has faith . . . For in it the righteousness of God is revealed through faith for faith . . . As it is written, "the one who is righteous will live by faith" (1:16-17). Now read Romans 1:18-3:20.

The Human Condition: 1:18-3:20

After hanging the banner of "good news" over the text of his letter, Paul then reviews the human condition with the recipients of his letter. Paul believes the human condition of sinfulness without the gospel leads to ungodly living. First, he summarizes the experience of Gentiles whose knowledge of God, vague and nebulous as it may be, comes through observation of God's power and through nature. Even though they possess God awareness, Paul says, Gentiles have attempted to live without honoring and thanking God. With lives totally void of God, they worship the objects of God's creation giving devotion to idols. Paul's major concern is idolatry.

Some are controlled by their sexual passions, allowing the practice of sexuality to become an end to itself, which is the practice of idolatry. It is a reminder of the Epicurean way of life popular in the Roman culture in the first century: "eat, drink, and be merry, for tomorrow we die." Especially in this era of Roman history with Nero and other emperors possessing young male slaves to use and abuse sexually and the presence of public baths and brothels to satisfy sexual appetites, it would be remiss of Paul not to refer to this extreme form of immorality even though his knowledge is secondhand.

In his discourse about Gentiles, Paul describes behavior and activity that is fully centered upon self. In verses 26-27, he speaks of men and women who are involved in sexual activity that is unnatural, and he specifically mentions men with men. At no point does Paul make reference to sexual orientation, only unnatural sexual activity. Paul could be describing same-gender sexual activity among heterosexual persons. He very likely viewed all humans to be heterosexual with a few who chose to participate in same-gender sexual activity. For this reason, he may be declaring same-gender sexual activity to be unnatural. Consistent with his references to same-gender sexual activity in letters to the Corinthians and to Timothy, Paul is probably referring to sexual activity that occurs in brothels where male and female prostitutes are for hire. Gender matching in these arenas has no rigid pattern; anything goes. Paul describes sexual behavior that is promiscuous, a sexual episode not bound by a promise of love and faithfulness.

Although this passage has often been cited as condemning present-day homosexuality, it is unlikely Paul is addressing a homosexual community. His focus is on persons who are totally obsessed with sexual passion and behavior even with those of the same gender. First, the absence of any word about sexual orientation is significant. Being homosexual is first and primarily who a person is. The same is true in being heterosexual. To say that I am heterosexual does not mean that I am presently engaged in heterosexual activity or homosexual activity. More important, being heterosexual or homosexual has no connection with choice. I cannot recall a moment in my life when I chose to be heterosexual. According to my homosexual friends and acquaintances, the same is true for them. The lust and activity he describes likely involves heterosexual males and females, but there is no certainty of that conclusion either.

Second, this passage is clearly not referring to same-gender couples who are living in committed, responsible, loving, and faithful relationships who desire to have their monogamous partnership framed with vows and validated by their faith community and supported by family and community as described in the previous chapter's ethical situation. The term *unnatural* does not automatically make an action sinful or evil. When medical doctors use life-support equipment or machinery to extend a person's life, they are using a procedure that is unnatural, not necessarily evil.

Paul continues with examples of excessive ungodly behavior among some Gentiles. Some are filled with wickedness, filled with greed, filled with evil, filled with vice, filled with jealousy and committed to devising more plans of evil. They have no conscience, do not keep promises, and practice no kindness. In this section, note how often the absolute terms *filled* and *no* are used. These people know better, and yet they actually encourage others to behave in the same extreme way. Obviously, Paul is not referring to the average person on the street; he has created a prototype of behavior that can occur when sinful humans are left to their own idolatrous devices. Paul Achtemeier writes: "Rather, the wrath which God visits on sinful humanity consists in simply letting humanity have its own way . . . He (God) withdraws the gracious power of his absolute lordship and allows other lordships to prevail."[15]

Remember, Paul has had no firsthand exposure or experience with the Roman culture although he probably was exposed to facets of a similar Gentile lifestyle in Asia Minor and Greece that allows him to generalize. In these fifteen verses of the first chapter of Romans, Paul illustrates that living without God and practicing idolatry lead to an obsession with self-centeredness and licentious behavior. In fact, without God humans lose their greatest source of support in dealing with their self-centered condition. See chapter three of this book for more information.

Next, Paul uses twenty-nine verses to describe the Jewish dilemma, the people who claim belief in God. In the end, Paul feels they are no better than Gentiles. Once again, I think Paul is not speaking of all Jews; he is generalizing. It is clearer in this case: "Therefore you have no excuse, whoever you are, when you judge others" (2:1). Paul's tone becomes more conditional in this section rather than definitive as he was with his summary of Gentile behavior; nevertheless, he clearly emphasizes that self-righteousness that leads to judging others actually puts the Jew on the same behavior plane as the one being judged. Likely, Paul has in mind the judging attitude of the Jews toward Gentiles. He continues speaking to law-abiding Jews, suggesting what they really despise is the kind and tolerant nature of God. Once again, this could be an oblique reference to God's acceptance of Gentiles, causing the obedient Jew to become jealous and frustrated. A similar response is made by the elder brother in Jesus' parable of the prodigal son. Self-righteousness and a loving, gracious, and merciful God do not mesh well.

Sounding like Jesus, Paul says it's not only the external thing we do and revere that counts, like circumcision and the law. What is more important is the equipping of one's heart through the work of God's spirit. Once again, Paul's point is that both Jew and Gentile struggle with the condition of self-centeredness, and the effort to make oneself right with God through law leads to self-righteousness, the epitome of self-centeredness. When laws come first or stand alone, they lead us down a dead-end street. They treat the symptoms, not the disease. They do identify the problem and provide guidance for living.

In the end, law serves as a reminder of our sinfulness or self-centeredness, the human condition that needs to be acknowledged by all people. Bruce Bawer writes: "The fact is that most churches that seek to be churches of love need to acknowledge evil more often and more emphatically than they do . . . Unless one is a privileged person who has had a very fortunate life, one will eventually find such preaching inadequate to one's situation."[16]

God Acts with Grace

Read Romans 3:21; 11:36

Paul emphasizes that God provides an alternative to either a life of license characterized by his description of the Gentiles or a life of law characterized by his description of religious Jew. That alternative is concisely stated in Romans 3:21-31 and summarized in verse 24: "they are now justified by his (God's) grace as a gift, through the redemption that is in Christ Jesus." Paul states that doing what law requires does not make people right with God. God has taken the initiative in helping deal with our sinful condition that alienates us from God and from humankind. Through faith in Jesus Christ our relationship with God and with others is restored. Grace is God's alternative and becomes the highest way for us in the context of Paul's message to the Romans.[17]

In the remaining chapters, Paul stresses the importance of faith or trust as the important link that connects us with Jesus Christ, and consequently, with God. Even Abraham, the father of the Hebrews, discovered his relationship with God through faith. Paul then shows that Christ is God's expression of love for the human race. He becomes the second Adam, the second human. Unlike the first human and those to follow, Jesus remains faithful to God to the very end. As human beings are committed to Christ rather than law, they are set free to experience life as God intends, no longer enslaved by their self-centered condition, but in Christ human beings are inspired to look beyond themselves and grow toward the human (wholeness) God created them to be.[18]

Well, what about law? Paul encourages readers of his letter not to do away with law, but to uphold it (3:31); however, since we live under grace, Christ has taken the place of the law. As he said himself, "I have fulfilled the law" (Matthew 5:17). This means the law's role is secondary alongside the way, the mind, and the spirit of Christ. The law in no way makes us right with God. In chapters 6 and 7 Paul emphasizes that God's grace has set us free from enslavement to sin and sets us free to live the new life in Christ. He writes: "But now we are discharged from the law, dead to that which held us captive, so that we are slaves not under the old written code but in the new life of the Spirit" (7:6). The grace of God in Christ helps us maintain the perspective that law comes through God's grace and does not stand alone or above grace.

Paul now continues in his letter to show that God's spirit brings us into a life in union with Christ Jesus. This union enables us to move beyond the recycling mode of sin and death. In the place of law, Paul substitutes the grace of God as the most effective means to diminish self-centered behavior. Paul even says law increases sin (5:20). That is understandable because adherence to law requires excessive attention upon self, while grace compels us to focus beyond self to Christ. Throughout his ministry, Christ confronts legalism; he reminds the religious leaders that the Sabbath (law) was created for the wellbeing of human beings; human beings were not created for the Sabbath (law) (Mark 2:27).

In chapter 8 Paul teaches that God's spirit encourages and strengthens those who live in Christ. In a time and culture where people relied on laws supported by force and fear to counter evil and greed, violent acts, and exploitation, Paul says to the Roman Christians God's love is more powerful than any human force in all creation, "nor anything else in all creation, will be able to separate us from the love of God in Christ Jesus our Lord" (8:39). The real test of trust in Christ and this promise comes when Christians move beyond acceptance of salvation by the grace of God to the courage to live the Christian life by grace and love.

In the remaining passages of this section, Paul laments over the people of his heritage, the people of Israel, many of whom have relied upon perfect obedience to the laws of tradition as the means of being made right with God. He repeats the message of the good news of God's grace and love over and over again, declaring in faith that God's mercy, God's grace, God's love, and God's salvation are for all people, Jew and Gentile. Paul Achtemeier sums it up well: "God's motivation in all this? Grace! Paul apparently cannot overemphasize that point. He returns to it again and again."[19] In the end, Paul has faith that sometime in the future "all Israel will be saved" (11:26), for their stubbornness is not permanent. Paul then concludes his theological section with a salutation to God: "To God be the glory forever! Amen"(11:36). Now read Romans 3:21-11:36, again comparing it to this brief commentary that highlights God's grace over obedience to rules as the means of being made right with God.

Our Relationship with Fellow Humans: Ethical

Read Romans 12:1; 15:21

In this section Paul moves from an emphasis on living in relationship with God to a Christian relationship among human beings, from the vertical to the horizontal. At the onset of chapter 12, Paul makes it clear that a radical shift occurs. This shift requires total devotion to God: "present your bodies as a living sacrifice" (12:1). Living by law is linear and hierarchical where power and authority flow from the top down, where insiders are clearly discernible from outsiders, where morality is measured externally, where people have clearly defined roles in life, and where the emphasis is upon the individual rather than the community.

Paul uses the image of a human body to describe how followers of Christ are connected with each other and together are connected to their leader, who is Jesus Christ. He uses this same imagery in his letter to Christians in Corinth, Colossae, and Ephesus. Living by grace, first means living in community, a body. Second, Christians as individual members work together. Third, all members of the body are important as they work together for the good of the entire body. Fourth, all members of the body receive direction for their mission from the same source, the head, who is Jesus Christ. Living by grace then means working together as a team, affirming the gifts of all the different members of the team, and giving all an opportunity to use their gifts for the common good. William Easum writes: "If a church emphasizes spiritual gifts, it is essential that it also gives permission for everyone to use his or her spiritual gift. It is disastrous to encourage people to discover what God created them to do and then tell them they can't use their gifts; it is also unethical."[20]

Paul devotes the remainder of this section giving examples of living by grace and love rather than living by law. He encourages followers of Christ to care for and nurture one another, to respond to the physical needs of others, to pray for those who oppose you, to maintain a balanced concern for all people, to live in peace with all people, to leave the judging to God, to overcome evil with good, to be a supportive citizen to those called by God in secular positions of authority, to be sensitive to the spiritual needs of one another, to support the weak in the faith, to seek the highest good of all people, and to be hospitable and accepting. Love and grace do have concrete substance. If people were busy practicing love and grace, self-centeredness would significantly diminish.

Paul summarizes what it means to live by love and grace when he says: "Owe no one anything, except to love one another; for the one who loves another has fulfilled the law . . . Any of the commandments are summed up in this word, love your neighbor as yourself. Love does no wrong to a neighbor; therefore, love is the fulfilling of the law" (13:8-10). Much of what Paul says in the ethical section of his letter resonates with Jesus' Sermon on the Mount and his teachings and example of love and grace. All are examples that law emerges through grace in the form of love.

Also, for Paul there is no compromise concerning the move from living by law to living by grace and love. "It is clear from the opening verse that grace is to affect the whole of human life."[21] Do you remember the compromise, the trade-off Paul accepted at the Jerusalem Council described in Acts 15? For freeing Gentile converts from being circumcised, Paul consented to a letter written to them that forbade eating meat offered to idols. At the time of the Jerusalem Council, the early church was making a transition from primary focus on law as the means to salvation to a primary focus on grace as the means to salvation. Paul said yes to the letter containing the three prohibitions, but only for the time being. He did not remain with the compromise. It still contained too much law for living the Christian life. When he writes the ethical section of his letter to the Romans, Paul completes the transition from law to grace as the first and primary focus for Christian ethics.

In the fourteenth chapter, Paul displays the high ethic of gracious living in the practice of hospitality to those who are weak in the faith as well as those who are strong in the faith. "Some believe in eating anything, while the weak eat only vegetables. Those who eat must not despise those who abstain, and those who abstain must not pass judgment on those who eat, for God has welcomed them" (14:2). Then later, Paul says, "I know and am persuaded in the Lord Jesus that nothing is unclean in itself" (14:14). Very likely he is referring to meat offered to idols, the practice forbidden in the letter written to the Gentile Christians in Galatia (Acts 15).

In his letter to the Corinthians, Paul says the same thing about eating meat offered to idols (1 Corinthians 9:10; 10). In the book of Acts, we see the young church making a transition from law as a primary focus for ethics to grace and love. This transition creates great stress and tension because in the first century many Christians are Jewish who were nurtured on innumerable rules centered on the holiness code, ritual and ceremonial law, as well as the Ten Commandments. In their eyes, obedience to all law was the means for being made right with God. By the time Paul writes to the Roman Church, he regained the perspective of law coming through grace.

In this chapter about food and the observance of holy days, Paul shows that genuine grace and love will compel the Christian to be supportive to those who are weak in the faith, even if it means refraining from eating certain foods until the new Christian completes the transition from previous religious practices to the experience of union with Christ and the reality of grace. Such sensitivity reflects another aspect of the gracious hospitality of God, so that all may be included and nurtured in Christ's body. This high calling of empathy illustrates, once again, how the new Christ ethic of grace and love carry the Christian far beyond obedience to the law.

Some have mistakenly criticized the grace/love ethic to be void of absolutes. The absolute is very clear, to use the words of Paul, "for the one who loves another has fulfilled the law" (Romans 13:8). Love and grace become the absolutes in the ethic of Jesus and Paul with law a necessary servant of both, but the church through history has wavered in upholding this absolute both in profession and practice, in theology and ethic by giving more allegiance to the secondary absolutes contained in law. Now, reread Romans 12:1; 15:21.

Conclusion

Read Romans 15:22; 16:27

In the remaining verses, Paul returns to practical matters at hand: his desire to visit Rome soon, his imminent trip to Jerusalem with an offering for the poor, his request for prayer, his greeting to numerous friends in Rome, his appeal to avoid division, and his salutation. Paul, likely, writes this letter *en route* to Jerusalem while concluding his third missionary journey. His mind is on the future, "Where do I go from here? Rome and Spain are next, but I must do first things first and take the generous offering of these Christians to the church in Jerusalem."

As Paul goes toward Jerusalem, he seeks the prayers of his friends in Rome for two reasons: first, because the Jewish leaders who opposed the Christian movement strongly dislike Paul because he is a traitor to their cause and his life will be in danger; second, so that his Christian service will be honored by God's people in Jerusalem. Paul Achtemeier has a good point in his commentary. He suggests that Paul is concerned about how the Jewish Christians will receive the monetary gift from fellow Christians who are mostly Gentiles. To this point, it has been the Jewish Christians who have shared their spiritual blessing (Christ) with the Gentiles; now the offering enables the Gentile Christians to share their blessing with the Jewish Christians. "This means they are mutually indebted to one another and are on equal footing within the people of God . . . And if the people of God are unified, then there are in fact no second-class citizens. Then racial origin will make no more difference than one's gender or social standing as far as one's Christian status is concerned: all will be one in Christ" (Gal. 3:28).[22] In this practical sense we see how the power of grace unifies all the differing parts.

In his final salutation, Paul concludes with emphasis on God and the good news embodied in Jesus Christ. That same positive, uplifting spirit is the way Paul began this letter that emphasizes that God has taken the initiative in Christ and has done for us what we cannot do for ourselves: in the spirit of grace through trust in Jesus Christ we are made right with God, incorporated as full members into Christ's body, and are called to live by grace and love.

The Church Today: Grace/Love and Law

I believe at the onset of the new millennium the church and Christians are more threatened and baffled by the grace of God than any other facet of God's nature. Some would say this message is too good to be true and then dismiss its possibilities of truth. As mentioned in the introduction, grace runs counter to secular messages of self-sufficiency and pride in saying, *I earned it and deserve it.* Very likely, most threatening is the duel nature of grace: we receive salvation as a free gift from God, not because we have earned it, but at the same time we are called and enabled to live by grace. In the Reformed tradition grace that provides forgiveness and salvation has been termed *justification,* and grace that enables us to live a new life has been termed *sanctification,* which means we are enabled to extend grace to others as God has extended grace to us. We are to accept *sinful* others unconditionally as God accepts *sinful* us without conditions. That's threatening and difficult. Saved by grace, yes! Live by grace, sometimes!

We need all the help we can get to maintain congruency between what we say we believe and how we live out our profession. This chapter, first, enables us to see the strength of grace in the life and ministry of Jesus Christ. Second, it reveals the difficult transition the early church made with the help of the Holy Spirit's presence to move away from being a Jewish sect bound by thousands of ceremonial and purity laws to become the Church of Jesus Christ continuing his ministry of love and grace. Third, this chapter reviews the strength of grace in Paul's letter to the Romans, written to assure them that salvation is a free gift of God through trust in Christ who frees them to live by grace. These three biblical sources provide support as we try to maintain integrity as people of love and grace when opposed from those who claim we are not being faithful to scripture. Nothing can be more biblical than being Christ followers who maintain a perspective for life embraced by God's grace.

I was in the practice of ministry in the Presbyterian Church for forty-one years. During this period of time I have served only two churches: one in Alabama during the turbulent sixties, another in Athens, Georgia since 1971. I have experienced firsthand the tension our denomination and other mainstream denominations faced in bearing witness to the grace and love of God by standing alongside powerless and/or oppressed people in our time. In the South we moved faster than our culture and some Christian denominations in practicing hospitality to all races of people and validating God's gifts for ministry among women as well as men.

As a result, a segment of our denomination became angry, declaring that we had forsaken biblical truth by reflecting secular values. In reality it was the secular values of exclusivity and elitism that were being challenged through the appeal of God's justice and love for minorities and women. More than forty years have passed; most in our denomination today applaud those decisions of justice as reflecting courageously the way of Christ, the head of church as well as the heart of biblical truth. It's interesting to me how much clearer the vision of the whole church of God becomes when a cause becomes acceptable to the majority. We know now that prior to the movement for civil rights for African-Americans and equal rights for women, the values of the church were enmeshed with the values of secular society.

The really great movements remembered in world history have often been those inspired by a religious faith that has the dignity and worth of persons as their underlying basis. The Protestant Reformation serves as a good example and was definitely inspired by God's grace and God's love for human beings. The influence of Mahatma Gandhi in achieving independence for India, the Civil Rights movement in the United States and in South Africa are other examples. In contrast, often when the church has sought power for self it has left a dark blot in history as witnessed by the Crusades in the Middle Ages, the Inquisition following the Renaissance, and second-class citizenship for women and the support of slavery and segregation in America. We are always living in a time when God's grace and love need to be the normative basis for decision-making, but too often the church takes refuge into law that can be manipulated to support self-serving ends. It can also be used to marginalize people.

God's grace and love revealed in the word written and the word who became human are powerful resources in helping Christian denominations take the lead in making decisions that not only support people in celebrating their full humanity, but also in strengthening marriage and the family. As always, it requires courage and faith as the church continues the ministry of Christ.

Has the church in these affluent times lost confidence in the power of God's grace and love? I hope not, because we live in a secular culture that relies upon laws and rules. The business community operates by legal contracts. Large corporations have their own legal counselors. Even marriage, to be recognized, begins with a civil contract between a man and woman. An athletic contest would evolve into chaos and confusion, and very likely violence if it were not monitored by rules and enforced by designated officials. Everywhere we turn we encounter rules: from driving an automobile to completing tax forms, from starting a business to building a home, and from hunting and fishing to using music written by another person. You name it; there is a law connected with it to assure that life is lived decently and in order. Yet laws have their limits, as seen in the extent of crime in the United States. From experience, we know laws have not been successful in making people live in healthy (right) relationships.

It seems to me, as our society becomes more dependent upon law the less it views love and grace as a viable option or powerful alternative. So our culture is saying, "People should get what they deserve either negatively or positively, earn their own way, reap what they sow." Laws and rules need to emerge from grace and love, and be enforced in the same spirit.

Why then are grace and love not chosen as the primary focus of corporate and civil life? Their differences may give a clue for an answer to that question:

1) Grace and love are personal and intimate; they have no life without relationships, while law often becomes an impersonal objective standard that can be used for judging; it sometimes separates people from one another. At that point it loses power and need for existence in personal and intimate situations; people normally do not need laws to motivate them to live in relationships.

2) Grace and love require trust; law demands accountability.

3) Grace and love are gifts given and received; law is imposed and obeyed.

4) Grace and love evoke gratitude; law creates ownership and pride.

5) Grace and love create interdependence and community; law encourages individualism and self-sufficiency.

Some feel that grace without law, without demands, without clear standards of morality is nothing but cheap grace. The Pharisees had the same reaction to Jesus' teaching and demonstration of grace. Both responses fail to see that grace enhances the quality of life and relationships. While law governs relationships, grace creates, sustains, and enriches relationships. Upon realizing that we are accepted by God through faith in Jesus Christ in spite of our self-centered condition, through gratitude we accept others as God accepts us. That's costly grace, because the Christian gives up self to continue the ministry of Christ. It's costly because it is discipleship, but it is grace because followers of Christ find genuine life by losing their lives in Christ. Saved by grace, yes! Live by grace, yes! Both are possible because of God's ever present help.

I am not suggesting that our culture needs to be law free. What I am suggesting is that when the law becomes the primary focus for living and seen as the solution to all the sinful ways of humanity, it in reality becomes part of the problem rather than the solution. The eradication of laws is not the answer. It does no good to go from one extreme to the other. Law needs a perspective, not stand alone as an end to itself. When seen emerging from grace, it serves a positive guiding purpose; it has spirit, it has passion, it has flexibility, it serves God, who is full of grace and truth.

American Christians live in two worlds. We are citizens of the United States that is governed by laws. We are also members of the body of Christ, the church. We have one foot in our culture and one foot in the church. Since we are surrounded by laws and rules designed to maintain order and protect human life in our society, we are naturally influenced to structure church life and the Christian life in the same pattern. To some extent we can do no other, and there is nothing wrong when both the culture and the church assume similar positions that are consistent to the ways of Christ and biblical truth. Nonetheless, there are times in the life of the Christian community when the grace of God appears lost. When viewed alongside the teaching and example of Christ, the experience of the early church, and the writings of Paul, the intense emphasis upon law in our culture today seems to have greatly influenced the church.

Since the mid-nineties, mainstream denominations have felt the growing influence of the legal perspective. I suspect the reasons are many and diverse. Since it is the way of our culture, legalism already has a comfort level that grace and love do not. Since the turbulent sixties when mainstream denominations were strong proponents of love, grace, and justice, their membership numbers have fallen, while churches of law have grown. So rather than being strong examples of love and grace, mainstream denominations are more receptive to the law which then influences the creation of orthodox theology.

Shortly before we moved in the twenty-first century rules were adopted by some denominations to prohibit ordination of officers and ministers who are in committed same-gender partnerships. Some of these denominations are now reexamining those rules in light of the fullness of scripture and are making changes.

When love and grace prevail, the church will be proactive rather than reactive. It will be a hospital for all sinners, not a country club for those sinners who think they are better than the other sinners. It will be the dynamic arms of hospitality reaching out and welcoming all, rather than being a gate dependent upon the gatekeeper whose views of right and wrong change with the blowing of the wind and the majority who rule and change the rules.

When love and grace prevail, like Christ, the church will go far beyond the requirements of law; sometimes the church will err in decision-making, but the church of love and grace will faithfully continue the ministry of Christ and will view all humans as unrepeated miracles of God's creation. The church of love and grace will help all people identify God's calling for their lives and will encourage them to nurture their gifts, so they may use them in service to God and for the wellbeing of all God's creation. In the concluding words of Paul to the Romans: "To the only God, who alone is all-wise, be glory through Jesus Christ forever! Amen!"

Endnotes: Chapter Five

[1] Morton S. Enslin, "The New Testament Times: Palestine," *The Interpreter's Bible Vol. 7* (Nashville: Abingdon Press, 1951), p. 112.

[2] William Barclay, *The Gospel of St. Matthew Vol.2* (Philadelphia: The Westminster Press, 1975), pp. 281-82.

[3] Ibid., p. 302

[4] Markus Barth, *The Sermon on the Mount: Smythe Lectures* (Decatur, GA: Society of Theological Scholarship, 1962), pp. 18-24.

[5] Ibid., pp. 32-43.

[6] Barclay, *Gospel of St. Matthew Vol.2*, pp. 45-57.

[7] Ibid., p. 30

8   Bruce Bawer, *Stealing Jesus* (New York: Three Rivers Press, 1995), p. 326.

9   Theodore P. Ferris, "Exposition," *The Interpreter's Bible Vol.* 9 (Nashville: Abingdon Press, 1951), pp. 107-117.

10 William Barclay, *The Acts of the Apostles* (Edinburgh: The Saint Andrew Press, 1961), pp. 67.

11 William Willimon, "Acts," *Interpretation: A Bible Commentary for Teaching and Preaching* (Atlanta: John Knox Press, 1988), pp. 128-29.

12 Ferris, "Exposition," *The Interpreter's Bible* Vol. 9, pp. 404-205.

13 John Knox, "The Introduction," *The Interpreter's Bible* Vol. 9 (Nashville: Abingdon Press, 1951), pp. 355-378.

14 William Barclay, *The Letter to the Romans* (Edinburgh: The Saint Andrew Press, 1955), pp. 1-8.

15 Paul Achtemeier, "Romans," *Interpretation: A Bible Commentary for Teaching and Preaching* (Louisville: John Knox Press, 1985), p. 40.

16 Bawer, *Stealing Jesus, p. 316.*

17 Gerald R. Cragg, "Exposition," *The Interpreter's Bible Vol.* 9 (Nashville: Abingdon Press 1951), pp. 431-33.

18 Knox, "Exegesis," *The Interpreter's Bible Vol.* 9, pp. 46-48.

19 Achtemeier, p. 189.

20 William M. Easum, *Sacred Cows Make Gourmet Burgers* (Nashville: Abingdon Press, 1995), p. 171.

21 Achtemeier, p. 195

22 Ibid, p. 231.

CHAPTER SIX

Common Ground: Created to Live in Fulfilling Relationships

Examining a Basic Need for All Human Beings

No man is an island, entire of itself; every man is a piece of the continent, a part of the main. If a clod be washed away by the sea, Europe is the less, as well as if a promontory were, as well as if a manor of thy friends or of thine own were. Any man's death diminishes me, because I am involved in mankind; and therefore never send to know for whom the bell tolls: it tolls for thee.
Meditation 17, "Devotions upon Emergent Occasions," John Donne

In a *National Geographic* article Joel Swerdlow indicates that many Chinese migrating to the United States move to Chinatown in New York City where cheap housing and jobs are found. Most important, in Chinatown they quickly become part of the community with fellow Chinese. Poverty, hard work, deprived and unclean living conditions are secondary to relationships. Relationship even rises above satisfying sexual needs; the word *sex* was not mentioned in the article, yet many husbands, wives, and families were separated, but that is not the end of the story.

One man says, "When I am here, my heart is in China." He has a telephone in his one-room residence that he uses to call his family in Fujian; his monthly telephone bill often exceeds his monthly bill for food.[1] Without batting an eye, we say that some of the basic needs for existence are food, clothing, and shelter, but what about a fulfilling relationship with fellow human beings? An intimate relationship with his family was obviously a basic need for this man from Fujian, China. In varying degrees all human beings have a basic need to live in a fulfilling relationship marked by love.

Four Relational Concepts in Scripture

Four biblical concepts, three originating in the Old Testament and one in the New Testament, appear to be saying the same thing. The first image is found in the first chapter of Genesis: "So God created humankind in his image, in the image of God he created them: male and female he created them" (Genesis 1:27). Karl Barth, interprets *image of God* to mean the ability to enter into relationship, a gift of partnership given by God, to be with God, and in partnership with fellow humans. It is God's blessing of being human, not possessed by humans but the very essence of being human.[2] Claus Westermann writes: "the uniqueness of human beings consists in their being God's counterparts. Relationship with God is not something that is added to human existence; humans are created in such a way that their very existence is intended to be the relationship to God."[3] This also means that humans are created to live in community with other humans, and so we have the origin and basic purpose of "family."

Barth and Westermann go one step further with the concept, *image of god*. Not only are humans created to exist in relationship with God but also with one another. Who I am as an individual is limited or expanded by fellow humanity; therefore, to grow toward my potential as a human, it is necessary to live in relationship with other humans.[4] Growth brings us back to the big picture of God, myself, and others. As I live in relationship reflecting the character of God, it enhances the spiritual growth of others, and as others living in relationship with me reflect the character of God, it enhances my growth. God, self, others—a dynamic picture of what it means to be created *in the image of God,* a beautiful concept of partnership.

The second image is found in the second story of creation following God's crafting the creature (*ha adam*) from the dust of the earth and putting the man (dust creature) in the garden to till it and keep it. "Then the Lord God said, 'It is not good that the man should be alone; I will make him a helper as his partner'" (Genesis 2:18). The experience of loneliness occurs before the experience of sinfulness. Once again, this image depicts a picture of incompleteness, a hungering and thirsting, a longing, a desperate unfulfilled need in being alone, outside an intimate relationship with another human. John Douglas Hall feels that this sense of loneliness is "the stuff (the condition) out of which some types of human suffering are made . . . not the filled, positive solitude that we experience as a part of the goodness of life."[5]

The crafting of animals from the dust of the ground was insufficient in fulfilling the need of community and relationship. Finally, the Lord takes the essence of the creature and creates another human, a female or woman. Some biblical scholars believe that the man (*ha adam*) remains a dust creature till the creation of the female. At that point, the man (*ha adam*) is a new creature (male) as well, which parallels the first story of creation of the male and female created simultaneously. I realize this creates a textual problem with Paul's statement to Timothy that the man was created first (1 Timothy 2:13-15).

Nonetheless, the text emphasizes that loneliness can only be addressed fully by living in relationship with another human, one of the same essence. In this second story of creation after creating a steward partner, the Lord God attempts to resolve the loneliness of man (*ha adam*). The Lord creates animals. That is not totally satisfying. Although the presence of animals contributes much to the quality of life for some, the sense of loneliness provides the inner signal that humans are created to live in relationship with those of the same essence. The female is then created from the man *(ha adam)*. They are of the same essence. At this point, the main concern is to resolve loneliness, so God creates a partner. Beforehand, no mention of marriage is made in reference to the creation of partners. When animals and birds are created to resolve the man's loneliness, pairs (male and female) are not mentioned.

Some people believe this account documents God's intention that intimate relational experiences should only occur in marriage among male and female. I believe the second major point of passage is to address the problem of loneliness by creating another human being who is female. Now that male and female are present, then the text describes the rationale for marriage and sexual intimacy in marriage: "that is why a man leaves his father and mother and is united to his wife, and they become one." This statement occurs outside the creation drama as an aside comment, like *by the way*. Also, it cannot be part of the drama because father and mother are mentioned. In the creation drama of satisfying man's *(ha adam)* loneliness, it is too soon for a mother and father to come on stage.

So to focus upon marriage in the second account of creation is to lose sight of its main point. Following the story of the first man and woman, there is nothing in scripture that dictates a particular matching of genders to respond effectively to the signal of loneliness. Providing the opportunity of relationship with humankind, whatever be the gender, was God's intention in creating woman (Eve). From my reading of scripture, I cannot recall the story of a human being living totally alone without a relationship with someone.

The third relational image found in scripture God likewise creates: "I will establish my covenant between me and you, and your offspring after you throughout their generations, for an everlasting covenant to be God to you and to your offspring after you" (Genesis 17:7). The covenant promise of God renewed over and over again with Israel and then fulfilled in Christ creates another important picture of relationship which God initiates with humankind.

In the covenant with Abram, relationships are broadened considerably, involving communities of people both male and female, young and old. From the divine/human relationship we have a model for relationships between human beings. The commandments given to Moses on Mt. Sinai were designed to enhance the quality of humanity's relationship with both God and humankind. Covenant, unlike the previous relational images, involves a promise or contract agreement between two or more parties. John Patton and Bryan Childs write: "It (covenant) requires true relationship and the acknowledgment of differences, and therefore also involves considerable creativity."[6]

The fourth relational image was created by the apostle Paul in describing the church: "Now you are the body of Christ and individually members of it" (1 Corinthians 12:27). The image of a human body clearly communicates the necessity of relationships if there is to be life and work. There is no way for the arm of the body to be the arm without most of the other parts of the body, and the same is true for the other members of the human body. In the body image there is no existence, purpose, identity, and development without the relationship of the individual members to the whole.

William Easum believes, "the Body of Christ is the best biblical image to connect with the *Quantum Age.* First, the Body of Christ points toward clear images from our common experiences with our own bodies; such images as cooperation, community, equality, mutual trust, networks, unity (but never uniformity or conformity) . . . Second, the Body of Christ is composed of networks and relationships that are in daily flux. New relationships are formed at will and networks emerge to fit the situation at hand . . . Third, Christians need to recover the continuity between body, mind, and spirit (the image of the body reminds us of the importance of its parts in connection with the whole, once again emphasizing communal relationships) . . . Fourth, the Body of Christ downplays the chauvinistic, male-dominated models blessed by many established congregations."[7]

There are other biblical images that likewise emphasize the importance of relationship such as: *household of God, kingdom of God, fellowship of believers, holy nation, family of God, and community and priesthood of all believers.* The importance of humankind created to live in relationships represents a major thread woven through every book in the Old and New Testaments. The many stories of faith included in scripture emphasize the value of living in a three-dimensional relationship to experience wholeness: relationship with the creator God, relationship with humankind, and relationship with self. These stories of faith struggle with the critical question: how is this done most effectively?

Guides for Relational Living: Law or Love

The Old Testament is not as concerned about the structure of human relationships as much as quality within the relationship, whatever be the structure. Structure, very likely, was cultural, for most of the nations of people in the Middle East possessed similar structures such as marriage, roles of husband/wife, slavery, and governance. Scripture attempts to give guidance in developing quality relationships within the given structure. So through grace God gives Moses the Decalogue as the general guide to be followed; it accompanies God's deliverance of the Hebrews from bondage in Egypt. Relationships are to be marked by love and responsibility toward God and toward one another. The key to all relationships begins with relationship with God: "Hear, O Israel: the Lord is our God, and the Lord alone. You shall love the Lord your God with all your heart, and with all your soul, and with all your might" (Deuteronomy 6:4-5). Although not part of this passage, Leviticus contains a summary of six commandments of the Decalogue: ". . . but you shall love your neighbor as yourself" (Leviticus 19:18b). As part of the Old Testament *holiness code* (Leviticus 17-26) this particular command is retained by Jesus, Paul, and the church as the umbrella over Christian ethics. Jesus, Paul, and the church dispensed with much of the *holiness code.*

The Ten Commandments were originally given to maintain unity and solidarity of the community of Israel, God's people, as well as guiding the people to live in fulfilling relationships reflecting the sacred quality of human life. Also, the laws were given for the sake of survival since God called Israel to be a light to the nations. In summary, the Decalogue was given by God as a means to an end: to serve the wellbeing of humans in their relationship with God and with one another.

When Jesus began his ministry the Decalogue and the laws in the Pentateuch were insufficient in the eyes of the religious leaders: the teachers of the law, the scribes, and Pharisees. They began to interpret the meaning and purpose of each commandment creating an endless list of rules that were included in a book called the Talmud comprising the Mishnah and Gemara. These rules became part of Jewish tradition, sacred and binding to every Jew, but impossible to obey fully, especially for the "people of the land" who earned their living by farming and raising sheep and cattle. For example, the religious leaders' definition of work from tying a knot in a rope to walking more than 100 yards made it impossible for these people to keep the Sabbath law. Since the people believed they had to make themselves right with God through obeying law, they were overburdened and felt cut off from God.

As emphasized in the previous chapter, by the time of Christ the law was now being used in a way that caused many Hebrews to feel excluded under the guise of being sinners or outcasts. H. R. Anderson, Jr., in an article in *The Presbyterian Outlook,* asks, "Do you know how it feels to be excluded?" He then tells a personal experience of worship, sitting in a beautiful sanctuary, singing familiar hymns, and passing the peace, creating warm feelings of belonging. The time then came to celebrate the sacrament of Holy Communion. The congregation was invited to come forward to receive the elements, but only those who were members. He was not invited to participate; he was excluded. The feeling of exclusion hit him like a ton of bricks.[8]

Anderson writes, "The church has to have rules. But I felt the suffocating reality of being excluded from the gift that Christ had given me, Himself, because of a law. I didn't realize how exclusion felt until I felt it in another church . . . One of the ways Jesus measured the truth of something was by considering the fruit it bore. Lois (wife) and I were denied Christ by a law, well-meaning, reasonable to those on the inside, intended to uphold righteousness. But what of all those who were excluded from Christ as a result?"[9]

Anderson continues, "I can't imagine how Nelson Mandela felt, excluded from his people and his country by a law supported by a Reformed church. I can't imagine how Rosa Parks felt, excluded in the back of a bus, forced there by a law many Christians supported. I can't imagine how Presbyterian women felt when their church excluded them from service and ministry in spite of their call by the Holy Spirit. I cannot imagine how men and women today, gifted by the Holy Spirit for service and ministry, but with a different sexual orientation from the majority, feel when they are excluded from a life as full and meaningful and enriched and committed as all others in their church. But I know how I felt when a church excluded me from coming in faith to receive Christ . . . I know that pain, that alienation. And I know it is wrong."[10]

Laws and rules created and imposed that exclude people from the religious community and the support that comes in that relationship was the very thing that Jesus challenged in his ministry of grace and love. The purity laws found in the *holiness code* of Leviticus were used to exclude people from the community of faith. Jesus challenged those laws when he said: "But to eat without washing your hands as they say you should, this doesn't make you unclean" (Matthew 15:20). When he touched a man with a dreaded skin disease, ate with outcasts, held the hand of Jairus' dead daughter, talked with a bleeding woman in public who was healed by touching him, entertained Samaritans, Jesus was violating the Hebrew purity laws and showing that people in the eyes of God are more important than rules. Throughout his ministry he confirms that God calls us to live in fulfilling relationships, and those relationships are more important than all the petty rules devised by the religious leaders, which often serve as walls excluding people from being with the very doctor who can give them wholeness.

Jesus leaves no doubt concerning what he believes is the ultimate purpose of God's commandments: "The first is, 'Hear, O Israel: the Lord our God, the Lord is one; you shall love the Lord your God with all your heart, and with all your soul, and with all your mind, and with all your strength.' The second is this, 'You shall love your neighbor as yourself.'" He then adds an important footnote: "There is no other commandment greater than these" (Mark 12:29-31). Matthew adds: "On these two commandments hang all the law and prophets" (Matthew 22:40). Jesus then helps us understand that our neighbor even includes those who are difficult to love and would be identified as the worst of sinners: the enemy who persecutes us (Matthew 6:43-48); and the one (Samaritan) who has left the faith and forsaken our sacred tradition by embracing another religion (Luke 10:27-40).

The apostle Paul also emphasizes the sacred nature of relationships in all of his letters. Following his image of relationships by creating the picture of the Body of Christ and the important gifts of all its members, Paul then says, "And I will show you a more excellent way: if I have every gift God has created but do not have love, I am nothing" (1 Corinthians 12:31; 13:13). In most of Paul's letters he makes specific references to the supreme value of the presence of divine (*agape*) love in relationships. "For the one who loves another has fulfilled the Law" (Romans 13:8). When a container is filled, completeness has been reached. No other laws are necessary to give the relationship additional meaning. The love of God is sufficient to equip us to live in fulfilling relationships. Paul, like Jesus, feels the food laws (purity) of Leviticus have run their course and are being used for the wrong purpose (Romans 14).

To assure the reader that I have not selected a few verses from two segments of the New Testament (the Gospels and the writings of Paul, as important as they are) at the exclusion of the other writings, consider the letter to the Hebrews. The first twelve chapters give strong emphasis to our relationship with God as understood through Christ, while the remaining chapter focuses on our relationship with others: "Let mutual love continue. Do not neglect to show hospitality to strangers, for by doing that some have entertained angels without knowing it" (13:1). Consider the letter of James. James does not share Paul's excitement about doctrine. Yes, he talks about faith in God and prayer, but he is primarily concerned about how our love for God energizes our love for fellow humans. "For just as the body without the spirit is dead, so faith without works is also dead" (James 2:26).

What about the importance of relationships in the remaining books of the New Testament? It is Peter who gives us some of those corporate images of relationships: "you are a chosen race, a royal priesthood, a holy nation, God's own people, in order that you may proclaim the mighty acts of him who called you out of darkness into his marvelous light" (1 Peter 2:9). It is Peter who says, "Above all, maintain constant love for one another, for love covers a multitude of sins. Be hospitable to one another without complaining" (1 Peter 4:8-9).

Peter expresses great concern about excluding people created in the *image of God* whose being is dependent upon a relationship with God and God's people, the priesthood of believers. I think Peter would say do not put a sign out front or a note printed in the bulletin that reads *everyone welcomed* if you do not really mean it.

What about the importance of relationships in the letters of John? Perhaps, in no other book in scripture are we exposed to the importance of loving relationships so intensely as in John. The very essence of God is love in John's belief, and we are God's children, but if we authentically respond by loving God we will likewise love one another. Likewise, if we live in love, we can be assured that we live in union with God. And the wonderful gift that accompanies love is courage which casts out fear (1

John 4). In the final two books of the New Testament, Jude encourages us to "keep ourselves in the love of God" (1:21), and in Revelation the author believes at the time of God's final judgment, it will not be wealth, fame, and power that impress God; what is important to God is faithfulness in our relationships. And the good news is this: "I will be their God and they will be my children, says the Lord" (Revelation 21:7). Throughout scripture, we are reminded of God's faithfulness and everlasting covenant.

So scripture emphasizes *agape* love as the basic ingredient of every fulfilled relationship. In his book, *Tuesdays with Morrie,* Mitch Albom conveys the basic philosophy of Morrie Schwartz. Morrie opened the window of learning and life to Mitch when he was a student of Morrie's at Brandeis University. Many years later, when he learns that his favorite teacher is dying of Lou Gehrig's disease, Mitch meets with Morrie every Tuesday and listens to life's greatest lessons. In one interview, Morrie says, "The most important thing in life is to learn how to give out love and let love come in. Love is the only rational act."[11]

To love others as God loves us through Christ means accepting others unconditionally; it means helping others in time of need. It means seeking the highest good of the other person and being an advocate of justice. It means encouraging that person's continued growth and development. Love creates relationships that recognize the need for one another, and yet at the same time respects each person's unique identity. Where relationships are bound by love, both community and individuation will be present.

Beyond the Law

Once again, it is important to return to the place of law and rules in the maintenance of our relationships. Now that love binds us together, do we revert to rules to keep us together? Of course, in rearing children rules in the context of love are necessary; children need to know their boundaries. Bill Ogelsby, past professor of counseling at Union Seminary in Richmond, would say, "Create only enough rules to assure the safety and wellbeing of your children, and always let them know the basis (spirit) for the rule. Then, as children mature, the rules are reduced, but the purpose (the Spirit) becomes the primary guidance for living. For example, we tell a child *do not lie, tell the truth*. We continue by saying, *for honesty builds trusting relationships. We can count on each other; our word is good. Honesty also makes us feel good about ourselves, while lying makes us feel false or phony.* The spirit behind honesty is the maintenance of good relationships and a healthy self-concept. As the child experiences this spiritual value, the rule becomes unnecessary. So eventually the rule is replaced by the spiritual value.

I think this is what Paul means when he says, "For the one who loves another has fulfilled the law" (Romans13:8). At this point of spiritual maturity, the Christian has moved far beyond the requirements of a legalized religion and society, and lives by the fruits of the spirit. At the same time, we are obviously "upholding the law," as Paul suggests to the Romans (3:31). A spirit-driven life then reflects the fruits of the spirit as suggested by Paul in some of his letters. In a sense, fruits of the spirit are also gifts of the spirit, beginning with love. When seen as part of the nature of God, love also includes justice. These two powerful aspects of the nature of God enable humans created in God's likeness to live in faithful relationships marked by both freedom and responsibility, community and individuation, giving and receiving, power and respect, play and work and mutual servanthood in the midst of diversity.

Such relationships will not be driven by laws and rules imbued by competition and a desire to prevail and be right; they will be energized by a common relationship with Christ, the servant of all, and by the presence of God's spirit, who empowers us to be servants to one another. As a result, the maintenance of our relationships will rely upon the spiritual qualities of "joy, peace, patience, kindness, generosity, faithfulness, gentleness, and self-control. There is no law against such things" (Galatians 5:22-23).

Paul says it a little differently in his letter to the Colossians: "So if you have been raised with Christ, seek the things that are above, where Christ is . . . As God's chosen ones, holy and beloved, clothe yourselves with compassion, kindness, humility, meekness, and patience. Bear with one another, and if anyone has a complaint against another, forgive each other; just as the Lord has forgiven you, so you also must forgive. Above all, clothe yourselves with love, which binds everything together in perfect harmony. Let the peace of Christ rule in your hearts, to which indeed you were called in the one body and be thankful . . ." (Colossians 3:1, 12-15). This counsel Paul gives to the Christians in Colossae contains much of what has been emphasized in this chapter. It is Christ centered rather than rule centered.

Paul uses the relational image of the body where members are different but work together for the good of all; Paul gives us hope by reminding us that in Christ we are a new creation (new self); and finally we are reflectors of God's image in us by responding to the presence of God's spirit, thus clothing ourselves with the fruits of the spirit, thereby enriching our relationships, and likewise developing a healthier and happier self.

Here we have another example of living by grace rather than the law. In reality, the law has been fulfilled and far surpassed, but there will be times when it appears that the written law has been broken even though its purpose has been upheld. This will occur because law maintains perspective through grace, and the spirit of the law, as Jesus shows, takes precedence over living by the letter of the law. I believe this remains true for our method of biblical interpretation as well as our patterns of living. Grace reminds us how we reach our goals is equally important to the goal itself. As the practice of grace reflects the grace of Jesus Christ, it will be costly; it will not be cheap, for it reflects the conviction of Christ that every human being is valuable in God's sight and is created to live in fulfilling relationships. As John Buchanan writes, "There is a Christian word that desperately needs to be spoken about the value of every human life, the amazing grace of God in Jesus Christ that reaches out to each individual."[12]

What about Sin?

A word about sin needs to be spoken in the context of grace. As children, we were taught that we commit sins by breaking God's laws or even our parent's rules. In church we learned early "that sin is any want of conformity unto or transgression of the law of God." Once again, if this definition stands alone it becomes an example of *saved by grace but live by the law.* However, when sin is seen in the context of grace, it is best perceived as self-centeredness or selfishness. Grace creates a picture of unconditional graciousness, acceptance, and self-giving, the contrast to selfishness. The act of Adam and Eve in the garden is self-centered; they want to be like God. The spirit of self-centeredness actually prompts the act of disobedience. As a result, we have an internal condition that serves as the catalyst for the external action. We have sin (condition of selfishness) spelled with a capital *S* before we deal with sins (disobeying rules or selfish acts) spelled with a small *s*. Once again, we are dealing with the internal spirit or heart of the human, which lies at the core of sinful behavior. Jesus deals with this same image concerning the nature of humankind in a debate with the teachers of the law when he says: "For it is from within, from the human heart, that evil intentions come" (Mark 7:21).

So if as Jesus says the core of sinful acts lies within the condition of the human heart, a heart infected with selfishness, then healing of the heart needs to be the primary focus of the church. In this case, the church has a wonderful opportunity to be proactive rather than reactive, to be positive rather than negative. For the church can then help its people be visionary as it encourages its people to grow toward their potential by focusing upon Jesus Christ and the fruits of the spirit. Once again, laws imposed against negative behavior will have little impact on the human heart.

When a person is sick, it is like treating the symptom, the fever, rather than the infection, the core of the physical illness. Granted, there are times when the symptoms have to be treated when a person is sick; the same is true with sinfulness in a crisis situation until the condition receives treatment. We know from the history of Israel, when law becomes the primary force to encourage right living, it creates a small exclusive group of self-righteous insiders devoted to protecting their purity and status. It also creates a large divided group of outsiders who feel excluded, who become hopeless and apathetic.

What is the tragic consequence of sinful behavior prompted by the condition of selfishness? It impairs the sacred quality of our relationships. It wounds the heart of God, thus impairing our relationship with God, not that God shuts us out, but our self-centeredness compels us to shut God out because the light of God is too self-revealing for us. Recall the story of Adam and Eve; they hide from God out of shame, but in this anthropomorphic picture of God, the creator searches for Adam and Eve.

Sin wounds their relationship with God, but it also impairs their relationship with each other; they become competitive placing the blame elsewhere. This selfish act also wounds their self-image; with self-awareness they express shame for their nakedness, being seen for who they really are. Like air, like food, like protective shelter and clothing, the very thing we need the most for a healthy spiritual life and fulfilling relationships we impair and sometimes destroy. That is the tragic consequence of our self-centered behavior.

In response, the greatest portion of the biblical story describes the relentless nature of the spirit of God to heal the human heart. In Christ we are given hope God continues to stand behind the ancient covenant promise and provides the means to address our loneliness through other human beings. In Christ we believe we are created in God's likeness with the capacity to experience God's spiritual presence of love and justice, and God calls us into an intimate relationship with each other and Christ as members of Christ's body.

Christians may have different beliefs concerning biblical doctrine and ethics, but we share common ground in the belief that God created us to experience fulfilling relationships. This belief is validated from a variety of human experiences. One example is seen in the desire of many to remarry following divorce. In their book on marriage and the family, John Patton and Brian Childs indicate, "According to some studies, one-third of those people between the ages of twenty-nine and thirty-five who were married in 1979 will experience divorce. A total of 80 percent of these people will remarry."[13] In spite of the pain experienced in the loss of an intense relationship and the failure associated with it, these facts point to the powerful need to have relationships. Humans will transcend their pain and loss to reenter another marital relationship. "Human relationality is just that powerful."[14]

The Church Today and Relational Living

The New Testament from beginning to end emphasizes the belief that human beings are created to experience a fulfilling relationship with God and fellow humans. When the church fails to value the importance of relationships more than rules and institutions, like marriage, it is not in a good position to help its members when they experience a crisis. For example, this could occur when family members become estranged, or a daughter gets pregnant outside of marriage, or a son does not want to go to college, or the relationship in marriage crumbles, or someone in the family comes out of the closet and announces that he or she is gay or lesbian.

Sometimes the family's pastor tries to find the perfect verse from scripture to set the situation straight, seeking to preserve the institution of marriage or a legalistic or orthodox system at the expense of helping the family see that the maintenance of the persons in the relationship is the clearest and most consistent reflection of what is biblical and Christ-centered. Too often the ones who are experiencing the most pain, who are powerless and wounded, are offered as the sacrificial lamb in behalf of an ancient Hebraic law that is no longer practiced by the Jewish community of faith today. They are sometimes sacrificed to preserve an institution God originally created to serve them.

In contrast, a relational response could sound like this: *we are in this together and no matter what happens, we will seek your best interest as human beings created in God's image and sustained by God's spirit of love and justice that we share with each other.* In this response, we see the presence of all four relational concepts woven through scripture: *image of God, addressing potential loneliness, covenant promise, and the body where we are linked together, working for the common good.* It is clear in New Testament teachings that persons are more important than a rule or an institution, or orthodoxy to be preserved. When faced with stressful examples like those given at the beginning of this section, the individual needs a word of grace, the absolute assurance of support from accepting, loving, and caring relationships. God has created human beings to live in fulfilling relationships.

Divorce and Remarriage

In the remaining portion of this chapter I will review two lifestyle patterns where relational needs are paramount and seek to be satisfied. In the first example, *marriage and divorce,* mainstream Protestantism has come a long way in providing pastoral care in supporting those who have been severely wounded by the experience of failure and loss when a marriage relationship crumbles. It concerns me to hear someone make slurring personal generalizations about the growing number of divorces: *so many people in our time don't take marriage seriously at the onset. If it doesn't meet their self-centered needs, they'll bail out,* or *when the sexual fun runs its course, they are ready to run to someone else.* In my experience of ministry I never encountered an engaged couple who did not take their forthcoming marriage seriously. In fact, many young adults are reluctant to marry because their expectations are unrealistically high, or they question their preparedness. Many asked for more than the four one-and-half-hour premarriage sessions, which I required as the officiating pastor.

More so, I have yet to witness a divorce that has not been a painful experience accompanied by loss and grief and many other forms of pain. John Patton and Brian Childs write: "Divorce is the most significant loss of relationship, which to a great degree involves the intentional moving away from relationship."[15] I find it hard to believe that a large number of people step into marriage with an indifferent attitude about the possibility of failure and the painful and wounded identity that comes with divorce as well as the relational loss.

First, the institution of marriage is extremely important and serves a valuable purpose. It provides structure to support the husband and wife in relationship. In the context of the church community, the bonding of two people in marriage receives the blessing of the body of Christ, a diverse relational unit that provides unique support. Because marriage is a civil institution in our society, couples in marriage have the blessing and support of family, friends, and community. These external and public means of support compel the couple to invest more of their time and energy in making their relationship fulfilling. The external support also provides fellowship centered on common needs.

Second, it is more important to remember that the structure of marriage has been created to serve the relationship of the persons in marriage. Mainline Protestant denominations have waited many years to move away from the legalism (preserving the structure) of marriage to affirming ultimate importance of the persons involved in the relationship. There are times, whatever be the reasons, when a marriage relationship dies. "It is central to Christian tradition to face and acknowledge death, including the death of relationships."[16]

So some Protestant churches, including the Presbyterian Church (USA), "have recognized divorce as legitimate, not only on grounds of adultery or desertion but also 'where a continuation of the legal union would endanger the physical, moral, or spiritual well-being of one or both of the partners or that of their children.'"[17] Not only under these same conditions is divorce legitimate for members of the church but also for the officers and ministers of the church. Once the issue of divorce was settled by the church, the question of remarriage was also sanctioned.

The important question is this: how can the church remain faithful to biblical teaching and also declare that divorce and remarriage are legitimate? In his response to the Pharisees and their questions about divorce, Jesus did not see divorce as legitimate, except for adultery, and he said those who remarry are committing adultery: "but from the beginning God has made them male and female. For this reason a man shall leave his father and mother and be joined to his wife, the two shall become one flesh. Therefore, what God has joined together, let no one separate. Whoever divorces his wife and marries another commits adultery against her; and if she divorces her husband and marries another, she commits adultery" (Mark 10:6-12). Jesus makes a similar statement in the Sermon on the Mount (Matthew 5:31-32).

These are not words from Paul or James; they do not come from the *holiness code* of the Old Testament. These are words from Jesus Christ. Based on such a clear directive, what was the biblical basis for making divorce and remarriage legitimate? First, Jesus refers to the second story of creation and adds that God originally intended marriage of male and female to be permanent and lasting. We know also the partner was created primarily to address the relational needs of aloneness. Second, if the relationship in marriage is no longer marked by love and justice and the fruits of the spirit, the union of the two has lost its creative relational purpose.

Third, without the presence of sinfulness, the self-centered condition, all would have been well, but now we have to deal with the reality of self-centeredness, which creates havoc for the wellbeing of the persons in the relationship, which could also include children. Fourth, Jesus himself places the value of humankind above institutions, legalistic systems, and orthodoxy. His actions on the Sabbath and his references to Sabbath law (Mark 2:27) are good examples. But he also has something to say about laws concerning offerings made to God when he speaks to the Pharisees and scribes, "Woe to you scribes and Pharisees, hypocrites! For you tithe mint, dill, and cumin, and have neglected the weightier matters of the law (love): justice, mercy, and faith" (Matthew 23:23).

So after the church examined the teachings of Christ in light of his great commandment of love, the church concluded: it is the quality of the relationship in marriage that matters the most; after all, marriage was created for the welfare and happiness of humankind. But what about remarriage? Jesus says that people who remarry following divorce (on grounds other than adultery) are committing adultery, that is the seventh commandment in the Decalogue. Adultery means unfaithfulness to the marriage partner by possessing another human being sexually in heart or in body.

Once again the church falls back upon the biblical teaching that to be human is to live in relationships of love and justice that grow with the practice of the fruits of the spirit. For many, marriage or an intimate partnership provides the ultimate experience of wholeness. It is believed that God created life to be lived on the high plane of relationships; that is one of the central themes woven through scripture. Through God's grace, those who experienced failure in one marriage relationship are forgiven. They are a new creation seeking to continue their spiritual growth not only in relationship with God but also the practice of God's love and justice in relationships, perhaps in another marriage relationship.

John Patton and Brian Childs believe that it is important for those who remarry "to affirm that readiness publicly to the church and to the state. The public nature of the marriage is more important to recognize in remarriage than in the first marriage because it affirms, in spite of previous sin and the failure of a committed relationship, that the remarrying person believes that he or she is prepared to make a commitment again."[18] Concerning marriage and remarriage, Protestant mainline denominations now proclaim the *good news* of a gracious God who creates human beings to live in relationships of love and justice, who forgives us when we mess up and encourages us not to give up on relationships that matter, but try again so that we can give, receive, and experience wholeness.

But one thing puzzles me. After 400 years, what has encouraged mainline denominations to break from legalistic captivity on this particular issue when they remain captive to the law on other ethical issues? As I wrote in chapter one, we are eager to be saved by grace, but living by God's grace is difficult because in grace we are expected to treat others as God has treats us. What has encouraged us to stand by those who have experienced brokenness in the most intimate relationship God has created?

Is it because we are willing to assess situations from the wholeness of the biblical message rather than from a few verses that have been quoted over and over again, often not addressing the issue at hand? Is it because following Christ means to treat with compassion and hospitality those who are wounded and have been pushed to the side of road (marginalized) by the abuser? Is it because divorce and remarriage have come close to the norm in our society, more acceptable, thus no longer considered abnormal? Is it because divorce is happening to us, the leaders and ministers in churches, forcing us who are the policymakers to see this situation in life from another perspective? What has encouraged us to break away from legalistic captivity on this issue of divorce and remarriage and to live by God's grace affirming that God creates us to live in relationships of love and justice supported by the fruits of the spirit? Very likely, all the reasons plus others have had a liberating influence.

Same-Gender Partnerships

Now let's examine the second lifestyle pattern where relational needs are paramount but partially satisfied. In response to this second example, gay and lesbian partnerships, mainline Protestantism is fearfully failing to provide pastoral care in supporting both the relational needs of these persons and incorporating them into the mainstream of church and society so they can use their gifts in service to God and humankind. At this time, in the United States only a few mainline Protestant churches as well as states validate same-gender unions. To identify the union as a *marriage* has made this issue more complex.

Church denominations began debating vigorously the morality of the gay/lesbian lifestyle approximately thirty-five years ago. Prior to that period, the gay/lesbian lifestyle was either publicly demonstrated in districts of large cities or was closeted (hidden and privatized) out of fear of losing a job, of being rejected by family and church, and of becoming victim to physical abuse by those who are homophobic. But for the most part, because of their sexual orientation or lifestyle they withdrew from community and church involvement and often moved away from their families to retain anonymity.

For a variety of reasons, in recent years many homosexuals began revealing their true identity. Some in partnerships desire to have their relationships blessed by the churches to which they belong, and some desire to continue serving their church as a minister or officer. Many people connect homosexual orientation and lifestyle as if the two words carry the same meaning. When homosexuals began revealing their identity, Church denominations appointed *Theological Task Forces* who created guides on issues related to human sexuality to be studied by congregations in order to broaden understanding and continuing the conversation on this issue. Church governing bodies soon created rules prohibiting same-gender couples from being officers or ministers. More will said about this issue in a later chapter.

Response of the Church

How is the church responding to the homosexual issue in contrast to divorce/remarriage? It seems contradictory. As noted in chapters two and three, scripture says very little concerning same-gender relationships and scripture says nothing about validating committed same-gender partnerships.

At the same time, we read many more passages in scripture concerning marriage and divorce, especially in the New Testament. The major passage of concern in responding to divorce and remarriage were the clear words of Christ speaking against both divorce and remarriage. In responding to homosexual concerns, Jesus gives us no guidance. He says nothing about homosexual orientation or activity. He does say a great deal about accepting those who are different and *loving our neighbor as we love ourselves and do unto others as you would have them do unto you*, but says nothing that would give reason to treat homosexual persons differently than we treat anyone else.

If the church, through the practice of grace, allows divorcees to continue to be full members, it seems the church would be overjoyed to give full membership to two people of the same gender who live in a committed, faithful, and loving partnership. The scripture and the teaching of Jesus emphasize strongly and consistently that human beings are created to live in meaningful relationships. Jesus makes it clear that grace takes precedence over rules, laws, rituals, and institutions. Those who are saved by grace are to follow him and live by grace. This saves grace from being cheap and phony.

In dealing with divorce, the church made its decision on the basis of grace and the biblical teaching that to be human means living in relationships of mutual love and justice. That was the key biblical truth in resolving the *divorce/remarriage* issue: "divorce is legitimate where a continuation of the legal union would endanger the physical, moral, or spiritual wellbeing of one or both of the partners or that of their children."[19] Without the presence of love and justice in the relationship, the physical, moral, and spiritual wellbeing of everyone is jeopardized. The health of the marriage relationship stands above all norms mentioned in scripture, even the specific words of Christ on divorce in Mark 10:1, Matthew 5:31, and 19:1-11.

In responding to present-day homosexual concerns, many church leaders have reversed their biblical course and have retreated into the grips of legalism. They prefer to be deadlocked by six verses of scripture that obliquely condemn same-gender acts that actually occur in the context of worshiping pagan gods in cults of prostitution. When these six verses are understood in their context, it reveals that many churches are making decisions of exclusion based on rules that do not address the present-day situation. This approach to biblical guidance is diametrically opposed to the approach used to settle the *divorce/remarriage issue.*

Reflect for a moment and answer this question: when did you make a decision about your sexual orientation? That is to say, when did you decide to be heterosexual or homosexual? Very likely your response is: *I never made a choice about my sexual orientation.* Being heterosexual or being homosexual is who we are. It is not something that we chose to be. I am not sure how my sexual orientation came into being. For our purposes, the answer to that question is not essential. What is important involves realizing that the relational needs for a homosexual person are the same as they are for a heterosexual person.

What we have in common is the belief that God has done something about our relational needs as human beings—heterosexual and homosexual. According to the second story of creation in Genesis, God responded to the loneliness of the first human by creating another human, someone of the same essence. So for both homosexual and heterosexual persons, it is necessary to live in relationships of love and justice supported by the fruits of the spirit. Both will then experience the wholeness of being human and will overcome loneliness, which Henri Nouwen says is "one of most universal sources of human suffering today . . . the root not only of an increasing number of suicides but also of alcoholism, drug use, and emotional disorders."[20]

The highest expression of completeness for some heterosexuals is found in a *marital partnership,* the spiritual and physical union of male and female. Based on the experience of some homosexuals, a committed *same-gender partnership* provides the highest form of completeness for them. Who am I, a heterosexual, to question what is real for them? Two things puzzle me. First, if God ordained human relationships as the means for wholeness, why is the church working to oppose the highest experience of completeness for homosexual persons that the church supports, promotes, and protects for heterosexual persons? Second, why is the church returning to captivity to the law on this issue, when scripture supports receiving homosexual persons into full membership of the body of Christ, enabling them to use their gifts in service to God and humankind?

Is the church opposing the blessing of a committed monogamous same-gender relationships because it genuinely believes such partnerships are inconsistent with scripture as a whole and is contrary to the will of God in Christ? Or is it because there has been a return to using the scripture as a rule book where one or two verses referring to a subject overrule the prevailing spirit of the biblical message and becomes a sanctified mechanism for controlling purposes? Or is it because the church is bringing fear and prejudice to this issue, therefore preventing an openness to God's spirit and God's written and incarnate word? Or is it because this issue is volatile, and mainline denominations are afraid if they stand with this minority group they will lose members and money? Or finally, is it because many still believe that most homosexual persons choose to be homosexual and need to repent and become heterosexual? Very likely all these reasons plus others have had their influence.

In the end, hopefully the whole church agrees that it is important to reach a decision that is most faithful to the wholeness of scripture as seen in the context of Jesus' ministry, lifestyle, and teaching. In the Bible there are approximately 1,151 pages containing sixty-six books with about 1,189 chapters and at least 31,173 verses. It does not make sense to rely on six or eight verses that make oblique references to same-gender sexual acts among people, who very likely are not homosexual, as the means for excluding Christians in committed monogamous same-gender partnerships from full membership in the Body of Christ. The church has a unique opportunity to bear witness to God's grace in this time when many are inviting the church to join with them in blessing their *same-gender partnership* and in creating an ethical structure of values that will provide the same expectations and give them the same credibility and support from the church that is received by heterosexual persons in a *marital partnership*. What is more, the blessing of the church enables them to become *people with a promise.*

O for a world where everyone respects each other's ways,
Where love is lived and all is done with justice and with praise.
We welcome one world family and struggle with each choice
That opens us to unity and gives our vision voice.
Miriam Therese Winter

Endnotes: Chapter Six

[1]   Joel L. Swerdlow, "New York's Chinatown," *National Geographic Vol. 194, No. 2* (Washington: National Geographic Society, 1998), p. 72.

[2]   Karl Barth, *The Doctrine of Creation: Church Dogmatics III, Part 2* (Edinburgh: T&T Clark, 1960), p. 429.

[3]   Claus Westermann, *Genesis1-1* (Minneapolis: Augsburg, 1974), pp. 151-58.

[4]   Ibid., p. 160.

[5]   John Douglas Hall, *God and Human Suffering* (Minneapolis: Augsburg Publishing House, 1986), p. 54.

[6]   John Patton and Bryan H. Childs, *Christian Marriage and Family: Caring For Our Generations* (Nashville: Abingdon Press, 1988), p. 134.

[7]   William E. Easum, *Sacred Cows Make Gourmet Burgers* (Nashville: Abingdon Press, 1995), pp. 39-40. Note: Easum feels that our society is in a new era influenced by quantum physics and microprocessors. "Both disciplines approach knowledge and reality in a radically

different way from classical physics. Quantum physics seeks to understand the system as well as the relationships that exist between the parts. The whole is understood to be more than the sum of the parts because of the *relationships* between the parts . . . That objects exist is less important than that they are in relationship. What a person *is*, is less important than what a person is *becoming*," p. 22.

8   H. R. Anderson, Jr., "How Does It Feel to Be Excluded?"; *The Presbyterian Outlook*, September 27, 1999 (Richmond: The Presbyterian Outlook, 1999), p. 7.

9   Ibid., p. 7.

10   Ibid., p. 7.

11   Mitch Albom, *Tuesdays with Morrie* (New York: Doubleday, 1997).

12   John Buchanan, *Being Church, Becoming Community* (Louisville, KY: Westminster-John Knox Press, 1996), p. 91.

13   Patton and Childs, *Christian Marriage and Family: Caring for Our Generations*, p. 190.

14   Ibid., p. 191.

15   Ibid., p. 164.

16   Ibid., p. 185.

17   *Marriage: A Theological Statement*, A paper adopted by the 120th General Assembly of the Presbyterian Church in the United States (Atlanta: Materials Distribution Service, 1980), p. 11.

18   Patton and Childs, *Christian Marriage and Family: Caring For Our Generations, p. 192.*

19   *Marriage: A Theological Statement*, p. 11.

20   Henri Nouwen, *Reaching Out: The Three Movements of the Spiritual Life* (New York: Doubleday, 1975), p. 135.

CHAPTER SEVEN

Human Sexuality: Beyond Eroticism

Come, Spirit, come, our hearts control,
Our spirits long to be made whole.
Let inward love guide every deed;
By this we worship and are free.
Hal Hobson

Introduction

We who are Christians are grateful to God, who is "gracious and merciful," for it is by God's grace and not because of our good works that we are members of God's family. As Paul reminds the Ephesians, we therefore have no reason to boast; however, we do have a mandate from Christ to live by grace, which means being as hospitable or accepting of others as God has been accepting of us. Chapter five focuses on the importance of living by grace. God's grace has a high purpose. God's spirit of unconditional acceptance not only opens the door to enjoy a relationship with God but also with fellow human beings.

When we live in fulfilling relationships, we experience God's created intention of wholeness. This was the theme of chapter six, but toward the end of the chapter I asked, "If God ordained human relationships as the means for wholeness, what about persons who are homosexual? Do they not have the same need to experience a fulfilling relationship as heterosexual persons?" The answer, of course, is yes. Some desire to experience a committed and validated *same-gender partnership*, similar to but not the same as a *marital partnership*. More will be said about that distinction in the next chapter.

Many in our society and in religious institutions are opposed or uncomfortable with same-gender partnerships. In the first chapter of this book, I created an ethical situation that exists in many churches and other religious groups in our culture. *Two people of the same gender have been housemates for many years. They have also been active in their church for the same number of years, teaching in church school, serving as youth advisors, active on committees, ushers and greeters in worship, and participants in the program of their church. They are well liked by all, enjoying the friendship of many. They have lived invisible lives because they are homosexuals not by choice any more than most people choose their sexual orientation. They have enjoyed a committed monogamous, caring relationship, but they remain invisible out of fear: fear of losing their jobs, fear of being marginalized by their community and church family, no longer welcomed to be youth advisors or church school teachers, no longer qualified to be an officer, or to continue to use their God-given gifts.*

In chapters two and three, I examined the biblical references to same-gender sexual activity. None of the passages conclusively address this ethical situation. John Boswell writes: "The effect of Christian scriptures on attitudes toward homosexuality could be described as moot."[1] Although scriptural passages are critical of same-gender activity within cults of prostitution and in violent acts in the same way scripture condemns heterosexual acts of the same nature, the scripture does not present an ethic on same-gender committed relationships. Nonetheless,

I believe the authority of scripture is the major norm alongside Jesus Christ in providing guidance for faith and practice.

I, therefore, feel it is important to examine same-gender sexual activity first by biblical standards before examining homosexuality from an experiential level to seek understanding of this facet of human sexuality. As we formulate a just and compassionate response to the ethical situation, I think it is necessary for us to seek God's will for our lives as sexual human beings. What is the nature and purpose of sexuality in general and what is the basis of the homosexual experience in particular?

Many who hear the word *sexuality* envision the latest movie they saw that had erotic scenes, or they may think that about telling their children about the *birds and the bees*, or words like *Viagra, sex abuse, or pornography* come to mind. So immediate responses to the word, *sexuality* go on and on. If these are common responses to the term *sexuality* then responses to the term *homosexuality* may be more physically graphic. Surely sexuality means more than a physical performance and body images.

I agree with John P. Burgess, who writes in *The Presbyterian Outlook* that first it is important to examine what God asks us to do with the sexual dimension of our lives before we can adequately deal with the two poles of current debate about homosexuality: biblical authority vs. hospitality.[2] Another important reality needs to be challenged alongside the question of human sexuality: are we in the religious community (all faiths) and in culture genuinely ready to move beyond patriarchal and hierarchical models to a model of mutuality among male and female, and clergy and layperson?

As seen in the next chapter on marriage, it is these two superior/ inferior models that have influenced church and society's relational practices in both marriage and sexuality. Until those models are replaced by mutuality, tension on all subjects of human relations will exist. Men will continue to attempt to dominate women in marriage and the marketplace and will use the female body on demand to satisfy erotic desires. This patriarchal/hierarchical attitude then greatly influences any objective discussion about same-gender and individual (singles) relational needs. The purpose of this chapter will show that human sexuality goes far beyond erotic desires.

Sexuality Leads to Self-Identity

Sexuality not only involves what males and females do or say or look like; it also involves who they are as humans. The whole being of sexuality is so mysterious that both who we are as sexual beings and what we do as sexual beings interact with each other shaping us spiritually, physically, psychologically, and mentally. "It includes the total sense of ourselves as male or female. Sexuality suggests personal identity and reflects cultural role definition. The nature and purpose of our sexuality are inseparable from the nature and purpose of our humanity."[3] Sexuality is more than gender or erotic desire when beholding another person, or great physical strength, or birthing another human being. Sexuality includes all these tangible realities, but much more. Perhaps most important, sexuality is the capacity to relate with fellow humans with kindness, love, joy, peace, patience, goodness, faithfulness, self-control, compassion, justice, honesty, and a listening ear. Our sexuality also gives us the capacity to relate to God who is spirit. As we perceive the fullness of sexuality, we can begin to identify what it means to be the human being God created us to be, and we can join with the stories of creation in Genesis by declaring sexuality is a good gift from God.

A Good Gift from God

In the first account of creation the text says, "So God created humankind in his image . . . male and female he created them" (Genesis 1:27). As was discussed in the last chapter the *image of God* is a relational model. Humans have the capacity to relate with God, who is a relational spirit, but we also are created to relate with fellow humans in the same spirit the creator God relates with us. God enables us to relate to others with the gifts and fruits of God's spirit.

These are good gifts from God, who enables us to be the person God created us to be, but that is only possible as we live in relationships with other males and females and with all creation. Only then comes the physical image of sexual expression between male and female: "God said to them, 'Be fruitful and multiply'" (Genesis 1:27). This act of creation concludes: "God saw everything that he had made, and indeed, it was very good" (Genesis 1:31). Note that the text speaks positively about sexuality and the act of procreation. The church has often forgotten this at points in its history, as will be discussed in the next chapter.

In the second story of creation the gift of sexuality is mentioned in a different way. In the process of the creation of human beings, God begins with a creature of dust. Realizing that it is not good for this creature to be alone, from the creature of dust God makes a woman. The creature of dust is no longer the same; so in a sense, in the creation of the woman, God also creates the man, both of the same substance but different.

The point is the dust creature is not fully human in being alone. He needs another being of the same substance to achieve wholeness as both man and woman live in relationship with God and with each other. In the drama of this creation nothing is said about husband and wife. That comes later as commentary.

At this point, the second creation account corresponds with the first. God creates male and female; these sexual beings are created to live in relationship with each other that satisfies the anguish of aloneness. Then comes the commentary: "therefore a man leaves his father and mother and clings to his wife and they become one flesh. And the man and his wife were both naked, and were not ashamed" (Genesis 2:24-25). This passage is not part of the drama of creation. The reference to family, *leaving mother and father,* indicates that these last two verses are an interpretation of the preceding act of creation.

The actuality of family cannot be part of the initial drama of the creation of male and female. The commentary describes a relationship that is sexually intimate and transparent where the two expose their whole selves to one another. In this sexual openness, each is a mirror helping the other experience self-identity. James Nelson writes: "We believe that human sexuality, while including God's gift of the procreative capacity, is most fundamentally the divine invitation to find our destinies not in loneliness but in deep connection."[4] Other relationships with males and females also help with self-identity and the development and discovery of sexual awareness.

Development and Discovery of Sexual Awareness

Long before marriage, as we live in relationships in family, among friends, at school, in the community of faith, among males and females, we become more aware of the person we are. In these different relational communities, friends and family help us identify our God-given gifts; they provide support in nurturing these gifts and using God's gifts. These gifts are more than what we normally identify as talents.

Without communal relationships, how do we nurture patience or practice honesty? How do we see the value of listening or demonstrating compassion? Without communal relationships how do we perceive God's call to serve others as a social worker or a doctor or in commerce or as a religious leader? The list goes on and on. So as we live in relationship with others, we begin to develop as a human being and realize who we are as a human being. We also come in touch with our maleness or femaleness as we live in community or relationships with males and females.

We are able to identify similarities and differences among those who are part of our relational communities. All this helps us discover who we are as sexual beings created by God, and the diversity affirms our differences rather than compelling us to dislike ourselves or to lose touch with self through self-denigration or conformity. At the same time, in relationships I discover the humanness of others created in God's image. I experience in relationships that I am an agent of God supporting them in being the person God created them to be. What is remarkable is that no two of us are identical. This is God's good creation of human sexuality, but that is not the end of the story.

This mirror reflecting the ideal human community has been broken by sinfulness, or better stated, by selfishness. Its origin is summarized in the story of Adam and Eve, man and woman, in the garden of Eden in the third chapter of Genesis. They are not content in being human creatures. They are tempted to be like God, so they put themselves first (selfishness) and act upon their self-centered desires. Rather than becoming like God, they fall. They fall below the intentions God has for humans. They miss the mark or target God has set for them. This dilemma faces every human because of the condition of self-centeredness within us.

What are the consequences? Relationships suffer as depicted in the drama in the garden. The man and woman hide from God; their relationship with God is not the same. They cease being responsible and honest with themselves as individuals by blaming others for their act of selfishness. Their relationship with each other has also been impaired. A desire to be clothed prevents natural self-disclosure. Finally, mutuality between male and female, husband and wife, is lost. Selfishness leads to competition for domination: "To the woman he (God) said . . . 'Yet your desire shall be for your husband, and he shall rule over you" (Genesis 3:16b).

Where there is selfishness, relationships suffer. Since it is through relationships we become who we are and we discover sexual awareness, then self-centeredness affects our sexuality. We misuse sexuality; we manipulate and hurt persons sexually for self-serving purposes. We use sexuality to dominate others; it becomes a symbol of power in relationships and a major source of commerce in society. It is sold and bought in the marketplace from theaters to department stores, from brothels to the job market. Where there is selfishness, relationships suffer, and self-identity is veiled by a dark cloud.

For some reason, the early leaders of the Christian church, in focusing on the fall or the advent of self-centeredness, lost sight of the big picture of human sexuality: the human being God created us to be. They failed to see sin as humans missing the mark God has set for us to live in loving, caring, just, and merciful relationships. They began to identify sin as a sexual drive out of control; therefore, sexual intercourse was sinful or impure, representing a lower base within the human creature. It's both ironical and tragic. The gift God has given us for the capacity of relatedness and creativity was demonized by the early church leaders. Why was this the case?

Perhaps it was because the Judaeo-Christian faith moved from Palestine, where the Hebrews viewed the sacred within the physical, to the Greco-Roman world where the physical was separated from the spiritual, whereas the physical was considered the lower part of the nature of humanity. The spiritual was perceived to be the highest source of goodness, whereas the physical was impure and the spiritual was pure. Two philosophies that had significant influence in the early church were Gnosticism and Stoicism. Both embraced the dualistic view of the physical and spiritual, where there were good and evil forces warring for control of humanity's soul.

Ironically, it was in the Greco-Roman world where sexual immorality was commonplace, where prostitution was not only permitted but was taxed for revenue and also served a cultic religious purpose. Perhaps church leaders became fearful of such sexual license and for practical purposes created a theology that tied sexuality with sinfulness, using Paul's letter to the Corinthians as a biblical base. Then, because of the influence of Stoicism, which combines self-denigration with sacrifice, they believed that any form of sexual pleasure was the most dangerous force in distracting the soul from its spiritual course.

Another dualistic group, the Manicheans, opposed all forms of sexuality. Saint Augustine was a member of this group before his conversion to Christianity.[5] Augustine taught that God created sexual desire and activity but that it was sinful to move the body or derive any pleasure from the act. Referring to Saint Augustine's sexual ethics, Eric Fuchs writes: "As a result, all of Christian ethics became almost fixated upon sexuality as the very symbol of the idolatrous covetousness of man. From this point on and for many centuries, sexuality could not be spoken of without simultaneously evoking the thought of sin.[6]

It was at this time that clerics taught that virginity among women and celibacy among men were the highest spiritual states achieved by humans; both were superior to marriage. For example, John Chrysostom writes, "a virgin marries God."[7] It was also believed that sexuality and love were incompatible because sexuality is aligned with sin. All these views of sexuality grew to reach their peak of power during the medieval period of Christian history. To some extent, these views still persist today, partly clothed in the church's reaction to the sexual revolution of the 1960s.

So as the church became fixated on sexuality as the big sin, I think it has become extremely difficult to get the church to discuss the subject even from a biblical perspective. Many of our views today concerning sexuality and marriage have been tainted by St. Augustine and medieval theology. As a result, we have shot ourselves in the foot, disabling one of the most significant gifts God has given humans for communal relatedness, for satisfying our sense of loneliness, for self-identity, for developing and discovering sexual awareness, all of which help us experience human wholeness.

We and they have forgotten that the *fall* of Genesis 3 is not the end of the story. God became a sexual being through the incarnation of Jesus Christ, the second Adam (human), to enable us to be the human (sexual being) God created us to be. In Christ, we who remain self-centered are given a taste of paradise. We, as males and females, are empowered spiritually to serve one another in relationships marked by mutuality and the fruits of the spirit; for in Christ, figuratively speaking, we are no longer male and female.

We are children of God, each different from the other as sexual beings, but each embracing the same need to live in fulfilling relationships, giving and receiving, serving and being served, speaking and listening, forgiving and being forgiven, and mutually demonstrating justice and compassion. In that arena of spirituality, we not only discover our sexual orientation, but we are also set free to be open and honest with ourselves and our community of faith in both revealing and accepting this important dimension of self-identity.

Sexual Orientation and Self-Identity
Who am I?

Some may be asking, why doesn't scripture address sexual orientation? Why are we left with the moral dilemma of figuring out what to do with this issue at this particular time in history? Well, to skirt a direct answer to the first question, there is much in life scripture does not address directly and specifically. Scripture does not address the institution of slavery directly, nor the institution of marriage, as will be seen in the next chapter. Scripture did not directly challenge the secondary position of women in society, nor does it address issues of science and government and science as we know it today.

The writers of scripture, inspired by God, accepted the worldview of their day as they communicated divine principles that can be applied to ethical issues we face from generation to generation. God came in Christ, revealing the great commandment of love by which all other biblical principles are to be assessed. Scientific and technological developments through the ages have revealed new knowledge and awareness of the cosmos and human nature, compelling the church to make responsible use of the ethical principles set forth in scripture and by Christ. This is one reason God's written word and incarnate word are timeless.

Concerning sexual orientation, like birth control and artificial insemination, there is nothing specifically mentioned in scripture. It was believed in that day that human beings were created male and female, and that these two genders were universally attracted to each other sexually for the purpose of procreation. That was seen as the natural order of things. Yes, men and women were also attracted to each other as friends and comrades. A good example in scripture is the relationship between David and Jonathan. One of the few times love between two people is mentioned in the Old Testament occurs in David and Jonathan's relationship with each other. In fact, their relationship is so special, it is bound by vows: "Jonathan made David swear again his love for him; for he loved him (David) as he loved his own life . . . he (David) bowed three times, and they kissed each other, and wept with each other" (1Samuel 20:17, 41).

Another biblical example is the relationship between Ruth and Naomi. Their relationship was likewise bound by promises made by Ruth. Those promises were put to lyrics and sometimes sung today in weddings. It was actually more common for men to spend time with men than with women. We have Jesus and the twelve disciples, the shepherds and wise men visiting the infant Christ as examples. Women may have devoted time with each other as well, as seen in the company of women at the cross and the empty tomb, but normally women remained close to home with the children.

In Greece through the third century, the purest and highest spiritual relationship occurred among men who at the same time were married with a family. Some of these relationships may have been physical, but little can be documented because it was the relationship that was important. Known same-gender sexual activity in Hebrew history occurred with prostitutes in pagan religious cults in the worship of the goddess Asherah (mentioned often in the Old Testament).

In the Greco-Roman world, same-gender sexual activity was common in public brothels and temples such as the temple of Aphrodite in Corinth. Sexual orientation was not a consideration because it was generally assumed that the participants were by nature attracted to the opposite gender for sake of procreation; therefore, it was assumed men chose to be with those of the same gender as spiritual friends (platonic love) or to use prostitutes or slaves for physical pleasure or sexual exploitation and abuse. By today's standard their sexual orientation was likely heterosexual.

As we move into the third millennium we know much more about human sexuality than was known in biblical days and the life of the early, medieval, and reformation church. Social sciences and physical sciences have greatly broadened our knowledge about human beings. At the same time this diversity of knowledge does not mean that we fully understand the nature of humanity. The terms *homosexual* and *heterosexual* were nonexistent before 1892 when they were placed in the dictionary.

Prior to 1950, if a person moving through the physical, emotional, and mental development of teens to adulthood began to ask "Who am I," he or she was left with two alternative answers: *I am a man* or *I am a woman*. What if the woman examined her body and concluded, *I am supposed to be a woman, but I am not attracted to men like my female friends are; I am attracted to women*. Prior to 1950 this woman was in serious trouble. Society would tell her she is psychologically sick, a queer, a deviate, a dike, sinful; she needs to get her head on straight and change (today, rather than change some are saying *be healed*). These diagnoses are not only coming from peers and friends but from family, the church, the medical profession, and the media. If you were this woman, how would you feel about yourself and your self-identity? In this context it would be difficult to achieve human wholeness.

Who am I? Prior to 1970 a young man who was attracted to men and a young woman who was attracted to women very likely said to themselves, *Who I feel I really am must not be true. If it were true, I simply will not accept it, and the last thing I will do is share my personal perception with anyone, especially my minister and my mother and father*. Some may have left home to find a support community only to be swept into counter-culture groups experimenting with drugs and sex. Suicide has become the option for some.

As a Presbyterian minister I supported and grieved with persons who are suffering from the consequences of choosing one of these three options because they did not feel free to accept who they were. I also supported and grieved with their families. Not one of the options is healthy; not one leads to wholeness. That was the offering of our society prior to 1970. This was a *cultural* worldview and religious institutions prior to 1970 bought into it in the same way the church bought into slavery, segregation of the races, and women as second-class citizens living in subjugation to their husbands, all neatly supported with verses from scripture.

Much has happened in America since it lost its innocence when the U2 spy plane flown by Gary Powers was shot down by the Soviet Union in May 6, 1960, and President Eisenhower first denied its existence but had to admit lying when Power's confession came across the television media all over the world. Before that time, no one would believe Americans would spy and presidents would lie. Since that time, we probably have learned more about the reality of the great institutions of our country than is healthy.

Our religious institutions, likewise, have not escaped exposure. The Roman Catholic Church is presently reaping the consequences of some extremely rigid and quasi-biblical rules about required celibacy for priests, whose roots go back to the medieval age. Protestant ministers, on the other hand, cannot declare total innocence. Novels like *Rabbit Run* by John Updike and *Catcher in the Rye* by John Salinger written in the sixties and folk music with its festivals communicated messages exposing phony aspects of our culture. It's time to be honest and not ashamed of who you are, whether red, yellow, white, or black, straight or gay, or lesbian or transsexual. *Freedom to be who I am* was the message ringing from college campuses all over the United States in the 1960s and 1970s.

Truthful Answers Emerge from the Question: Who am I?

Doors and ears began to open, enabling people who were questioning their sexual orientation to be heard. We remain in that block of time where understanding and resolution have not been reached by a consensus of our religious institutions as well as our country. We have come a long way in fifty years. Richard Lovelace, in his book *Homosexuality and the Church*, presents the following chronology: in 1948, Alfred Kinsey's study of male sexual behavior reports that on a continuum from zero (exclusively heterosexual) to six (exclusively homosexual), 5-10 percent registered a five or six while 25 percent registered more than *incidentally homosexual.* In 1951, the first comprehensive study by an acknowledged homosexual was published. In 1954 the Anglican Church of England produced the first report on the subject of homosexuality, to be followed in the 1970s by studies done in the United States by the Presbyterian, Lutheran, United Church of Christ, Episcopal, Methodist, and Quaker/Mennonite denominations. In 1968, Troy Perry, a conservative Pentecostal minister who admitted to being gay, was pressured to leave his church and family only to start the Metropolitan Community Church of Los Angeles as a Christian ministry to homosexuals. In 1973, the American Psychiatric Association voted to remove homosexuality from the category of mental illness.[8] As doors and ears began to open, more homosexual persons have elected to *come out of the closet* and share with family and friends their truthful answer to the question, *who am I?*

The topic of homosexual orientation now has faces and personalities. It can no longer be an impersonal, indifferent, objective debate concerning what scripture says or does not say, or what science or sociology reveals, or how the tradition of the church responded to this issue years ago. We are now dealing with more than an issue; we are making decisions about the lives of human beings. These decisions of inclusion or exclusion affect more than the subjects being discussed. They affect mothers and fathers, brothers and sisters, the extended family, and friends.

For example, where would you stand if a son or daughter demonstrated the courage to *come out* and reveal his or her homosexual orientation to you? Would you embrace your loved one with the same unconditional love and acceptance you displayed when the doctor placed this child in your arms following birth? I know where I stand, and the word *embrace* is not strong enough to express the support I would demonstrate for such a loved one. I suggest that every parent or close friend of someone consider where you would stand if a loved one *came out* with the truth about his/her homosexual orientation. Then extend that unconditional acceptance to include all God's children we have been called to love.

After serious consideration, if you feel the obligation to change rests with your loved one rather than unconditional acceptance on your part, I suggest that you continue reading. Hopefully, legitimate and well-informed reasons will be given to encourage you to reconsider your position.

What causes one person in a family to be homosexual and another heterosexual when both have been reared in the same environment and the same parents? Hear the following stories:

> *In the Philippines, I was born into and grew up with a very religious Catholic family. I am sure I said my first prayers before I could even read and write. In London, where I pursued postgraduate studies, I finally came to terms with my homosexuality. I never lost my Christian faith, and it was in these moments when I would find myself talking with God. I never expected miracles to happen, but the mere process of prayer was enough to boost my spirit and infuse my being with determination to carry on.*
>
> —*C. Gonzales*[9]

> *I am a lesbian. I have come to accept and embrace my sexuality after denying it for twelve years (until age twenty-eight). I thank God for the acceptance I have from my*

family and a growing number of trusted friends. I thank God for the counseling I received from my home minister at First Presbyterian. I thank God for God's care of me throughout my life, but especially in the last three years as I've quit denying who I am.

—Yours in Christ[10]

The Presbyterian Church promised me in my college years what I could not find in the fundamentalist denomination in which I was reared. I struggled as a Baptist, accepting Jesus over and over again with the hope that God would take away my homosexuality. I believed that God had the power to change me, so when that did not happen I quietly accepted my "thorn in the flesh." The Presbyterian Church helped me understand that my quest for justice for other marginalized people grew out of my own sensitivity at being "unacceptable."

—Chris Glaser[11]

A letter to Abigail Van Buren reads: *I am a twenty-five-year-old lesbian Learning to accept my homosexuality was difficult. While I am finally happy about my life, misinformation about homosexuality continues to appall me. I am one of three girls raised in a loving family, as close as you could get to the sitcom families of the fifties. I have never had a bad experience with a male. No one tried to convert me to lesbianism. For years I thought something was wrong with me. I tried desperately to be straight. I even contemplated suicide. I feared my family would reject me, but in the end they turned out to be very supportive. There was no significant difference in the way my sister and I were raised. Genetics, nature, or God's will is my explanation for my orientation.*

—Name withheld

These four situations have much in common. The four people grew up in stable, middle-class, loving families who were active in the practice of the Christian faith through their church. They have brothers and/ or sisters and enjoyed a compatible relationship with them. In the late teens they struggled with their sexual orientation, knowing they were different from the same-gender friends with whom they spent time. They denied their homosexuality, but at the same time they sought God's help in changing how they were feeling. At the onset, because of ashamed feelings they did not share their struggle with family or anyone.

When they came out to their family and church family, they did not receive the same degree of understanding and support; however, when these case studies were written all remained active in their church. They came to terms (accepted) with their homosexuality before they became involved with someone of the same gender. When they developed a relationship with someone of the same gender, it strengthened their self-worth, which was close to bankruptcy.

Consider the Causes of Homosexuality

Their honesty, along with the openness of thousands of other homosexuals, has helped everyone with questions like: *how did this happen? What caused you to be this way? Did you choose to be homosexual?* The social and physical sciences have attempted to seek definitive answers to these questions with marginal success. These sciences focus in two areas: the biological and the psychological. Biological studies imply that persons are either innately homosexual, or they were born with a predisposition to be homosexual. The research has been done by comparing hormone levels, brain structure, and characteristics of the inner ear between heterosexuals and homosexuals. Although differences emerge, there are no definitive answers to causality that would clearly indicate that homosexuality is biological like being left-handed or right-handed. Nonetheless, what has been discovered in scientific research strongly supports a biological cause.

Psychological and sociological studies emphasize homosexuality is learned because of family experiences, role modeling, and interaction with siblings while growing up. Once again, in this research no consistent patterns of development have been connected with those who are homosexual, especially the popular assumption that gay men were likely smothered by their mothers and neglected by their fathers. In conclusion on homosexual research, Joseph Nicolosi writes: "Recently, we have begun to realize that biology and psychology cannot be so neatly separated but are in-separately linked."[12]

What is the cause? There is another possibility: the theological response. Some homosexual persons believe God created them with their sexual orientation. When compared with biblical experience and interpretation, this response is difficult to dispute because it is a faith statement. In response, some who disagree may say God is not responsible for something God does not intend for creation. God is only responsible for that which is natural. Heterosexual is natural and homosexual is unnatural.

The natural/unnatural response is inadequate when placed alongside biblical stories of faith. In the Bible, nothing is more natural than procreation: "Be fruitful and multiply." Sarah, Rachel, and Hannah were barren for a long period of time. Nothing could be more unnatural for ancient Hebrews, yet they believed God was responsible for their barrenness. "Sarai said to Abram, 'You see, the Lord has prevented me from bearing children . . .'" (Genesis 16:2). Jacob speaking to his distraught wife, Rachel, asks, "Am I in the place of God, who has withheld from you the fruit of the womb?" (Genesis 30:2). Concerning the plight of Hannah, the text says, "Though the Lord closed her womb." These women of faith prayed to God to change the course of their sexual lives. Paul had a "thorn in the flesh"; it must have been unnatural because he asked God to remove it.

Throughout the Old Testament it was believed God was responsible for various kinds of adversity, some of which were unnatural. Upon awakening every morning, it was customary for the ancient Hebrew male to express gratitude to God that he was born a male rather than female. If God is responsible for one's gender, cannot God be the cause behind one's sexual orientation? As Chris Glaser said, *I quietly accepted my "thorn in the flesh."* So there are those who, in faith, believe God is the cause of their sexual orientation. If God is the cause, they feel free of whatever guilt is imposed upon them by church and society. They are then liberated to seek wholeness through a committed partnership in the same way heterosexuals seek wholeness. This response to the question of cause should make sense to those Christians who readily attribute the hand of God to whatever happens in their lives.

What is the cause for homosexual orientation? There is a third response, which is the one I embrace. I do not know the cause; knowing the cause is not that critical for me because I have not spoken to a homosexual person who says *I chose to be homosexual.* I have not read the story of a homosexual person who has chosen to be homosexual. As I reflect upon my sexual development, I cannot recall making a choice to be heterosexual. What about you, the reader? Did you choose your sexual orientation? If we didn't choose our sexual orientation, why would we assume homosexual persons choose theirs? That assumption reveals little contact and openness with homosexual persons. The anguish, the denial, the fear, the loneliness, the struggle one describes in accepting a homosexual orientation rules out the absurdity that one would choose it.

Whatever be the cause of our sexual orientation, we are not responsible, any more than we are responsible for the color of our skin, our gender, or being left-handed. The question is not *why* am I homosexual or heterosexual. The critical question to answer is *how.* Knowing my orientation, *how* am I going to deal with it, accept it, and continue to reflect the glory of God?

Endnotes: Chapter Seven

1   John Boswell, *Christianity, Social Tolerance, and Homosexuality* (Chicago and London: The University of Chicago Press, 1980), p. 11.

2   John P. Burgess, Rethinking Sexuality, in *The Presbyterian Outlook* (Richmond: Outlook Publishers: February 25, 2002), p. 8.

3   *The Nature and Purpose of Human Sexuality:* A Paper Adopted by the 120th General Assembly of the Presbyterian Church in the United States (Atlanta: Materials Distribution Center, 1980), p. 4.

4   James B. Nelson, *Sexuality and the Sacred: Sources for Theological Reflection* (Louisville: Westminster/John Knox Press, 1994), p. xiv.

5   Boswell, p. 128-129.

6   Eric Fuchs, *Sexual Desire and Love: Origin and History of the Christian Ethic of Sexuality and Marriage* (New York: The Seabury Press, 1983), p. 116

7   Ibid., p. 99.

8   Richard Lovelace, *Homosexuality and the Church: Crisis, Conflict, Compassion* (Fleming H. Revell Company: Old Tappan, NJ, 1978), pp. 29-31.

9   Sylvia Thorson-Smith, *Reconciling the Broken Silence* (Louisville: The Presbyterian Publishing House, 1993), p. 18.

10   Ibid., p. 19.

11   Ibid, p. 20.

12   Joseph Nicolosi, "What Does Science Teach About Human Sexuality?" in *Caught in the Crossfire,* edited by Sally B. Geis and Donald E. Messer (Nashville: Abingdon Press, 1994), p. 67.

CHAPTER EIGHT

Homosexuality: Response of the Church and Society

Help us accept each other as Christ accepted us;
Teach us as sister, brother, each person to embrace.
Be present, Lord, among us and bring us to believe
We are ourselves accepted and meant to love
Fred Kaan

Answers That Isolate A Choice

Someone says, "I am gay and it is not by choice." "I am lesbian, but I did not choose that orientation." What are some of the responses from church and society? I believe the response that represents the largest segment of our population, especially within the church because of the generalities coming from pulpits connecting homosexuality with sin, is *"You are wrong, I believe your orientation is your choice as well as your lifestyle, and both are sinful."*

Even in the Presbyterian Church, I have heard on numerous occasions when this subject is discussed that the Bible teaches clearly and unequivocally that homosexuality is a sin. That comment makes the state of being homosexual sinful, which means the homosexual person is sinful beyond the condition of selfishness that all humans share. So a large segment of church and society have much to learn or perhaps unlearn because of what they had heard from the pulpit in their religious facility or from the pulpit on television and radio. They believe one becomes a homosexual person by choice rather than by discovery or awareness of one's homosexual orientation. Likely, many of these people have not had a close positive association with a homosexual person.

Be Healed

Those who believe homosexual orientation is a choice likewise feel the persons need to repent and turn from their sinful ways. For them, with God's help, they need to be healed. The booklet, *Healing for the Homosexual,* presents ten principles to help a person move from a homosexual lifestyle to a heterosexual lifestyle. The principles focus primarily on changing the behavior of the homosexual person through confession of homosexual sin, repentance, following specified disciplines, and being connected with a caring community.

The conviction is that homosexual perversion is an abomination to God, that the wound should not be treated lightly, and that firm love calls for radical surgery. The goal is to remake homosexual persons into heterosexual persons. Like becoming addicted to alcohol, drugs, or cigarettes, the homosexual first chooses to participate in the lifestyle and then becomes homosexual. The five case histories in the booklet present persons who are first immersed in sexual orgies, alcohol, drugs, social dependence, and pornography. Each is then led into homosexual behavior.

Perhaps this is a stereotypical picture of a homosexual person in the eyes of many. It is evident that healing is needed. What is not evident is a clear delineation between homosexual orientation and homosexual behavior. One fact presented in *Healing for the Homosexual* says: "By succumbing to temptation, heterosexuals may become homosexuals."[1] The five persons in the case histories could well be heterosexuals. Once they are freed from their self-destructive behavior patterns, their sexual orientation may be more evident to them.

Various forms of therapy are available for those who elect therapy out of an acute psychic discomfort being homosexual. Joseph Nicolosi writes: "Therapy for a male does not imply a magic cure; its goal is to improve a man's relating to other men and to strengthen masculine identification."[2] The goal in this approach is not the eradication of homosexuality but to allow space so that the homosexual person may have a choice to leave the gay world if that is possible and preferable.[3] This is a form of "reparative therapy."

The 211th General Assembly of the Presbyterian Church (USA) affirmed that medical treatment, psychological therapy, and pastoral counseling should be in conformity with recognized professional standards. If we are supporting counseling that conforms to recognized professional standards, we will not lay claim to changing sexual orientation. One professional organization, the American Psychiatric Association, feels the risks of reparative therapy are too high. It can be the source of anxiety, depression, and self-destructive behavior, and there is virtually no scientific evidence that it is effective. Other professional organizations also do not recommend reparative therapy.[4]

Celibacy

When a person *comes out* and says *I am gay* or *I am a lesbian and I did not choose to be*, another segment of the church and society concede, *"If you say you did not choose your orientation, we believe you, but we expect you to remain celibate."* There are two facets of the demand to be celibate. First, it means do not get sexually involved with someone of either gender. The person who has this expectation for homosexuals very likely lives by a double standard. With friends or children who reveal in different ways their heterosexuality, it is unlikely this person would verbalize such an expectation.

Second, to be celibate also means do not marry, because marriage is reserved for a man and a woman and is a sexual relationship. So the demand to remain celibate is like a doubled-edged sword: have no sex and have no spouse or partner. This is *required celibacy*.

When the medieval church required celibacy for its priests, John Calvin expressed opposition because it was unnatural. He would say people are sexual beings, and their sexual nature compels them to connect with others physically. Celibacy stands in the way of that which God has created. Not only is *required celibacy* unnatural, as John Calvin emphasized, it stands in opposition to the church's historical teaching about celibacy. Celibacy has always been considered a *special spiritual gift (charism)*. Fr. Richard Rohr, a Franciscan writes: "You cannot possibly order someone to have a *charism*, the "gift" of celibacy. It is an oxymoron and an insult to our theology of grace and gift.[5]

The Protestant Reformation spoke clearly in opposition to *required celibacy* because it was unnatural and became a facade for celibate monks who had concubines. Very likely this same law in the Roman Catholic Church today is the source of numerous cases of sexual abuse of children (boys and girls) and sexual exploitation of women. To fall back upon celibacy as a response to some who *come out* revealing homosexual orientation is a strong call.

The church needs to reexamine what the Bible really emphasizes about the legitimate basis for intimate sexual experience between two people: is it a formalized civil marriage for the procreation of children bound by economic commitment, or can it also be a committed relationship bound by economic support? There is a difference. People of faith in the Bible and in the church prior to the Reformation experienced both options. I believe history reveals that *required celibacy* is like putting a Band-Aid over a deep cut. Many have and will experience deep suffering. Surely there must be a healthy response that is not directed to one group but includes the entire community of faith and society in a redemptive way.

Responding to the Answer in Support Acceptance

Upon hearing many stories of anguish from people who faced the realization of their homosexual orientation, the last thing I want to do is make this option seem simple, because it is not. On the personal level, it is much like the journey of anguish experienced in accepting the death of a loved one or the death of a marriage. It's tough, it's painful, and the journey is often long and lonely, accompanied by the fear of being totally rejected and isolated with the loss of the same communities that have helped shape your whole being.

Based on the stories I have heard, there is confusion, a near loss of self-esteem, a feeling of *what is wrong with me*, a response of *surely this is not true*, denial, and the fear that someone may find out. At the awareness point, many homosexual persons are driven into the depths of despair and the dark cave of aloneness. Yes, there is also self-pity, which is dangerous because it pushes the person even deeper into the darkness of despair, away from the comfort and companionship of loved ones. Some experience extreme guilt for having feelings of attraction toward those of the same gender.

Some feel they have let God down, or God has let them down. Some are quick to be angry with God and especially the church if they belong to a church, because they feel they already know how the church will respond. Most leave the church for different reasons: guilt, discomfort, anger, and the sense of not belonging. I cannot adequately describe the anguish many people experience as they face the realization of homosexual orientation.

This orientation will have great impact upon their sexual identity, which encompasses who they are as human beings created in the image of God—an identity that has been crafted and nurtured through the relationships of their lives to this point. In anxiety, many are fearful of the loss of those relationships as they continue their journey in nurturing self-identity. When these burdens become cumulative, some even consider taking their life; suicide is very high among those who are homosexual.

Despite legitimate fears, those in counseling recommend *acceptance* and moving to the question *how:* how am I going to make a life for myself in light of who I am? Those of us who do not face this difficult experience in life need to realize that much of the anguish of this experience occurs because of the way church and society respond. I am not only referring to homophobic responses that may be the easiest for homosexuals to cope with as long as they are not violent.

Homophobic people are communicating their own fears and anxieties that homosexual persons can identify with. It is the loss of support and relationship that creates the greatest source of anguish; therefore, sometimes friends and family are not trusted with the truth until the homosexual person has established a same-gender relationship or at least a community of homosexual friends. For this reason some who have no idea of the journey of this anguish reach the conclusion that it was contact with homosexuals that caused the person to choose to be gay or lesbian.

For acceptance to be healthy, it requires more than self-acceptance on the part of the one who has accepted his/her homosexual orientation. John Boswell reminds us that homosexuals grow up at a time when church and society declare that homosexuality is condemned by God as sinful; to God it is an abomination, it is unnatural, the homosexual is perverted, a deviate, and sick.

Unlike ethnic minorities who have experienced rejection by their communities, gays and lesbians are not born into gay and lesbian families; they do not have a support group readily available to them. They suffer rejection and oppression alone and individually without emotional support from family groups. Throughout history their situation is more like those born left-handed or blind who are dispersed throughout the population rather than having been born into racial or ethnic groups that may be victimized by prejudice.

Homosexual persons are dependent upon the popular attitudes of the community. If those attitudes are hostile, they have to become invisible, as one close lesbian friend has reminded me. Also, homosexual prejudice has been longer lasting than any communal prejudice history has experienced, and this prejudice is strongly supported by the major religions of the world with only the Christian and Jewish religions challenging the prejudice within its religious structures, thus creating great division.[6] Unlike the journey of anguish necessary to reach the point of acceptance in the death of a loved one or the death of a marriage, homosexuals often do not have the confidence of the support of their closest communities: family, friends, and the church.

Not only do gay and lesbians who *come out* need the unconditional acceptance and support of their close communities, but if those who *come out* are young adults, their parents usually need a great deal of support too. At sixteen when Adam Ellis told his mother and father, Jeff and Patti, that he was gay, it turned their life upside down. Adam and his brother Austin grew up with a healthy family life and were active members of a church.

At first the parents were devastated and thought their teenager was confused. They went into denial. Patti, Adam's mother, said she felt trapped between love for her son and the teachings of her church. Everyone stayed in the closet and their house became a tinderbox of denial, depression, and anger. No one knew what to do. Jeff and Patti were torn between a loving son and a society that said homosexuals were perverted and sexual deviants. They shared their anguish with friends, and the friends quit calling.

They were afraid to seek help from the church because their church denomination just voted 2–1 to retain their position that homosexuality is incompatible with Christian teaching. Adam said that position hardly makes a gay person feel welcomed. Jeff and Patti were miserable and were advised by a counselor to attend the support group Parents, Families, and Friends of Lesbians and Gays, which they did. Patti and Jeff have accepted their son's sexual orientation and now have their own website in an attempt to be supportive of other families who have gay/lesbian children.[7] The haunting question that surfaces in my mind is this: Where was the church and its denomination when this family needed unconditional acceptance and support?

The Church and Homosexuality
What the Scripture Teaches

At this point it may be helpful to recall the ethical situation in the first chapter about two female church members who are more than housemates but lesbians in a monogamous relationship for many years. Only the two of them know this. Out of fear they have lived invisible lives. Is the church in a position to support their relationship if they *come out* of the closet? What I write in this section generally represents the position of most mainline denominations (Presbyterian, Episcopal, Methodist, Lutheran, American Baptist as examples). The sources of authority for guidance in faith and living for the church are Jesus Christ, the scriptures of the Old and New Testaments, the guidance of the Holy Spirit, and church tradition. Because of its commitment to these sources of authority, the church first seeks their light and wisdom for guidance.

In chapter one of this book, the ethical situation was assessed alongside the specific passages of scripture that mention same-gender sexual activity. First, these scripture passages do not address all facets of homosexuality; in fact, the passages say very little if anything about homosexuality. As I said earlier the word *homosexual* was not created until 1892. Second, these passages are likely expressing concern about participating in pagan cultic practices with both male and female prostitutes. Also, they are neither attempt to present a sexual ethic, nor do they address present-day ethical situations where two people of the same gender are living in a committed monogamous relationship.

Many biblical scholars, having done thorough research, reach the same conclusions. Nonetheless, for different reasons, some feel the church should not change its prohibitive position on homosexual practice that was developed in the seventies and eighties. In response, Peter Gomes writes: "What is at stake is not simply the authority of scripture, but also the authority of the culture of interpretation by which people read the scripture in such a way as to lend legitimacy to their doctrinaire prejudices. Thus, the battle for the Bible, of which homosexuality is the last front, is really the battle for the prevailing culture, of which the Bible itself is a mere trophy and icon."[8]

I think Gomes has a significant point. I remember what it was like in the 1950s as a teen. The word *homosexual* was not commonly used in those days, but other words were, such as *queer*, *sissy*, and *fag*. It was common to label guys with those names if they did not fit the model of masculinity designed by the *in group*. I do not recall if female teens were scrutinized in the same way. What I do know is this prejudice had no substance; it was a worldly prejudice, because the church (mainline) was still a good distance from dealing with the topic of gays and lesbians. It was not until the latter part of the 1970s that the church began biblical studies on homosexuality. Interestingly the church's conclusions supported the prevailing attitude of culture. Some of the reasons were:

1) At this time very little research among self-avowed homosexuals had been done; therefore, little was known about the nature of being homosexual. It was generally believed that homosexuals were heterosexuals who chose that lifestyle and pattern of behavior, so it was believed that homosexual persons were mentally and emotionally sick.

2) These studies and decisions were made close to the time of the sexual revolution, which began in the 1960s, which depicted in magazines and on television young adults countering traditional sexual values and morality, often in public. The church was in a catch-22 situation: to support the validity of homosexual relationships (few committed partnerships were made public

at this time) could be seen as supporting the counterculture movement; to support traditional views would be supporting the existing worldview.

3) Biblical studies did reveal a few scriptural passages opposing same-gender sexual activity outside of committed relationships (religious cults of prostitution). Even though Jesus did not address this issue, nowhere does scripture affirm intimate same-gender relationships.

4) Other more practical reasons, likely, influenced decision-making, such as maintaining the *status quo* until evidence requires a positive position; more time is needed for study; an affirmative position will upset the unity of the church and reduce the financial support from its members; some even embraced Paul's position mentioned to the Corinthian church: "Do not cause your neighbor to stumble, even if what you do is not wrong." What then is the position of the church on the issue of homosexuality?

What the Church Says
Background

By 1970, national governing bodies of mainline denominations began receiving overtures concerning homosexuality seeking guidance for congregations The first responses were general in nature because of the lack of knowledge biblically, scientifically, and socially. The initial responses viewed homosexuality as a departure from the natural structure of God's creation. Very soon, denominations recognized the need to appoint a task force to provide research and preliminary studies for congregations and governing bodies.

The studies and decisions of the Presbyterian Church will be used as the model. Other mainline denominational studies are similar. The preliminary study for each national Presbyterian body (Presbyterian Church, US and USA) was prepared in 1977 so each General Assembly could respond to the study at its annual meeting in 1978. *A position or policy paper* was then drafted and adopted by each General Assembly. The studies of both bodies were similar, and both assemblies adopted a major portion of the studies that became a *position or policy paper*. The decisions are not constitutionally binding on the congregations in the two denominations; they are simply the voice of those particular general assemblies hoping to provide counsel and guidance for congregations and other governing bodies of the Presbyterian Church; however, in some instances the authority rose to *definitive guidance*. More will be said about that concerning officers and ministers in the church.

General Conclusions

The studies believed that 5 to 10 percent of the population is predominantly homosexual and that it is caused primarily by psychological and social factors, with some possible influence from biological factors. Most homosexual persons do not consciously choose their affectionate preference (sexual orientation). It is believed that the creation of humankind, male and female, to be the fundamental pattern of relationship and appropriate context for genital sexual expression. Same-gender sexual intimacy is seen as a *contradiction of God's wise and beautiful pattern for human sexual relations*. This is not to say that God intended to limit the possibility for a meaningful life to heterosexual marriage.

At this point the study is referring to celibacy using Jesus as an example. Concerning the nature and cause of homosexuality, the study admits that it cannot give a definitive answer. The study does conclude that *homosexuality is not God's wish for humanity. It is a sign of brokenness in God's world rather than willful rebellion*. It is also believed that some people freely choose to demonstrate homosexual behavior; however, where homosexual orientation is not a choice, it is neither a gift from God nor a state or condition like race: it is the result of our living in a sinful world. The point being made is that God is not the author of homosexual orientation.

It is believed the practice of homosexuality is a sin, but the studies do not speak of the condition of the homosexual to be sinful, but it is believed that the condition of being homosexual is the result of sin as emphasized earlier. At the same time, the studies remind the reader that all persons are sinful and no one has a spiritual basis for feeling self-righteous. The sin of *homophobia* is strongly discouraged. The studies reflect the belief that homosexuals can make use of the *resources of grace and receive God's power to transform their desires and arrest their active expression.*

Biblical Conclusions

Since scientific studies are inconclusive concerning the origin of homosexuality, the study and position papers rely upon scripture as the primary way to understand God's intention for human sexuality. The basic biblical passages for reference are: Leviticus 18:22 and 20:13, Romans 1:26-27, 1 Corinthians 6:9-10, and 1 Timothy 1:9-10. Conclusions from one or more of these passages are:

1) homosexual behavior is sinful and an abomination to God
2) homosexual passion and behavior are unnatural (contrary to God's created intention for humans as described in Genesis 1 and 2) and dishonorable
3) homosexual practice is incompatible with the Christian faith and life
4) Jesus affirms godly celibacy for those who do not engage in a marriage covenant
5) the teaching of scripture indicates that genital sexual expression is meant to occur in the covenant of a heterosexual marriage.

Church Membership

Those who manifest homosexual behavior should be treated with the same respect and pastoral care due all God's children. Since the church is a hospital for sinners, all sinners, then the church is called to welcome homosexuals in its membership, hoping that in the context of a loving community homosexual persons can arrive at a clear understanding of God's will for their sexual expression. In summary, "homosexual persons who sincerely make a profession of their faith and obedience should not be excluded from membership" (pp. 206-07, "Homosexuality and the Church: A Position Paper").

Ordination

The *position paper* reads: *For the church to ordain a self-affirming, practicing homosexual person to ministry would be to act in contradiction to its charter and calling in scripture. The repentant homosexual person who directs his or her sexual desires toward a married heterosexual commitment or can live a celibate lifestyle can certainly be ordained to office. Our present understanding of God's will precludes the ordination of persons who do not repent of homosexual practice.*[9] These conclusions concerning ordination of officers have been reaffirmed by succeeding General Assemblies of both Presbyterian bodies in the form of *definitive guidance*. Some have attributed more authority to *definitive guidance* than to other policy statements that have come from General Assemblies. Normally, only statements in the constitution have binding power in congregational life and lower judicatories. As a result, *definitive guidance* became a source of debate and challenge, leading to the adoption of a constitutional statement.

In 1997 a majority of the Presbyteries in the Presbyterian Church (USA) gave approval to adopt and add to the Book of Order the following paragraph to the chapter on *the church and its officers: G-6.0106b Those who are called to office in the church are to lead a life in obedience to scripture and in conformity to the historic confessional standards of the church. Among these standards is the requirement to live either in fidelity within the covenant of marriage between a man and a woman, or chastity in singleness. Persons refusing to repent of any self-acknowledged practice which the confessions call sin shall not be ordained and /or installed as deacons, elders, and ministers of the word and sacrament.*[10]

Although this statement does not specifically mention partnerships between two people of the same gender, the primary purpose for crafting the statement is to address sexual intimacy among people of the same gender. In governing bodies, discussion of the phrase *chastity in singleness* has focused solely upon homosexuals. Virtually nothing has been said about *chastity in singleness* for heterosexual singles. The last sentence refers to *refusing to repent of any self-acknowledged practice that the confessions call sin shall not be ordained.* In the Presbytery (governing body) to which I belong, nothing has been said about that important sentence in a time when Sabbath-keeping has become a joke even among ordained ministers and officers. Much is said in the confessions of the Presbyterian Church as well as scripture about the importance of Sabbath-keeping.

In 2001 the General Assembly sent to Presbyteries an amendment to delete this paragraph from the Book of Order and to terminate any binding authority in the phrase *definitive guidance.* This amendment did not receive a majority of the votes of Presbyteries; therefore, it was defeated. In 2003 and 2004, the General Assembly voted not to act on an overture to delete paragraph G-6.0106b.

In 2010 the general assembly sent an overture to its Presbyteries recommending a substitute statement for G-6.0106b. This time the Presbyteries approved the deletion of the *fidelity in marriage or chastity in singleness* statement and replaced it with a more constructive and universal statement that everyone can embrace. This change in the constitution of the Presbyterian Church still does not give a minister the privilege of blessing the union or marriage of two people of the same gender.

Problems with What the Church Says
Introduction

I was a commissioner to the 1979 General Assembly when the position paper was recommended for adoption. I voted for it. What were some of the reasons? First, commissioners are given a huge volume of information that has to be read and processed prior to the meeting of the General Assembly. I could not find the time to do an in-depth study on this subject that I knew very little about. Second, it was impossible to be a faithful member of the committee to which I was appointed and attend the hearings of the committee handling this report. I attended some but not all. The hearings provide a wonderful opportunity to hear other sides of the issue. Third, as a result, it is assumed those serving on the committee dealing with this issue would have done in-depth study and research; therefore, unless there was a glaring reason (strong minority report), I was prepared to support the recommendation of the committee, which favored passage of the *position paper.*

Fourth, at that time I did not distinguish between homosexual orientation and behavior. I assumed most people chose to be homosexuals. Fifth, at this time in American history, my greatest exposure to same-gender relationships was viewed in the media as a counter-culture revolution. Sixth, I thought it would be in the best interest of youth to support this position. Seventh, the popular worldview I had embraced when growing up was congruent with the conclusions of the *position paper,* although the position paper opened my eyes to the complexity of the problem.

Eighth, I felt good about the positive emphasis in the *position paper,* and I thought it dealt with the subject with compassion and sensitivity, especially the emphasis on acceptance in church life. Ninth, the understanding of scripture as presented and interpreted in the *position paper* was the major influence for voting in its favor. I felt Jesus Christ, who nowhere says anything affirming same-gender intimate relationships, and the scripture are the primary sources of authority for guidance in faith and practice.

What is the Problem?

What then is the problem with what the church said before 2010? Since 1979 I have had an opportunity to study the scripture for myself. To read the seven or eight verses in the scripture referring to same-gender sexual activity was easy. To review the story of Lot in Sodom was not time-consuming. What was time-consuming involved taking time to see these passages in their immediate contexts and to read the entire story of Israel from Genesis through the prophets to be introduced to their major concern with sinfulness, which was practicing idolatry by worshiping pagan gods. The pagan practice mentioned most often beginning with the exodus from Egypt to captivity in Babylon is the worship of the goddess, Asherah, a fertility cult with male prostitutes who serviced males, as well as female prostitutes who serviced males. Nowhere in the Old Testament do I recall a prostitute (male or female) servicing a female.

I then read the New Testament and passages referring to same-gender sexual activity. That was followed by word studies. I discovered that the word *homosexual* is not even in scripture, although the new versions beginning with the Revised Standard incorrectly inserted the term *homosexual* for the Greek terms *malakoi* and *arsenokoitai*.

Decisions being made by the church today on this subject are still being supported by studies done nearly thirty years ago. Many in the church today are still saying scripture clearly condemns homosexuality. Some in the church are not even willing to reexamine the definitive term, *clearly* or *unequivocally*. Even today many churches are categorically declaring all same-gender intimate relationships to be sinful. These decisions are either based on personal prejudice similar to what I embraced between 1950-1980 or upon the studies done by church denominations in the 1970s. Why is this a problem?

I think all would agree that it is wrong for the church to prohibit a person from responding to God's call to serve as an officer or minister based on secular or social prejudices. The study papers in no way deal with the powerful nature of social prejudice toward homosexuals. Most everyone in the church in the 1970s grew up during a time when homosexuality was not only considered a pathological disease, but we also believed homosexuals were really heterosexuals who elected to be involved in same-gender sexual activity. The studies do condemn homophobia, but not widespread social prejudice that at that time in history implicitly influenced nearly everyone.

What about making decisions today based on those studies done nearly twenty-five years ago? I will give some examples where research and experience call into question some portions of the *position paper* adopted in 1979 based on studies that began in 1975. The paper says that *most authorities now assume both heterosexuality and homosexuality result primarily from psychological and social factors affecting human beings during their growth toward maturity . . . and some possible influence from biological factors.*

Since 1975, research shows a growing biological influence connected with orientation and less psychological and social. Through interviews with homosexual persons, it is learned that the social and psychological context has had little influence on their orientation. Concerning the cause of orientation, homosexual persons are as baffled as those who are doing the research. As a result many attribute their orientation to the creator God. Since orientation is not learned, it is now believed that contact with homosexuals will not make a person a homosexual. This is even true of a child growing up with parents who are same-gender partners.

The learned theory (social and psychological) in the *position paper* leaves people with the impression that homosexual orientation can be unlearned, and to be successful it requires a desire from both the homosexual and the therapist. I call this *choice by reverse,* leaving the full responsibility for orientation on the back of the homosexual person through healing. In the end, the consequence of this is no different from the view that homosexuals choose to be homosexual. If that is the case, orientation is not an issue, because in reality it does not exist.

The position paper does not provide success/failure data concerning the option for reversing homosexual orientation through healing or therapy, but it does place responsibility upon the homosexual person by emphasizing that success is dependent upon the client's desire to be healed. At the present time, it is generally accepted that healing for those who are exclusively homosexual is virtually impossible and can actually be spiritually and psychologically damaging. Even among those whose homosexual orientation is not as dominant, healing usually means changing behavioral patterns rather than orientation; in many cases it leaves the person confused and depressed, struggling with deep guilt about same-gender attraction. The position paper does not deal with these issues about which we are more knowledgeable today.

The position paper also concludes that *homosexuality is not God's wish for humanity. It is a sign of brokenness in the world.* The paper states: *homosexuality goes against God's created intention of male and female, created to become one flesh as described in the first two chapters of Genesis.* I do not believe that God is responsible for homosexual orientation, but at the same time I would not attempt to enter the mind of God by indicating that homosexuality is a sign of brokenness, any more than heterosexuality is a sign of brokenness.

Why are some people right-handed and others left-handed? Why are some people more practical minded and others more ethereal? Why are some people very musical while others cannot carry a tune in a bucket? Is it necessary to attribute difference to brokenness? I think this theological conclusion treads on thin ice and offers little help and no consolation to the homosexual person. Yes, according to scripture and Jesus Christ, God wants human beings to experience wholeness, but a person does not have to be heterosexual to experience wholeness. Wholeness comes through loving God, one another, and self, and through fulfilling relationships embraced by the fruits of the spirit. Homosexual persons are not broken any more than heterosexual persons. They can experience God's created intention of human wholeness.

To make a decision that excludes people from full membership of the church based on studies done twenty-five to thirty years ago, I think, will be viewed with disdain in years to come. The *position paper* indicates that its major conclusions come from biblical study as it relies upon the preliminary study on homosexuality ordered by the 1972 General Assembly of the Presbyterian Church (US). The preliminary study does acknowledge and share options for interpreting the seven biblical passages that specifically refer to same-gender sexual activity. The study also examines the context of the mentioned same-gender sexual activity. The study, however, reveals limited knowledge about the distinction between homosexual orientation and practice.

Concerning the three New Testament passages, the study refers to homosexual persons mentioned in these passages. The 1 Timothy and 1 Corinthian passages do not say these persons are homosexual. In the text, each person is described by specific sexual activity, not orientation. One person, *malakoi,* is passive, so is either a prostitute or young boy (slave); the other person, *arsenokoitai,* is active, and very likely a rapist similar to the men in Sodom. There is no indication that either of these people is homosexual as we understand that term to mean today: one whose orientation causes attraction to those of the same gender. Those mentioned in the New Testament are likely heterosexual by orientation.

The study paper refers to them as homosexual persons, which is misleading and contributes a strong bias to the conclusions. It also confuses what is meant by natural/unnatural in Paul's letter to the Romans (1:26-27).[11] See the third chapter of this book where the study is done on these verses as well as other passages referring to same-gender sexual activity. As mentioned throughout this book, these passages make no attempt to address situations in the church today where two people of the same gender desire to live in a faithful monogamous relationship.

The *position paper* also refers to the seven biblical passages where same-gender sexual activity is mentioned but does not share different views of interpretation, nor does it refer to the context, yet it concludes: "the New Testament declares that all homosexual practice is incompatible with the Christian faith and life."[12] One thing is clear about the Romans, 1 Timothy, and 1 Corinthians passages: they are addressing specific kinds of same-gender sexual activity and are not presenting a sexual ethic concerning homosexuality. The above conclusion is not correct biblically.

The *position paper* then attempts to give more credibility to its conclusion by referring to human creation and natural law: "Biblical revelation . . . in both the Old and New Testaments and confirmed in nature, clearly indicates that genital sexual expression is meant to occur within the covenant of heterosexual marriage."[13] I think a more accurate statement reflecting biblical teaching and practice sounds like this: in both the Old and New Testaments, genital expression is meant to occur within relationships marked by faithfulness, economic support, and love (New Testament).

Monogamous relationships were not realized until the church moved into Greece and Rome where monogamy was already practiced, but even then monogamy did not exclude concubines for the husband. So what is wrong with what the church says today? Its conclusions are based on studies done twenty-five to thirty years ago that need to be reexamined and corrected. The new studies also need to involve the people in the pew; it could be a phenomenal biblical experience for everyone.

The Task of the Church

First, I suggest that mainstream denominations unite by creating a joint taskforce. This interdenominational taskforce needs to create a study guide on human sexuality for congregations. The study guide needs to contain differing points of view of science (biology, genetics, psychology, and sociology), theology, and biblical studies. I believe people in the pew who have to cope with human sexuality every day have much to contribute in reaching conclusions about marriage, family, and sexuality. Reports and suggestions need to be made to higher judicatories indicating that such studies have been done and that their contributions will be honored and will make a difference.

Second, leaders in the church need to be honest about what we know and do not know concerning the biblical passages referring to same-gender sexual activity. For a leader to stand before a congregation and say *scripture clearly and unequivocally condemns all homosexual behavior* is simply not true. The Bible does condemn some forms of same-gender sexual behavior in the same way it condemns some forms of heterosexual behavior. I have yet to hear anyone say scripture condemns all heterosexual behavior since it does condemn some. Honesty and consistency are important if the church is going to maintain integrity and have moral influence.

Third, I believe the church needs to delineate clearly between homosexual orientation and homosexual behavior, and let it be known that orientation is not a choice, either for homosexuals or heterosexuals. I feel that a majority of the population in this country still believe people choose to be homosexual. In the past twenty years, I have spoken to or read about at least 200 gay and lesbian persons who have been asked: *did you choose to be homosexual?* Not one of those persons said yes. One hundred percent said they gradually became aware of their sexual orientation. Who is in a better position to know than those who are lesbian and gay persons? Many of these people denied their homosexuality to themselves for months and years.

Fourth, I believe thorough, unbiased research needs to done concerning *therapy for gays and lesbians* who are seeking help. The word *healing* is unacceptable because it implies sickness. I realize some persons are not happy in having a homosexual orientation. In many cases, therapy has created additional problems such as depression, guilt, denial, loneliness, and repression. All forms of therapy need to be monitored by the professional codes of the American Psychiatric Association. Whatever gays and lesbians elect to do about their orientation, it is extremely supportive for society to be loving, open, and accepting, providing an environment where they, like all people, are free to identify their gifts, nurture them, and use them fully as they live in meaningful relationships marked by the fruit of God's spirit.

Fifth, I appeal to the church and its leaders, especially *evangelical*, to correct previously incorrect statements, stereotypes, and conclusions about homosexual persons, such as *to be homosexual is a choice, a disease, or an addiction like alcoholism, or learned by repeated sexual activity, sinful in the eyes of God. Gays and lesbians can be healed with God's help if they really want to be healed. Scripture clearly condemns homosexual persons.* The church needs to challenge public statements that are incorrect and create prejudice as the one appearing in the August 6, 2001, issue of *Newsweek* in an article about the Boy Scouts: "In the Bible, it's a sin to be gay."

Sixth, since the church is the body of Christ and people of grace, it needs to respond to all people in a spirit of grace so they, like a flower exposed to sun, will be exposed to God, who provides spiritual nourishment, enabling them to blossom and enrich the lives of those around them. As people of grace, the church first attempts to find a biblical and Christological reason to be inclusive rather than seeking a means to exclusive. When God's grace comes first, all God's people will be drawn into community and unity. God's grace continues to be a more excellent way.

Seventh, it is critically important for the church to affirm over and over again that it is a community, a family of God's people. All people have one need in common, whether conservative or liberal, homosexual or heterosexual, male or female, young or old. We are not complete without living together in fulfilling relationships. God essentially said, "It is not good for any<u>one</u> to be alone." This can be said more strongly than the theological statement "God created male and female; only in that union is intimacy permissible." Nowhere is that concluding phrase found in scripture; in fact, that statement is invalidated throughout scripture. It is God's gift of sexuality that attracts us to another to live in a fulfilling relationship.

Scripture teaches that physical and spiritual wholeness are experienced through a fulfilling relationship with God and with fellow humans. This is true for both homosexual and heterosexual persons; therefore, when either realizes that a committed relationship addresses that need, it reflects the will of the creator God. For this reason, *partnership* needs to be the formal relational title shared by both male/female and same-gender committed relationships with both retaining their uniqueness with the subtitle *marital partnership* for male and female couples and *same-gender partnership* for couples of the same gender.

This saves the partnership for the homosexual person from becoming an appendage to marriage. It also preserves and enables the church to continue to define a marriage as the union of a man and a woman. The *partnerships* for both homosexual and heterosexual couples are beyond being erotic. Both *partnerships* are fulfilled by mutual relationships of love, commitment, support, responsibility, creative expression, and adventure. The following chapter provides the basis for not identifying partnerships among people of the same gender as a marriage.

Endnotes: Chapter Eight

[1]   Betty Schonauer, Brick Bradford, William Showalter, Leonard LeSourd, Catherine Jackson, Robert Whitaker, *Healing for the Homosexual* (Oklahoma City, Presbyterian Charismatic Communion, Inc., 1978), pp. 5-51.

[2]   Nicolosi, p. 75

[3]   Ibid., p. 76

[4]   Tricia Dykers Koenig, Letter to Editor of *The Presbyterian Outlook* (Richmond: The Presbyterian Outlook Publishers, August 2-9, 1999), p. 2.

5   Richard Rohr, "Where the Gospel Leads Us," in *Homosexuality and the Christian Faith,* edited by Walter Wink (Minneapolis: Fortress Press, 1999), p. 86.

6   Boswell, pp. 15-17

7   Ralph Ellis, "Silent No More" in *The Atlanta Journal-Constitution* (Atlanta: Cox News Service, April 13, 2002), p. B1.

8   Peter Gomes, *The Good Book* (New York: William Morrow and Company, Inc., 1996), p. 162.

9   *Homosexuality and the Church: A Position Paper* in the Minutes of 119th General Assembly of the Presbyterian Church in the US (Atlanta: Office of the Stated Clerk, 1979), pp. 201-209.

10 *The Church and Its Officers: G-6.0106b* in Book of Order: Constitution of the Presbyterian Church (USA), Part II (Louisville: The Office of the General Assembly, 2001), G-6.0106b.

11 *The Church and Homosexuality: A Preliminary Study* (Atlanta: Materials Distribution, 1977), pp. 15-23.

12 *Homosexuality and the Church: A Position Paper*, p. 206.

13. Ibid., p. 206

CHAPTER NINE

Marks of Marriage: Old Testament Israel through the Early Church

O God, you give humanity its name,
Your covenant of grace remains the same:
Be with these two who now before you wait:
Enlarge the love they come to consecrate.
Fred Kaan

Introduction

Whatever be one's view concerning same-gender partnerships or cohabitation prior to marriage or divorce or arranged marriages or celibacy, most Christians believe God created human beings with a basic need to live in fulfilling relationships. At this point, Christians share common ground. Today, many Christians would also affirm God created marriage to be a major way to experience a fulfilling relationship.

We may be surprised to learn that the Church, in two-thirds of its history, did not see the primary purpose of marriage as the means for living in fulfilling mutual relationships marked by love, justice, compassion, kindness, and other fruits of the spirit. Likewise, the story of Israel and the church in scripture see marriage possessing multiple purposes, some different from the ideals of marriage in our time.

The night before I began writing this chapter on marriage, I read articles in *Newsweek* magazine describing the recent controversy in the Roman Catholic Church about priests being accused of sexually abusing children and teens, both male and female. Some feel the problem centers around the church's present laws concerning celibacy and marriage. Richard Sipe, a former priest who is now a psychotherapist, conducted a twenty-five-year study of celibacy, sexuality, and the clergy and estimates that at any given time 50 percent of priests, no matter what their orientation, are sexually active in some way."[1]

While the Catholic Church deals with the marital status of its priests, a fundamentalist preacher is telling the congregation that in marriage a wife should submit graciously to the servant leadership of her husband. In another arena of life, David Weinlick and Elizabeth Runze celebrate their first anniversary of an arranged marriage that is turning out happily. In a contest, David had friends pick a wife for him; two weeks before his wedding, he met Elizabeth for the first time. Although radical at this time in American history, this contest has an ancient and somewhat biblical ring to it.[2]

In many ways, the subject of marriage and sexuality have been on the forefront of the news media. American society wrestles with a divorce rate that borders on 46 percent of its marriages. In response, the governor of Louisiana in 2001 signed into law a new *covenant marriage* bill. Couples in that state can now opt out of *no-fault divorce* and elect *covenant marriage,* which requires both premarital and predivorce counseling. At the same time, a recent study of Gen-Xers (people born between 1963 and 1981) reveals they are putting financial independence and career stability before marriage. Sexual relationships prior to marriage are agreed upon with no strings attached and are seldom accompanied by the expressed term *love*. Many of the Xers who embrace this attitude grew up with parents who were experiencing a bad marriage or were divorced, so these Xers see marriage as an enormous risk.[3]

In a letter to Abby Van Buren, its author says, "I am a gay man who is in the middle of a nasty divorce ending a ten-year marriage. I married to hide from my conservative religious parents and family the fact that I am gay. The divorce has been a terrible experience for both my wife and me, and we will bear scars of this broken relationship for many years to come. How I wish I had waited until I was strong enough to deal honestly with my sexuality instead of getting married . . . Abby, my effort to become a heterosexual was a total farce for me!"[4]

As humans seek ways to live in fulfilling relationships in such confusion, what does scripture actually say about marriage, and how was it practiced by the biblical people of faith? To begin with, very likely the ancient Hebrews adopted the same purposes and patterns of marriage as their neighbors in the Middle East since their origin occurs in the fertile crescent of Mesopotamia. This means they adopted the cultural patterns of their day with the specific belief that marriage was instituted by God during the act of creation. The book of Genesis presents two perspectives. In the first chapter male and female are created simultaneously and are commanded to "be fruitful and multiply and fill the earth." This picture of marriage or *the coming together of male and female* involves a sexual union.

The second chapter of Genesis is more descriptive in the creation of male and female. The Yahwist community sees creation beginning with a creature of dust infused with the spirit of the creator, Lord God. This creature is alone and therefore lacks wholeness. With the substance of this creature (the rib), Yahweh creates a woman. In this descriptive manner, the Lord God crafts male and female. It requires another creature of the same substance to satisfy loneliness and achieve wholeness. Then, in reflection upon this magnificent creation, this

Hebrew faith community concludes, "Therefore, a man leaves his father and his mother and clings to his wife, and they become one flesh."

Once again, this second picture of marriage depicts a sexual union. So the Hebrew community believed the primary purpose of the marriage of male and female was for procreation—a sexual union. This is strongly emphasized throughout scripture and the church until the Reformation.

A second purpose of marriage emphasized in scripture is to provide for the maintenance of the social order of families. Both father and mother assume responsibility for the nurture and support of the household, which includes, children, slaves, and the elderly. Third, marriage alongside procreation creates an heir so property can remain in the family. These three purposes of marriage serve a utilitarian purpose centered on economics: the creation, maintenance, and preservation of the household. Marriage, therefore, is not only a sexual union, it is also an economic union.

Finally, marriage responds strongly to the need for humans to live in a fulfilling relationship rather than being alone. Scripture does not elaborate upon this purpose other than what is said in the second chapter of Genesis, "It is not good for the man to be alone." Humans, according to scripture, cannot experience wholeness outside meaningful relationships. For this reason we are created to live within the intimacy of families, to enjoy friendships, and for some to experience the intimacy of marriage.

If God has created humans with this need of intimacy, how then does the church support homosexuals, for whom heterosexual marriage is false, personally destructive, and lacks integrity? One purpose of this chapter is to show that marriage is not the biblical paradigm for homosexuals. If the church has the courage and compassion to support homosexual persons in satisfying their God-given need for intimate relationships, it needs to create a new paradigm rather than blessing a same-gender union as if it were a marriage.

At the same time, the major purpose of marriage has changed considerably. In scripture marriage is first a sexual union between a man and a woman for the purpose of procreation. This was true for the church until the Reformation. Since the Reformation, the primary focus of marriage has changed from procreation to "an intimate union of man and woman marked by the commitment in fidelity and forgiveness that represents God's own covenant of love." The term *marriage* no longer describes the major purpose of the union of all males and females. For this reason, the title *partnership* best describes the union of male and female, as well as two people of the same gender.

Since marriage and sexuality still remain connected both in our culture and in the Christian church, its uniqueness is retained with the specific title of a *marital partnership*. To identify same-gender unions as marriages lacks biblical integrity. The term *marriage* does not reflect the primary purpose for unions among people of the same gender. They are united, not for the sexual purpose of procreation but for the purpose of living in a fulfilling relationship in order to achieve the wholeness that God desires for all creation.

As we examine the marks of marriage in the Old and New Testaments, the early and medieval church, and the Reformed church, I think it will be evident that same-gender unions need to have a life of their own, a paradigm that uniquely and clearly communicates their primary purpose. The union of male and female and two people of the same gender share the same major purpose: both are committed and fulfilling mutual partnerships marked by love and faithfulness, enabling one another to experience the happiness and wholeness of being the person created in the image of God.

Marks of Marriage in Old Testament Times
Responsible and Committed

In the present time, the words *love* and *happiness* are commonly associated with marriage. At the wedding, the officiating minister may say *marriage is instituted by God for the mutual welfare and happiness of husband and wife;* often, Paul's chapter on love in 1 Corinthians will be read. In biblical times those words were seldom used to describe the coming together of persons in the act of matrimony. In biblical history through the time of David, the word *love* is used approximately two dozen times to describe the feelings of one person for another. Three of those occasions describe Jonathan's love for David; another, Amnon's love for his sister Tamar whom he raped; and another, Shechem the Hivite, who loved Dinah, the daughter of Jacob and Leah, whom he also raped. The most familiar expressions of love among people described in scripture are Jacob's love for Rachel and the poem of two unmarried lovers entitled Song of Songs.

In this hierarchical age, marriages for the most part are arranged rather than determined by courtship, love, and free choice. This was a practice of many ancient Middle Eastern cultures. A good example is the selection of a wife for Isaac. Abraham sends a trusted servant to his relatives in Haran of Mesopotamia to obtain a wife for his son. Rebecca, the daughter of Bethuel, is selected. The servant bestows expensive gifts upon Rebecca's family and together they return to Canaan. At their first meeting, Isaac takes Rebecca into Sarah's tent.

It is assumed this private moment of intimacy consummates their marriage. The text also says that Isaac grows to love Rebecca, who comforts him after the loss of his mother (Genesis 24). At the point of marriage Isaac becomes committed to and responsible for Rebecca. For them marriage was a sexual and economic union. In the next mention of their relationship, the scripture says Rebecca has no children. So Isaac pleads with God and Rebecca conceives and gives birth to Esau and Jacob. For Isaac and Rebecca, marriage is a sexual union for the purpose of procreation.

Second, the story Jacob and Esau reveals the reason for having children, sons in particular. The oldest son in the family receives the birthright and father's blessing to assure that property and wealth remain in the family for future generations. Of course, Jacob, through trickery, steals both from his older brother, Esau. As a result, he flees for his life and goes to Haran, the birthplace of his mother, Rebecca. There he meets his uncle Laban's daughter, Rachel and falls in love with her.

He reaches an agreement with Laban. He works seven years for Laban to pay for the bride. On the wedding night he unknowingly sleeps with Leah and has intercourse. In this trickery, he learns in their culture the older daughter must marry before the younger. In this case, the marriage was arranged without Jacob's consent; their marriage is consummated by intercourse. When Jacob pledges to work for his uncle for seven more years, he and Rachel are married. Jacob is now committed to and responsible for two wives.

The marital drama does not end. Leah bears children, Rachel does not. To conceive a child, it is then permissible for Jacob to have intercourse with Rachel's maid, Bilhah, as it was for Abraham to have intercourse with Sarah's maid, Hagar. When Leah is unable to conceive, she gives Jacob her maid Zilpah, who also bears children. Before Jacob returns to Canaan, he has fathered twelve sons and one daughter by two wives and two concubines. The family dramas of Isaac and Jacob reveal many of the marital customs not only of Israel but also that part of the world till the time of Jesus. The first marks of marriage in the Hebrew culture are commitment and responsibility. It is unlikely in this context that love and happiness would be envisioned as they are today.

Life Together

Even though marriage brought husband and wife together for intimate sexual experiences, husband and wife did not spend much time together. There are many reasons for this. First, the wife was considered property of the husband to be used to bear children and care for the family and work in the fields. It was a hierarchal superior/inferior relationship. The value of the female in terms of money is seen in Deuteronomy: "If a man meets a virgin who is not engaged and seizes her and lies with her, and they are caught in the act, the man who lay with her shall give fifty shekels of silver to the young woman's father, and she shall become his wife" (22:28-29).

Individual rights for the wife were very limited. The husband could even demand that a wife terminate a vow given to God (Numbers 30:10-12). In some situations in the biblical story of faith, wives are given significant status like Rachel, Ruth, and Deborah; in other situations their names are not even mentioned, like Noah's wife and his son's wives. Sometimes they are used for protection, as in the case of Abram giving his wife, Sarai, to an Egyptian king as his sister (Genesis 12:10-20).

Second, husbands also spent much time away from home, usually with other males of equal status, bearing responsibility for the family's livelihood by farming, hunting, fishing, or caring for herds of sheep. Third, it was not uncommon for the husband to have more than one wife and a few concubines. For this reason, if possible economically, the husband had separate living quarters. In first-century Hebrew culture, polygamy was a not a popular practice, but the men who could afford it had concubines.

What then were the signs of faithfulness in the Hebrew culture? For wives who were property of the husband, faithfulness required no sexual involvement with other men. This was a violation of the seventh commandment on adultery. For the husband, faithfulness involved caring for the economic needs of the family, which may include more than one wife and concubines. Hebrew law states: "If he (a man) takes another wife to himself, he shall not diminish the food, clothing, and marital rights of the first wife" (Exodus 21:10). If the husband became sexually involved with someone else's wife, he would be committing adultery.

Fourth, how was intercourse between husband and wife regarded in Hebrew culture? Most often, when intercourse between husband and wife is specifically mentioned, pregnancy is the result; however, sexual activity between husband and wife is considered normal and positive under most circumstances. At the age of ninety-nine years, when Sarah hears that she will conceive and bear a son, she laughs and says, "After I have grown old and my husband is old, shall I have pleasure?" (Genesis 18:12). The love poem, *Song of Songs,* positively communicates sensual feelings between male and female, especially since the songs have been interpreted by the Jewish community to be a picture of the relationship between God and the community of faith.

On the other hand, some of the purity laws of the Old Testament give the impression the sex act causes the couple to be unclean. For example, a priest is required to marry a virgin and forbidden to marry a woman who was a prostitute (Leviticus 21:7). The text implies that only a virgin is ritually clean; therefore, by implication there is something spiritually unclean about sex and those who have engaged in it. The *holiness code* also says that after intercourse the man and woman must take a bath; they remain unclean until evening. It also states that anything semen touches is unclean (Leviticus 15:16-18). These laws, along with the inferior status of the wife as property, very likely contributed to the husband's involvement with prostitutes. Throughout the period of the monarchy (1030-586 BC), scripture mentions the influence of the pagan cultic worship in the temples of Asherah, which housed both male and female prostitutes. Very likely that is the concern of the references to homosexuality in Leviticus 18: 22 and 20:13.

Children

One of the major marks of marriage was bearing and nurturing children. The wife's personhood was dependent upon marriage and bearing children. The prophet Isaiah describes a time when many of the men of Jerusalem will be killed in war, leaving an imbalance of men to women in the population, so the women live on the verge of panic. "Seven women shall take hold of one man in that day, saying, 'We will eat our own bread and wear our own clothes, just let us be called by your name, and take away our disgrace'"(4:1). They are essentially giving up their most important legal right of survival—the economic support of the husband—in order to birth a child and maintain personhood through marriage. The eldest daughter marrying before younger sisters supports the importance of marriage for Hebrew females.

Personhood also hinges upon giving birth to children. This is documented over and over again throughout the Old Testament from Sarah to Rachel and Leah, and then expressed in anguish and sacrifice in the life of Hannah, who pledges to give her firstborn to the religious service of the priesthood. Perhaps the best known illustration of the importance of birthing children is seen as law in Deuteronomy 25:5: "When brothers reside together, and one of them dies and has no son, the wife of the deceased shall not be married outside the family to a stranger. Her husband's brother shall go in to her, taking her in marriage."

The purpose is to give the dead brother a descendent. Children are not only the source of support in old age, they are also the means for maintaining the life of the family, both materially (property and wealth) and spiritually (blessing of God). This passage is also found in Matthew, Mark, and Luke, used by the Sadducees, hoping to trick Jesus. Once again, the means by which to have children is sexual, emphasizing that *marriage is a sexual union* between male and female.

Separation

Finally, it is necessary to deal with the mark that separates marital partners, the grounds for termination of the marriage or divorce. Leviticus 20:10, "If a man commits adultery with the wife of his neighbor, both the adulterer and the adulteress shall be put to death." Not only is marriage in the Hebrew religious community considered an important sexual union, the misuse of that gift from God also becomes the basis for dissolving the union.

In summary, in the Old Testament community of faith the tie that binds male and female together in marriage is commitment and responsibility. Marriage served the utilitarian purpose for the procreation of children and for maintaining the social structure of the family or household, which has always been the nucleus of the Hebrew nation, Israel. None of this could have happened without recognizing and accepting the significant role sexuality plays in the marriage relationship.

Marks of Marriage in New Testament Times

Very likely the Old Testament pattern of marriage for the Hebrews remained the same during the life and ministry of Jesus Christ in the first century; nevertheless, what is introduced in Christ's teachings and lifestyle creates a new perspective on marriage. The same is true of the teaching of the apostle Paul, especially seen in his letters to the Ephesians and Corinthians. At the same time, we are not exposed to models of marriage that reflect what is envisioned in the New Testament.

We know very little about the marriage and family life of Peter, Paul, and others. Some feel that Paul at one time had a wife since he was a member of the Hebrew Council (Acts 26:10). Council members were supposed to be married. At the same time, in his first letter to Christ followers in Corinth he says he is unmarried: "It is well for them (widows) to remain unmarried as I am" (7:8). Apparently, the cultural pattern of marriage in the Old Testament continued during New Testament times. Let's examine some of the seeds for change as reflected in life and teachings of Christ and Paul.

Jesus Christ and Marriage

To begin with, Jesus was not married. That represents a significant departure from the expected customs of Jewish culture. It was expected of all Jewish males to be married by the age of twenty, unless they were students of the law. If they were not married at this age, they were in violation of the commandment "To be fruitful and multiply." For example, following the revelation of her first pregnancy in old age,

Elizabeth exclaimed: "Now at last the Lord has helped me. He has taken away my public disgrace" (Luke 1:25). Although Jesus was not married, he held marriage in high esteem, as did the Hebrew culture of the first century.

At the wedding feast in Cana of Galilee, he changed water into the finest wine. This enabled the festival to continue into the evening until it was time for the ceremony. Then the bride and groom were led by the wedding party to their new home through the streets by the lights of torches, enabling people of the community to extend their best wishes.[6]

John Witte writes: "Christ used the image of marriage and the family to teach the basics about the kingdom of God. 'The kingdom of heaven may be compared to a king who gave a marriage feast for this son.'"[7] On one occasion, Jesus referred to himself as the bridegroom when asked why he and his disciples do not fast like the followers of John the Baptist and the Pharisees. He responds, "Do you expect the guests at a wedding party to go without food? . . . As long as the bridegroom is with them, they will not do that" (Mark 2:18-19). At the same time Jesus did not believe that marriage comes before commitment to the ways of God's kingdom, nor do people marry in the kingdom to come.

Finally, it was Christ who referred to God's act of creation in setting forth the ideal principle of marriage. "Have you not read that He who made them from beginning 'made them male and female' and said, 'For this reason a man shall leave his father and mother and be joined to his wife, and the two shall become one flesh'? So they are no longer two, but one. No human being must separate, then, what God has joined together'" (Matthew 19:4-6). Jesus not only emphasizes that marriage is a sexual union; he adds a spiritual dimension to marriage, which like a seed will eventually germinate, take root, and blossom. But the seed remains dormant for many years in church history only to reach fruition following the Protestant Reformation.

In this same episode where Jesus is responding to an effort by the Pharisees to trap him on the subject of divorce, Jesus makes an interesting response to his disciples who are bewildered by his strong opposition to divorce. They assume it is then better not to marry and Jesus says, "There are eunuchs who have been so from birth, and there are eunuchs who have been made eunuchs by others, and there are eunuchs who have made themselves eunuchs" (Matthew 19:12).

It sounds to me, all three are sexual references. Two should not marry because they are unable to procreate. Some eunuchs were castrated to serve in a king's harem, as noted in the book of Esther; some eunuchs were born without procreative ability or desire. The third group are those who put the responsibilities of the kingdom of God before the responsibilities that accompany marriage and family, from which came the doctrine of celibacy among Christian priests.

I believe it is not only the spiritual references Jesus expressed about marriage that has made it more than a *sexual union;* it is also his sensitive treatment and mutual acceptance of women. He regarded them as equally human, thus violating many of the Jewish and Middle Eastern customs of his day. He not only conversed with them in public and treated them as friends, but women accompanied him and the male disciples in ministry. This new status would have profound influence on the formation of the New Testament church only to lose energy as church leadership becomes more hierarchical from the second to the sixteenth century, reflecting the patterns of Western society. During Jesus' ministry, the Jewish community retained its Old Testament patterns of marriage, but the early church under Paul's leadership began to expand its view of marriage.

Paul and Marriage

Paul, a Jewish scholar was trained in the law by one of the best teachers, Gamaliel. Paul, a Pharisee, who took it upon himself to persecute the early followers of Christ, sees the light and becomes an evangelistic missionary of the good news of Christ. Steeped in Jewish tradition, a scholar of Old Testament law, Paul moves beyond tradition and law to apply Christ's spiritual emphasis to marriage, likewise planting seeds that will not germinate until after the Reformation.

In the New Testament, Paul uses the model of Christ and the church in describing the relationship between husbands and wives, but first he introduces an image of mutual servanthood as the result of mutual commitment to Christ. "Be subject to one another out of reverence for Christ" (Ephesians 5:21). This is a radical break from the patriarchal view that the husband owns the wife, whose major role in the relationship is to provide and care for children. From this point, everything Paul says about husband/wife needs to be understood within this preamble of mutual subjection or servanthood, which sounds much like the message given by Christ to his disciples, "Whoever wishes to be great among you must be your servant" (Mark 10:44).

Using a Christological model, Paul then says: "Wives, be subject to your husbands as you are to the Lord" (5:24). Then Paul says to husbands, "Husbands love your wives just as Christ loved the church and gave himself up for her . . . He who loves his wife, loves himself" (Ephesians 5:25, 28b). In this Christological model, Paul communicates the importance of mutual subjection. Paul sees in Christ the restoration of wholeness for all God's created order. In Christ, husbands and wives can now live in fulfilling relationships of love where each seeks the highest good of the other. In our mutual relationship in Christ, the second Adam, we are able to return to paradise and begin the journey of life anew. Jesus possesses the power to conquer sinfulness so that its consequence, as expressed in Genesis 3:16, is eradicated and relational life begins anew on a higher plane.

In Christ, God's pronouncement has been radically altered from, "Yet your desire shall be for your husband, and he shall rule over you" (Genesis 3:16), to "there is no longer Jew or Greek, there is no longer slave or free, there is no longer male and female; for all of you are one in Christ Jesus" (Galatians 3:28). "So if anyone is in Christ, there is a new creation; everything old has passed away; see, everything has become new!" (2 Corinthians 5:17).

In Ephesians, Paul concludes that the deep mystery between the union of Christ and the church also applies to husbands and wives, thus enabling love to be central to the relationship. In his letter to Titus, Paul teaches "older women to encourage younger women to love their husbands" (Titus 2:4). In both cases, *love* (agape) describes commitment and seeking the highest good for the other. In his model, Paul places Christ in the center of the marriage relationship, which broadens the spiritual dimension, providing divine substance to the sexual union.

At the same time, Paul, like the Old Testament, recognizes the importance of the sexual dimension of marriage. To Timothy he writes: "Yet, she (woman) will be saved through childbearing" (1Timothy 2:15). On the one hand, Paul does not depart from the importance of marriage for procreation, but on the other hand, Paul's geographical context has a strong Greek influence. It frees him to consider the spiritual dimension of marriage and sexuality using Christ's relationship to the church as a model.

At the same time, the Greek influence apparently creates great caution when he writes to the Christians in Corinth where respectable women were seldom seen in public. When they were outside their separate living quarters, they were accompanied by a servant and were covered by a veil from the head to the feet. Marital purity was demanded by the husband, who enjoyed sexual license in the Greek culture. On the acropolis overlooking the city of Corinth stood the Temple of Aphrodite, which housed both male and female prostitutes who freely roamed the city streets.[8] Prostitution was a legalized business servicing men both married and unmarried.

When Paul wrote to Corinth, it was a man's world where marriage was primarily for procreation and taking care of the home. Wives were virtually prisoners in their homes to care for their legitimate children.[9] Margaret A. Farley writes: "Marriage for both Greeks and Romans was monogamous. In Ancient Greece, however, no sexual ethic confined sex to marriage. Hence, there was what some have referred to as sexual polygamy within marital monogamy."[10] This unwritten law, of course, refers to the husband, not the wife.

Paul's references to marriage and sexuality in his letters to the Corinthians need to be understood in this context. Also, like Christ, Paul gave priority to faithfulness to God's kingdom over marriage and the family. Likewise, Paul believed the close of the age and consummation of God's kingdom were imminent. All these factors contribute to understanding Paul's movement away from marriage to recommendations of celibacy to the recipients of his letter in Corinth. In the seventh chapter he tells the Corinthians, "Those who are married need to satisfy each other fully; each is the master of the other's body. To those who are unmarried and to widows, it is better to remain unmarried (celibate), but it is better to marry than burn with passion. I wish that all of you were (celibate) as I myself am."

Because of his belief in the imminent coming of God's kingdom and the closing of history, Paul actually encourages those who are married to live as if they were not married (celibate), so they can devote their full time to God's work of ministry (1 Corinthians 7:25-39). When seen in their social context and Paul's belief about the end of the age, these passages should not be taken as general commands about marriage and sexuality, but as specific recommendations to the Corinthian situation. Paul actually says, "This is said by way of concession, not of command" (1 Corinthians 7:6).

So when the biblical story of the New Testament church concludes, marriage continues to be a sexual union for the purpose of procreation and the social maintenance of the family; however, marriage is also seen as a mystical union where husband and wife love one another in servanthood in the same way that Christ gave up his life in love for the church, his body. In scripture, very little is said about the partners in marriage becoming one in flesh as a pleasurable experience of love. Song of Songs in the Old Testament communicates physical delight between male and female, but there is no evidence they are married.

Marriages in biblical Hebrew history begin with commitment, responsibility, and Christlike love. The fullness of mutual love (agape/eros/phileo) and happiness has not yet become a pattern conceivable for a culture that is strongly patriarchal and hierarchical and perceives women to be inferior to men. This is not to say that some in marriage did not grow to the fullness of love for one another. At this point it was left to the church and its leaders to translate these patterns that originated from a Hebraic mindset to a hierarchical culture that was governed by Roman law but with strong Greek philosophical roots. So what does the early and medieval church do with its inheritance from the scriptures concerning marriage, *the two shall become one flesh*?

Marks of Marriage in the Early Church

During the first 300 years of the Christian church, there were many voices representing its beliefs and practices. The church gradually moved from a democratic process of arriving at decisions in their geographical areas to church councils in order to have one voice concerning beliefs. This was necessary so the young church could present a consistent message to the world. In these first centuries, the church was primarily concerned about prostitution, because young boys and girls were so easily thrust into it.

There were many schools of thought about marriage, but early in the life of the church some began to question marriage as a calling because of the uncleanness of sex. Others, like the early church father Clement, defended marriage as instituted by God and necessary. He concluded that husbands may cohabit with wives with self-control but only for the purpose of begetting children. To have sexual intercourse without intending to have children was a violation of natural law.[11]

These views concerning uncleanness of sex likely came from a worldview strongly influenced by Greek philosophy, which identified the material or physical with the lower nature of humankind while spirit, mind, and ideas were identified with the higher nature of humankind.

These attitudes did not originate from the scriptures at this point in church history. They were already present in the Greco-Roman world in the philosophical thoughts of Stoicism and Gnosticism.

During this early period of the church, marriage was administered and governed by Roman law, and some Christians followed Roman customs that allowed for concubines.[12] Roman law declared procreation to be the only purpose for marriage. Roman society believed marriage and *passion love* were incompatible or antithetical. Though marriages were arranged in Roman culture, marriages were validated by mutual consent, after which the wife was taken to the husband's house.[13]

When Christianity became the adopted religion of the Roman Empire under Constantine, ecumenical councils were held from 325 to 451 AD to resolve theological issues and to adopt the canon (New Testament). During this period, the practice of marriage became a major concern for church leaders. It was at this time the power of the church gradually shifted from Constantinople toward Rome.

The leading Greek father, St. John Chrysostom (345-407), believed marriage was created by God for two major purposes: to make people chaste and to make people parents. He felt that marriage was a natural remedy to prevent fornication. At the same time Chrysostom felt that love between husband and wife provides harmony for the family, and this creates a solid society. Chrysostom did not embrace Paul's view of mutual subjection between husband and wife.

The wife is second to the husband in authority. In a hierarchical society and with the church moving in that direction, Chrysostom could not fathom a democratic marriage.[14] At the same time, he sought to retain the love perspective of marriage introduced by Paul. In reality this is difficult to do when one person in the relationship is subservient to the one in authority and is told that *it is God ordained.*

On the Roman side of the church, St. Augustine (354-430) emerged as the leading authority. In marriage he merged the natural and spiritual into the act of procreation and called it the glory of marriage. He believed marriage to be the mysterious (*sacramentum*) bond of permanent union.

At the same time, it is Augustine who strongly emphasized the spiritual superiority of virginity and chastity, teaching that sexual intercourse is sinful and likely the means of original sin. In marriage, intercourse should only occur for the purpose of procreation, with the couple deriving no pleasure from it. If passion and pleasure were associated with intercourse, it became a sinful act.

Christopher Brocke writes that Augustine had a concubine but never gave her a name; in sorrow he sent her away when his mother gave him a wife. Before marriage he took another mistress. [15] The writings of St. Augustine on the subject of marriage and sexuality were going to have profound influence on the medieval church and God's call to celibacy. He saw marriage as a sexual union in a way never expressed by scripture because of his personal views on sexual intercourse.

Endnotes: Chapter Nine

[1] Jon Meacham, "A Case for Change: Celibacy and Marriage," *Newsweek*: May 6, 2002 (New York, NY: Newsweek Inc., 2002), p. 29.

[2] The Atlanta Journal-Constitution: June 13, 1999. p. D6

[3] Joanna Soto Carabello, Article in the Athens Banner Herald,

[4] The Atlanta Journal-Constitution: January 26, 1999. p. B5.

[5] Marriage: A Theological Statement, *A Paper Adopted by the 120th General Assembly of the Presbyterian Church in the United States,* (Atlanta: Materials Distribution, 1980), p. 15.

[6] William Barclay, *The Gospel of St. John Vol.1* (Philadelphia: The Westminster Press, 1975), p. 196.

[7] John Witte, Jr. *From Sacrament to Contract* (Louisville, KY: Westminster/John Knox Press, 1997), p16.

[8] William Barclay, *The Gospel of St. Matthew Vol.1* (Philadelphia: The Westminster Press, 1975), pp. 153-55.

[9] Nikos A. Vrissimtzis, *Love, Sex, Marriage in Ancient Greece* (Athens, Greece, 1995), p. 21.

10 Margaret A. Farley, "Sexual Ethics," *Sexuality and the Sacred,* ed.
    James B. Nelson and Sandra P Longfellow (Louisville: Westminster/
    John Knox Press, 1994) p. 57

11 Eric Fuchs, *Sexual Desire and Love: Origins and History of the
    Christian Ethic of Sexuality and Marriage* (New York, NY: The
    Seabury Press, 1983), p. 87-92.

12 Christopher Brocke, *The Medieval Idea of Marriage* (Oxford: Oxford
    University Press, 1989), pp. 39-47.

13 Eric Fuchs, pp. 93, 105

14 John Witte, Jr., p. 21

15 Christopher Brocke, p. 63

CHAPTER TEN

Marks of Marriage: From the Medieval Age to the Present Time

Marks of Marriage in the Medieval Age
Courtly Love

At the beginning of the medieval period, an interesting movement began outside religious circles. It was called courtly love, *the love of the couple who are willing to lay down their life for one another, who are drawn to each other without procreation on their minds.* It is an attraction marked by passion and mutual love, and it is highly spiritual. Those who embraced courtly love had disdain for marriage because marriage was primarily a contract that stridently subjects the wife to the desires of her lord and master purely for the purpose of procreating his children and carrying on his name and wealth. Courtly love accepts the woman for who she is: a person. In courtly love the woman is liberated to be the man's friend. This was not so with marriage up to this time nor after.

Abelard and Heloise experienced this dimension of love (agape-divine, phileo-friend, and eros-erotic) in the twelfth century, but their marriage, not love, was dissolved when Heloise went into the nunnery and Abelard was castrated as a priest. The medieval church strongly rejected this form of love because it placed male and female, husband and wife on a mutual plane. It also challenged the church's spiritual hierarchy, which had elevated the celibate priest to the top of spiritual ladder wedded to Christ, with men superior to women.

Marriage

Prior to St. Augustine, the church had no jurisdiction over marriage, nor did the church conduct a formal wedding ceremony. Marriages were designed and regulated by civil authority. Augustine introduced vows to be spoken before a priest in the presence of witnesses, but marriage was still governed by Roman law, which required common consent. Following Augustine, more emphasis was placed upon the spiritual quality of virginity, which began to cast a shadow on both marriage and sexuality. Following the division of Christendom into East (Orthodox) and West (Roman Catholic) in the eleventh century, the Roman church gradually assumed jurisdiction over marriage. Canonical law required nuptial blessings by the church, so liturgy for ceremonies was created. Sexual intercourse validated the consummation of marriage.

John Witte writes: "From the twelfth century forward, the canon law of marriage was also systematized, first in Gratian's Decretum (c.1140) . . . Marriage was conceived at once (1) as a created, natural association, subject to the laws of nature; (2) as a consensual contract, subject to the general laws of contract; and (3) as a sacrament of faith, subject to the spiritual laws of the church."[1]

As the church formally systemized marriage and formed laws of marriage, it became clear how closely marriage was aligned with sexuality in the eyes of the church. By *natural association*, the church believed male and female were created "to be fruitful and multiply";

that is to say, to beget children, which of course occurs through sexual intercourse. To give additional emphasis to sexuality, the church believed after humanity's fall into sin (Genesis 3) that marriage also served to save humanity from lustful passion, providing a healthy outlet for sexual expression. At this point the church was greatly influenced by the words of Paul to the Corinthians: "It is better to marry than to be aflame with passion" (1 Corinthians 7:9b). Marriage became an obligation for those who may be tempted by sexual sin. Of course, this belief about marriage opened the door to emphasize the spiritual superiority of virginity and celibacy.

In the eyes of the church, marriage was more than a natural association subject to the laws of nature. It was also a *consensual contract,* which means through mutual consent the couple makes known their intention to enter into this indissoluble bond that involves authority over one another's body and the common commitment to beget children. This consensual contract was legally binding. By canon law, marriage was also declared *a sacrament.* Since marriage was a sacrament, it was now fully under the spiritual jurisdiction of the church. In accordance to Paul's words to the Ephesians, the church believed, like Christ's bond to the church, the bond between husband and wife was indissoluble and eternally binding. In the eyes of the church, marriages could no longer be dissolved.

Canon law also identified three stages in the consent of marriage: *betrothal* or promise to marry, days or months later a promise of marriage *now,* and *consummation* of marriage through sexual intercourse. If sexual intercourse occurs before the second stage during the betrothal stage, by canon law the couple was married.[2] Now, in the laws of the church, we see the close association between marriage and sexual union. At this time in history, when the church was not only seeking power over its parishioners but also the state, the decision to declare marriage a sacrament has been perceived by many to be self-serving.

As the church moved out of the medieval age and experienced a renaissance, it experienced a growing tension with its laws concerning marriage. Laypeople became dissatisfied with the rigidity of church law concerning divorce, that marriage was indissoluble whatever the grounds, even adultery. Those who were most seriously affected by this canon law were women since men still possessed freedom to have sexual relations with concubines. Laypeople were also unhappy that clandestine marriages (without parents' consent and without a priest) were prohibited since all that was required for hundreds of years was consent between male and female. According to canon law their marriage could not be dissolved but at the same time was not permitted without parents' consent; this contradiction was a threat to the social order because by the sixteenth century canon law had jurisdiction over marriages throughout the Western world.

Finally, another serious contradiction weakened the church's moral authority, the practice of the clergy. The clergy interpreted celibacy as a calling from God not to marry, taking the words of Christ in Matthew 19:12 literally and at face value: "There are different reasons why men cannot marry . . . there are eunuchs who have made themselves eunuchs for the sake of the kingdom of God." Jesus did not literally mention sexual relations but marriage. This interpretation is ironic in light of the church's (clergy) close correlation between marriage and sex: marriage is a sexual union. It raises the question: if it is impossible in the eyes of the church for a person to be married without sexual consummation, is it likewise impossible to have sexual intercourse and remain unmarried?

Eric Fuchs writes: "As we know, at the end of the fifteenth century, the great majority of priests were living with concubines. Clergy at that time interpreted celibacy as an obligation not to marry, but not as an obligation to renounce living with a woman."[3] The church began to lose power and authority in all areas of morality but especially in promoting the virtues of virginity and chastity. As the Roman clerical hierarchy sought more and more authority and yet failed to apply it to itself, a receptive climate for reformation began to grow among laypeople. The catalyst for reformation was ignited not from without the church but from within on a parchment with ninety-five theses written by an Augustinian monk whose name was Martin Luther.

Marks of Marriage in the Reformed Church
Matters of Consensus among Reformers

The Protestant Reformation did not produce a singular voice on marriage and its many ramifications in life; nevertheless, many of the conclusions coming from Martin Luther, John Calvin, and others were much the same. All looked for biblical models that would provide guidance for the church. As a reflection of the sixteenth century society and the support of biblical passages, the reformers reaffirmed the authority of the husband over the wife with the husband being the head of the family as Christ is head of the church. In the plan of God, they believed this hierarchical pattern maintained unity between husband and wife.

Since unity between and wife is primary in the minds of the reformers, adultery is a forbidden act. Reformers believed the relationship between husband and wife greatly influences the future of individuals and society; therefore, it needs to be protected from everything that can threaten it. So reformers begin with the value of the couple when identifying priorities in marriage rather than embracing the traditional model of procreation as the primary reason for marriage.

Although procreation was not declared as the primary or singular purpose of marriage, reformers retained the view that the natural consequence of marriage is procreation. They also retained the practice of marriage as a voluntary union formed by mutual consent of the couple. Reformers, however, rejected marriage as a sacrament, but rather a social institution created by God for all people who desire to assume this commitment despite their religious practice.

The legal jurisdiction of marriage, consequently, was returned to the state, where it had always been even in biblical times. The reformers felt civil law, not canon law, should govern marriage. Because people lived under God's law of love, the church counseled those preparing for marriage. The church also offered a spiritual blessing for those who elected marriage.

Reformers opposed celibacy as higher spiritual station in life than marriage. They felt required celibacy goes against the law of nature and encouraged concubinage.[4] They believed God willed human beings to use their sexuality because sexuality is a facet of being human. Humans, as stewards of God, are expected to create a healthy context for sexual expression where there is mutual consent and mutual commitment to one another. They see healthy sexual activity encompassing all three facets of love: *eros*, *agape*, and *phileo*. When sexual activity between husband and wife is balanced with these three facets of love, then the unity of the couple is greatly enhanced.

Two other major areas of change by the reformers were in the area of birth control: *contraception* and *abortion*. Respecting natural law, the Catholic Church forbids any form of *contraception* and recommends abstinence from sexual intercourse if conceiving children is not the primary purpose. In contrast, reformers placed priority upon the unity of the couple. They believed humanity is called to be God's steward over the natural order, so they were advocates for the couple to make responsible decisions for birth control.

The subject of *abortion* is different. The Catholic Church forbids abortion for the same reasons it forbids contraception. Protestants on the other hand are not of one mind on abortion, but all agree that while contraception prevents conception, abortion destroys a fertile egg and is irreversible. Some say a third party, the fetus, is involved in the decision of abortion. So all Reformed groups begin by recalling the gravity of abortion,[5] but most leave the decision to the woman and support the woman when her life is threatened or for other extremely critical reasons.

Although the Protestant reformers shared similar views concerning the basics of marriage and sexuality, they created different models of marriage. John Witte says Lutherans created a *social* model grounded in the earthly kingdom of creation, primarily for human ends. Calvin and reformers established a *covenantal* model that sees marriage as sacred acts and promises of the community, which includes the betrothed, the minister, the magistrate, the congregation, the family, and friends, all who witness this holy union in the presence of God.

Anglicans designed a *commonwealth* model that includes the social and covenantal and the sacramental, affirming that marriage serves the common good of the couple, the children, the church, and the state all at once. Some of the specifics of each of these models have changed through history to the present time. I will examine the *covenantal* model more thoroughly.[6]

The Covenantal Model of Marriage

The author of the *covenantal* model of marriage was John Calvin; it was designed and redesigned while he lived in Geneva from 1536 to 1564, with a three-year absence while in Strasbourg. Although believing strongly that the state should have legal jurisdiction over marriage, with the church exercising spiritual authority, Calvin spent much time influencing the city council to accept the church consistory's rules and laws of marriage. These legal reforms met with much resistance in Geneva. Calvin's jurist background in France greatly influenced his approach in establishing the covenantal model of marriage.

His theology of marriage began with the biblical concept of covenant. God initiates relationship with humanity, as with Abraham, through a promise and mutual agreement called covenant. It was a well-known and accepted theological concept in the Christian church. Calvin viewed marriage, not as a contract between a man and a woman, but as a sacred covenant between three parties: man, woman, and God. God, the creator of marriage, presides as a spiritual partner in the marriage and draws the husband and wife into a covenant relationship with each other bound by promises.

God works through the community to uphold those being joined together. So the couple's parents are present and give their consent to the marriage; at least two witnesses are God's priests to the two being married to attest to their union; the minister of the word blesses the union; and the magistrate registers the marriage, making the union legal. Prior to marriage, the couple announces their intention and become betrothed. John Witte writes, "Betrothals seek to safeguard against secret marriages, to seek the consent of the couple, their parents, and the broader community to this vital first step of intimate union . . . a formal church wedding had to follow within three to six weeks of betrothal."[7]

In the covenantal model, a marriage is considered permanent, "Till death do us part," but there were grounds to legitimize separation. The marriage could be annulled upon proof that one person withheld critical information about self, like a familiar relationship (relative), or an incurable disease, or if it were discovered the wife was not a virgin (apparently men are not held accountable for their virginity), or if sterility or impotence became known. When a marriage was annulled, both parties were free to marry someone else. Divorce, on the other hand, could be enacted on the grounds of adultery or desertion.

Calvin strongly pushed the city Council of Geneva to adopt many laws concerning marriage primarily for the protection of children and wives. Calvin's legal formulations were strongly opposed by many people in Geneva, but most were eventually adopted as law by the council.

What then was the primary purpose of marriage in the covenantal model? Calvin believed marriage was rooted "in the creation and commandments of God and in the law and order of nature to be a lifelong union between man and woman for three interlocking purposes: 1) the mutual love and support of husband and wife, 2) the mutual procreation and nurture of children, and 3) the protection of both parties from sexual sin."[8]

This covenantal model, which has remained strong in the Reformed church, contains for the first time in church history a purpose that focuses upon the spiritual well-being and unity of the couple with mutual love and support, as emphasized by Paul in the fifth chapter of Ephesians. At the same time, two of the three major purposes for marriage are strongly sexual, procreation of children and to satisfy humanity's sexual drive to avoid sexual promiscuity. So as we move out of the Reformation period, marriage remains a sexual union. What is the position of the reformation church today?

Marks of Marriage for the Twenty-first Century

In Reformed churches in general, the marks of marriage have not changed considerably since John Calvin created the covenantal model. The major change has occurred in emphasis and priority. Consistent with biblical times through the early church and then the Reformation, in the covenantal model legal jurisdiction for marriage is left to the state. This is the case in our country. States determine what constitutes a valid marriage between two people. States, through their laws, licenses, and court actions, regulate marriages from their beginning through their end if divorce is necessary.

During the medieval period the Roman Catholic Church assumed full jurisdiction over marriage, which represents the only time in Western history that has been the case. Civil jurisdiction returned during the Reformation; however, John Calvin and the Reformed church in Geneva wrote many of the marriage ordinances that the city council in Geneva eventually enacted as ordinances. Present-day Reformed churches in the United States leave full civil jurisdiction to civil authorities. For example, a minister may officiate at the wedding of a man and woman but they are not legally married unless they have a license from civil authorities. On the other hand, a marriage may be solemnized from beginning to end in the civil arena. The church's involvement in marriage is spiritual and communal.

Marriage in the Presbyterian/Reformed church continues to be covenantal. It is more than a contract between two persons, but a sacred covenant that includes God, whose spiritual presence of love equips the man and woman to grow in their relationship. The Presbyterian Book of Order says: "For Christians, marriage is a covenant through which a man and a woman are called to live out together before God their lives of discipleship."[9] The covenant is communal in nature as the Book of Order says, "Christian marriage, a lifelong commitment, is made by a woman and a man to each other, publicly witnessed and acknowledged by the community of faith."[10]

Of course, covenant also includes the promises between the bride and groom. The exercise of one's will plays an important role in covenant. It creates a picture of mutual negotiation between husband and wife, with each sharing power and responsibility in the role of servants to each other, to use the imagery of Paul in the fifth chapter of Ephesians.[11]

The purpose of marriage becomes evident through what is believed to be the marks of marriage. The *first mark* of marriage involves a commitment a woman and a man make to each other to live in a relationship of mutual love and support as they are drawn to each other to be united in one flesh while at the same time retaining their unique personhood or identity. This mark of oneness accepts sexual unity as a good gift from God from the time of creation. The movement toward unity is greatly supported by the form of love called *eros,* a passion that includes our whole physical being similar to Christ's commandment to love God with our strength or body.

Love, however, does not stop at this point but includes that divine dimension where man and woman are called to love one another "as Christ loved us" (John 13:34), which is the same imagery as Paul's in the fifth chapter of Ephesians. This divine love, *agape,* provides spiritual energy for husband and wife to make sacrifices for one another, seeking the highest good for the other, sometimes at the expense of self-gratification. Divine love also introduces the spiritual quality of forgiveness, which helps maintain unity in times of stress and self-centeredness. A third facet of love, *phileo,* greatly strengthens the marital relationship, spiritually binding wife and husband as *friends* who are intent on developing common interests and activities they enjoy together.

In the first chapter of Genesis, the creation of male and female in the image of God is emphasized prior to being fruitful. As explained in the third chapter of this book, *image of God* conveys humanity's ability and need to experience a fulfilling relationship. The quality of their commitment to family will be determined by the quality of their relationship with each other. Likewise, the second chapter of Genesis first describes the steps the creator God took in addressing the loneliness of Adam, creature of dust. From Adam is created another human of the same substance so that through relationship the problem of loneliness is resolved. So the mutual care and love for one another comes first in the covenantal model for marriage. Once again, an important dimension of that mark involves the sexual dimension of the union, "and the two become one flesh."

The *second mark* of marriage is family. "Marriage is a gift God has given all humankind for the wellbeing of the entire family."[12] Note that the word *procreation* is not used in this statement, but procreation can be included in the meaning of the statement. Care for the entire family involves more than procreated children. Children may also be adopted or fostered or the result of blended families. Care for family also involves parents in the family who were involved in our conception; it involves individuals in the family who are not married. Family involves husband and wife even if they do not have children.

John Patton and Brian Childs in their book, *Christian Marriage and Family: Caring For Our Generations,* place emphasis on *care,* which describes God's call to have *dominion* over the earth. The call to care includes all individuals in the family, past, present, and future generations.[13] This calling resembles the importance the biblical community placed upon the family as a household (economy) for survival: protection and caring for physical needs.

Of course, marriage is also for the purpose of procreation, the *third mark.* The scripture and the early church until the Reformation put procreation as the first and most important purpose of marriage. That was possible in a time when marriages for the most part were arranged and support for the household was of major importance in order to survive. Wives were subject to the husband; husbands often had concubines, so the marital relationship was seldom marked by deep love and friendship. Society as a whole was hierarchical; therefore, people understood what it meant to submit to authority backed by power and sometimes physical force.

In our culture today, people enjoy freedom of choice in virtually every arena of life. This includes the choice to marry or to remain single, the choice of a marriage mate, and the choice to have children or not. Marriage does not automatically mean having children as the primary way to justify sexual intercourse. Sexual intercourse from a Christian perspective is no longer considered unclean as understood in Old Testament times and sinful as taught by St. Augustine and practiced by the medieval church. Nonetheless, since one purpose of marriage in the covenantal model involves the family, procreation occupies an important place, and marriage as a sexual union remains dominant.[14]

One purpose of marriage introduced by Augustine and remaining with the church through the Reformation but no longer stated in the present-day covenantal model, involves the protection of humans from sexual sin (words of John Calvin). Augustine and the medieval church described it this way: marriage serves to save humanity from lustful passion, providing a healthy outlet for sexual expression. This purpose originates with the words of Paul to the Corinthians: "it is better to marry than to be aflame with passion"(1 Corinthians 7:9b). Those who hold this purpose based on the words of Paul fail to realize that Paul is speaking to a particular situation in the Corinthian culture, greatly influenced by the belief of Christ's imminent return.

To use marriage as a way to avoid the temptation of sexual sin greatly reduces the significance of the first mark of marriage, which emphasizes the love and justice, faithfulness and forgiveness husband and wife render to one another. It sounds like marriage is simply used to legitimize sexual intercourse, making the sexual union of two people really more important than the marital love of two people. This purpose for marriage is no longer retained in the covenantal model of marriage

Much more could be said about marriage, but the major purpose of this chapter is to show that throughout history in different expressions and models marriage has remained a sexual union between a man and a woman, between husband and wife. Where marriage and the family will be fifty years from now, I do not know; however, the last chapter of this book will take a glimpse at the changing nature of marriage and the family as we move into the third millennium.

Conclusion

God created male and female . . . be fruitful and multiply (Genesis 1:27-28). The man leaves his mother and father and is united to his wife, *and the two become one* (Genesis 2:24). The same picture of marriage is expressed by Jesus, *and the two shall become one* (Matthew 19:6). The apostle Paul also presents this picture of physical intimacy.

To my knowledge, marriage vows between two Christian people have never been expressed with the intention of husband and wife remaining virgin to each other. Their marriage to one another is celebrated through physical union or sexual intercourse. This physical facet of marriage became so important in the medieval period that intercourse was required for marital consummation. If for some reason male or female could not engage sexually, the marriage would be annulled. Also, if one party in the marriage were sterile, the marriage would be annulled. Both practices emphasize the importance of procreation. Those positions are not accepted in the Presbyterian Church.

In my opinion, since procreation has assumed a historical role in the union of male and female in marriage, the term *marriage* does not adequately describe the primary purpose of a committed relationship between two people of the same gender. This of course does not rule out the possibility of children for them through other means. Some people I know who have partners of the same gender do have children, but the children were not conceived by the partners.

Relationship rather than procreation is the purpose of the union of two people of the same gender. This is not to say that two people of the same gender are not sexually attracted to one another, but what is most important for two people of the same gender involves experiencing a mutually fulfilling and committed relationship. This purpose creates the picture of *partnership.*

Throughout this book, I have emphasized that scripture teaches and most Christians believe God created human beings with a basic need to experience fulfilling relationships—*love God and love your neighbor as yourself.* Modern practice of psychology agrees with this conclusion, and I imagine if any of us were left on an island alone for more than a month, we too would agree with these conclusions. Once again, the term *partnership* beautifully describes a fulfilled relationship.

Even though historically a marriage has been closely connected with procreation and the sexual relationship between husband and wife, Reformation leaders broadened the meaning of marriage, especially in the *covenantal model.* The exercise of one's will plays an important role in covenant. It creates a picture of mutual negotiation between husband and wife, with each sharing power and responsibility in the role of servants to each other.

We have moved away from the hierarchical model of marriage where the wife is subject to the husband to the mutual model where they are *subject to one another* (Ephesians 5:21). Now, in marriage the term *partnership* likewise is the most appropriate title describing a fulfilled relationship. It describes the union more completely whether the husband and wife have children, adopt children, or do not have children.

Both same-gender committed relationships and male/female committed relationships can share the same title. *Partnership* becomes the title of new relational paradigm for both same-gender couples and male/female couples. At the same time, within this new institution both retain their unique characteristics. Both seek to become the context for meaningful relationships. There are many other contexts for meaningful relationships that usually do not provide the same degree of intimacy, support, and shared life such as friendships, church family, community, school, and vocation.

By reserving the term *marriage* for male and female, it should reduce tension in our society and open the door (minds and hearts) to support people entering into a validated committed *same-gender partnership* with the same rights and protection of a *marital partnership*. When the complete step is taken, both homosexuals and heterosexuals will be liberated to live together in a community of love, support, and servanthood.

Since the scripture from beginning to end strongly emphasizes that humans are created to live in fulfilling relationships, since homosexual persons are attracted to each other not of their choosing, and since the scripture does not deal with committed monogamous relationships between two people of the same gender, it seems to me that the church under the authority of what scripture does say has the responsibility of grace to validate the need, the intention, and the consummation of committed monogamous *same-gender partnerships*.

This conclusion is further supported in light of the reasons given by both Martin Luther and John Calvin to oppose required celibacy. It is a spiritual gift and calling from God and should not be imposed on people. When it is imposed, it goes against the law of nature; however, Calvin not only opposed required celibacy as unnatural, he also opposed sexual activity among those of the same gender for the same reason.[15] His rationale in opposing required celibacy and homosexuality is consistent, but he lived at a time when the world assumed all human beings were sexually attracted to the opposite gender. The words *heterosexual* and *homosexual* were not yet coined, so I can understand why Calvin felt that same-gender sexual activity goes against the laws of nature. However, in recent years we have learned that some people by nature are homosexual in the same way some people by nature are left-handed, some are right-brained and some are left, and some are heterosexual.

What would John Calvin, the rational Christian humanist who opposed required celibacy, say today about homosexual persons whose sexual orientation is as natural for them as his heterosexual orientation was natural for himself? Even more, he opposed required celibacy because it was unnatural for some humans, who by nature are sexually attracted to others. Based on what is known today about homosexual orientation, would Calvin enforce required celibacy on persons who by nature are homosexual? The same rationale Calvin used to oppose required celibacy for priests could be used to oppose required celibacy for persons who are homosexual.

Margaret Farley writes: "Calvin, too, saw marriage as a corrective to otherwise disordered desires . . . Calvin thought that sexual desire is more subject to control than did Luther, though whatever fault remains in it is 'covered over' by marriage."[16] Martin Luther assumed that sexual desire was a fact of life and good if channeled through marriage. He, like Calvin, comes close to saying that all should marry as a way to create an orderly structure for sexual desires. Although I disagree with the use of marriage for this purpose, could not this same logical argument be used today to insist that all homosexual persons bridle their sexual desires through committed relationships with someone of the same gender?

Although the Christian church believes God created the institution of marriage for male and female, it realizes the specific norms of marriage have been *cultural,* with civil authority exercising jurisdiction. This was true during Judaeo-Christian (Old and New Testament) history and church history, with the exception of a portion of the medieval period. Through the years the face of marriage has changed complexion to meet the needs of changing patterns of *culture.* That was also evident even during biblical times.

It seems to me that homosexual persons share the same basic needs with heterosexual persons. God created all humans to seek wholeness through fulfilling relationships. Marriage between male and female is now meeting that need for a large segment of the human population, but not for everyone. Jesus knew that marriage was not for everyone when he said to his disciples: "There are some eunuchs who have been so from birth"(Matthew 19:12a). By the term *eunuch,* Jesus was referring to a person who did not have the sexual capacity or sexual desire to unite in a marriage between a man and a woman. If marriage is not the natural way of supporting these persons to experience wholeness in a fulfilling relationship, what then is the way? I suggest *validating same-gender partnerships* as the next chapters describe.

Endnotes: Chapter Ten

1   John Witte, Jr. *From Sacrament to Contract* (Louisville, KY: Westminster/John Knox Press, 1997), p. 24

2   Ibid., pp. 22-33

3   Eric Fuchs, *Sexual Desire and Love: Origins and History of the Christian Ethic of Sexuality and Marriage* (New York, NY: The Seabury Press, 1983), p. 135.

4   John Witte, pp. 2-5.

5   Eric Fuchs, p. 163-165.

6   John Witte, pp. 4-10

7   Ibid., p. 83, 85

8   Ibid., p. 96

9   Book of Order, *Marriage* (Louisville, KY: Materials Distribution, 2001), W-9000

10   Ibid., W-9000

11   John Patton and Brian Childs, *Christian Marriage and Family: Caring for Our Generations* (Nashville: Abingdon Press, 1988), pp. 133-34

12   op. cit., Book of Order, W-9000

13   John Patton and Brian Childs, pp. 24-27

14   *Marriage: A Theological Statement: A Paper Adopted by the 120th General Assembly, Presbyterian Church in the U.S.* (Atlanta: Materials Distribution Service, 1980) pp. 5-9

[15] Margaret A. Farley, "Sexual Ethics," *Sexuality and the Sacred,* ed. James B. Nelson and Sandra P Longfellow (Louisville: Westminster/ John Knox Press, 1994), pp. 63-64

[16] Ibid., p. 63.

CHAPTER ELEVEN

Singles Seeking Relationships: People Wanting a Promise

Called as partners in Christ's service, called to ministries of grace,
We respond with deep commitment, fresh new lines of faith to trace.
May we learn the art of sharing, side by side and friend with friend,
Equal partners in our caring to fulfill God's chosen end.
Jane Parker Huber

Introduction

Very likely every religious congregation in the United States with more than a hundred members has a member who is homosexual or a family in which someone is homosexual. In some congregations there will be partners. In most cases no one, not even the pastor, is aware of these situations. A lesbian in our congregation once said publicly, *I am afraid to admit who I really am because I could lose my job, I may lose the opportunity teach Sunday school in our church, or serve as an officer. Concerning who I really am, I must remain invisible; it is extremely lonely.* John Boswell writes: "One of the most difficult aspects of being a lesbian or gay person is the phenomenon of pervasive invisibility; exclusion from any generally recognizable category. This usually happens with persons considered outsiders in some way by their contemporaries."[1] Congregations, whether they be conservative or mainline, fundamentalist or liberal, very likely have families with members living in such loneliness and isolation.

Prior to the 1960s this reality created no problems in congregational life because no one knew the truth. The *don't ask, don't tell* commandment was written in stone. These people would remain hidden in their families; some, following college, moved from their hometowns to cities to live isolated, anonymous, invisible lives, never returning to church. Tragically, some would marry thinking their homosexual orientation would go away. The decision to live a lie, of course, often created unhappiness for the spouse and children, sometimes resulting in divorce.

Since the 1960s, the sexual revolution has introduced honesty and counseling support; we are encouraged to come to terms with our true self and use our gifts for the common good. As a result, some gay and lesbian persons are coming out of the closet and putting a face to the subject. They are family and church members, teachers and doctors, senators and professional athletes, accountants and homemaker mothers, caterers and clerks, ministers and community leaders, and on and on.

They prefer not to call attention to themselves and their sexual orientation, yet at the same time, they want to live a fulfilling life in a significant relationship based upon who they really are. They want to live their life in mainstream society. Like their responsible heterosexual peers, they want to use their gifts and contribute to the common good in their religious and secular community; however, their known presence challenges long-held secular prejudices and stereotypical models.

Perhaps more than any other institutions in American culture, religious bodies have the best resources to support and incorporate lesbian and gay persons into the mainstream, so they can experience human wholeness and continue to be strong contributors to community life. These spiritual resources enable us to rise above our differences and prejudices to receive others with a spirit of hospitality. For Christians, those roots go back to the Christ. Yes, Jesus did not address same-gender attraction or partnership, but his ministry, his example, and his teaching give us a strong foundation to build a structure marked by his way, his truth, and his life. He reached out and welcomed all in spite of public rebukes. His close followers were beneficiaries of his grace, his unconditional love, and his vision of a community of compassion and mercy.

We learned in chapter two, following Christ's resurrection and ascension, Christ followers were given opportunities to continue his ministry of grace and unconditional acceptance. Peter, steeped in Hebrew tradition, was the first to come to terms with Jesus' new perspective of what constitutes genuine spiritual community.

In Joppa, Peter learns firsthand what Jesus meant when he said it is not the kind of food one eats which creates uncleanness; it is what comes out of a person's heart. It is how we treat people. Peter is told: "What God has made clean, you must not call profane" (Acts 10:15b). This experience with food prepared Peter accept a Gentile soldier, and respond to his spiritual needs. Gentiles were considered unclean; to touch or enter a Gentile home caused a Hebrew person to be ritually unclean. But now, looking through the spectacles of Christ, Peter sees that Cornelius is a child of God. Peter enters his home and baptizes him, saying, "God has shown me that I should not call anyone unclean. I truly understand that God shows no partiality" (Acts 10:29, 34).

The second significant spiritual experience occurs in Jerusalem (Acts 15:1-35). This experience includes many followers of Christ. A council of Christian leaders has been called to meet concerning Gentiles again. Many are responding to the *good news* of Christ. The question these Hebrew Christian leaders had to resolve was this: Do we make them like us before we accept them into the church; i.e., do we circumcise them so they become Jews? Under Peter's leadership, this first Christian council said no, they do not have to become like us to be a member of the body of Christ, the church. To be a member of the body of Christ means to be a full member. It is what exists in the hearts of people that unites them. Peter says, "And God, who knows the human heart, testified to them by giving them the Holy Spirit, just as he did to us, and in cleansing their hearts by faith has made no distinction between them and us . . ." (Acts 15:9, 11).

These two significant experiences in the life of the early Christian community validates the guiding power of the Holy Spirit, enabling the Jewish Christ followers to be authentic witnesses for Christ. They become a global community eventually, fully incorporating Jew and Gentile, Greek and Roman, free and slave, male and female, single and married, and yes, even people we now identify as gay and lesbian. Institutions of both society and religion today face the same problem the Corinthian church of the first century grappled with. How do we maintain unity without uniformity and diversity without division?

The apostle Paul had two responses. First, since this new faith called Christianity was to embrace all people everywhere, the new spiritual body of God, like the physical body of male and female, will have many different members. They will have different characteristics; they will have different functions. They will work together for the common good. Their unique life will depend upon being connected with each other in the common commitment to their lord or head. The *body of Christ* will be the symbol or image for the new paradigm, *validated committed partnerships.*

How can this dream be fulfilled? Common sense tells us that a spiritual power greater than ourselves is required to achieve such a ideal design and mission in a self—centered world marked by personal greed, ambition, prejudice, and fear. The reality of sin prompts Paul's 2nd response: "Strive for the greater gifts. And I will show you a still more excellent way" (1 Corinthians 12:31). In the next chapter, Paul identifies the still more excellent way to be: "Love which is patient and kind, not envious or boastful or arrogant or rude . . ." (1 Corinthians 13:4-5). What was true and necessary for the early church, I believe, remains true and necessary for the church today. A still more excellent way will enable the church to experience diversity without division and unity without uniformity. As Edwin Markham writes:

> He drew a circle that shut me out-
> Heretic, rebel, a think to flout.
> But love and I had the wit to win;
> We drew a circle that took him in. [2]

The Season among Us

Days come and go; they flow into weeks, and weeks into months, and months into years. In the midst of the flow of life we enjoy seasons. Their movement reminds me of the span of a lifetime from birth till death; however, in the scope of time (*chronos*) that comes and goes, there is another facet of time that cannot be governed and rule by the rising and setting of the sun. It is God's time (*kairos*), that special maturing moment like the ripening of fruit, when ears are prepared to hear God's word and hearts are nurtured to act upon what is heard.

It seems to me that this maturing moment is arriving for both the secular and the religious community to reexamine the best way to support one another to live in fulfilling relationships. Because of changing patterns of life in our technological culture, with life expectancy more than doubling since biblical times, the scope of committed relationships is changing whether the religious sector wants to have an influence or not. As stewards of God's creation, Christians have much to contribute in shaping ethical standards for the different forms of significant relationships, which are evolving.

These ethical standards will then enrich not only the quality of the specific relationship but the quality of the community as well. In both word and deed, Jesus Christ had more to say about relationships than any other important topic of his day. So the season has come (*kairos*) for the church to unite, to examine the global situation in the context of scripture under the lordship of Christ, so that diverse committed relationships will be validated, freeing them to bear much fruit for the benefit of all.

Time to Develop a Win/Win Paradigms
Peace with a Price

Often when the right time (*kairos*) comes, consensus has not been reached; therefore, those who respond in faith to this special time to act will likely face ridicule, anguish, and sacrifice, perhaps suffering as did Christ. The right time usually comes before consensus. It's much like hitting a fast ball in baseball. When the pitcher releases the ball, the batter begins the swing before the ball reaches the plate. That is the right time (*kairos*). If the swing does not begin before the ball reaches the plate, seldom will the bat connect and make the hit.

The time has come to develop a win/win paradigm, so that gay and lesbian persons (with partners or not) will be full members of their religious institution and society. The right time is the catalyst that leads to consensus, which eventually represents the popular opinion of the people. Martin Luther, the reformer, understood this dynamic from experience, so did Rosa Parks and Martin Luther King about 425 years later in getting the attention of the people of this country concerning civil rights for African-Americans.

The ultimate goal in practicing hospitality in the spirit of grace involves establishing peace so that those discriminated against will have the opportunity to experience wholeness and satisfy their relational needs, and so religious institutions and society can enjoy wholeness rather than being divided with violence both physically and verbally. This peace comes with a price, so that gay and lesbian persons, may be part of the wholeness of our society and religious institutions.

Although there are many faithful religious and Christian people who feel all forms of homosexual behavior are sinful according to biblical teaching, this negative feeling about homosexual persons and behavior existed long before the twentieth-century church studied the scripture for a ruling. Since cultural consensus was reached long before biblical study began, the seven biblical passages referring negatively to same-gender sexual activity easily validated cultural prejudice.

In the minds of those who were satisfied with this superficial ruling, nothing more needs to be said, no more biblical study, and no more discussion. The matter is settled once and for all time. The effort to create a win/win paradigm will have to come at a time when it is not popular, because there is strong opinion that scripture is definitive about this issue. Even some mainline denominations have taken this position.

Biblical Integrity

Important issues that radically alter the lives of communities of people seldom come easily. I think that's good. Change for change's sake seldom enhances the quality of life for anyone over a long period of time. Since the passages in scripture that refer to same-gender sexual behavior are expressed in the negative, I have tried to show that this paradigm is clearly supported by biblical integrity.

First, in chapter one I examined the seven biblical passages that refer to same-gender sexual activity; I attempted to understand their meaning and purpose in their context using the accepted norms of biblical interpretation in the Reformed tradition. The Old Testament passages mentioning same-gender sexual activity are likely referring to rape (Sodom) and pagan cults of prostitution. In the New Testament, Paul's references to sexual behavior are in specific areas such as rape (pederasty), prostitution, and adultery. Idolatry rather than sexual activity is more likely the underlying basis for passages in Leviticus and the New Testament. They are not written to provide sexual ethics.

Walter Wink concludes: "There is no biblical sex ethic. The Bible knows only a love ethic that is constantly being brought to bear on whatever sexual mores are dominant in any given country or culture or period."[3] The passages also give no clue to the sexual orientation of those involved in same-gender sexual activity. James Nelson writes: "We receive no guidance (from scripture) whatsoever about the issue of sexual *orientation*. The issue of homosexuality—a psychosexual orientation— simply was not a biblical issue. The concept of sexual orientation did not arise until the mid-nineteenth century."[4] These passages provide no guidance for two people of the same gender who live in committed and loving monogamous relationships. I believe it is important to refrain from making scripture say more or less than it is actually saying. Biblical integrity is lost when this happens.

We know from the study of Roman and Greek history that male same-gender sexual activity was common for the well-to-do, political leaders, and soldiers even though they were married with families. Robin Scroggs writes: "In the Greco-Roman world there was one basic model of male homosexuality: pederasty, the sexual use of boys by adult males, often in situations of prostitution and always lacking in mutuality."[5] The three passages in the New Testament referring to same-gender sexual activity are found in Paul's letters to people or churches in the Greco-Roman world.

Second, since scripture does not address same-gender committed relationships, I examined two basic themes that are consistently emphasized from beginning to end of scripture as a biblical basis for accepting homosexual singles and partners into the full life of the church. Both themes are considered most important revelations of God's mind by Christians who are conservative, moderate, and liberal.

The first is grace. Since we ourselves are recipients of God's grace and received as full members of God's family, then grace is a good place to begin with decisions that affect a person's membership into the body of Christ. As people of grace and members of the body of Christ, it is apparent we are called to extend that same degree of hospitality to all people.

The second dominant theme present throughout scripture is the verbally repeated and graphically illustrated truth that human beings are created to live in fulfilling relationships. We become the person God created us to be as we live in loving and faithful, just and compassionate, and merciful and accepting relationships. As Christ and both testaments emphasize, "We are to love God and love our neighbors as ourselves." I do not document this phrase because it is emphasized in nearly every book in the New Testament that magnifies the importance of relationships.

If loneliness (no significant relationship) is a primary concern in the mind of the creator God, why would we presume that God is only concerned that heterosexual persons fulfill their relational needs while it is sinful for homosexual to do the same? I have been told by gays and lesbians that the greatest spiritual and emotional anguish they experience is feeling so alone. I think there is a common belief among most Christians that God created human beings to live in meaningful relationships.

I believe the scripture teaches that it is God's will for all people to enjoy committed and faithful relationships, even those who do not marry. Biblical integrity requires looking at the fullness of scripture rather than being restricted by a few verses that address specific cultural situations of the first century. A win/win paradigm will have biblical integrity.

Hope with a Promise

At the present time many relationships that add meaning to our lives are bound by promises. These promises provide hope for those who share in the promises. Of course, the most common relationship bound by a promise is the *marital partnership* of a male and female. The bride and groom step into that relationship by giving themselves to each other. Since it is bound by promises made public, both persons are given hope for the future as they commit themselves in faith for the present. Promises are not uncommon for many other relationships.

In relationship with our country, we make a pledge of allegiance. In relationship to our church, we make a commitment or promise. When we baptize a child in the presence of the congregation, we make promises as parents in relationship to the child and to God; the congregation also makes promises to God concerning its relationship with the child. A Boy or Girl Scout makes specific promises to nurture and maintain quality relationships. Those promises demonstrate faith in the relationship in the present and hope for the relationship in the future. Hope is essentially faith in the future tense. Promises made public strengthen and solidify significant relationships.

The church offers no promises and blessing upon relationships between two people except the marriage of a man and a woman. The church offers nothing for two people who want to celebrate and bless a lifelong friendship, or the calling of a person to be a caretaker to someone who has a chronic illness, or the mutual committed love of two people of the same gender, or the mutual love and care of two older adults who do not regard their relationship a marriage, or the same for two young adults who do not feel ready for marriage. We have allowed fear of the sexual dimension to override scripture's ultimate emphasis on loving and faithful relationships.

Promises provide faith and hope. With love they create a spiritual bond for the relationship. Singles in our culture are not provided with an opportunity to strengthen their relationships with promises made public. This not only applies to two single people of the same gender who want to make a public commitment sealed with promises, but also to a single male and female who are not ready for marriage and yet want to strengthen their relationship formally with promises. As illustrated in the preceding paragraph, there are many other vocational relationships that could be strengthened by promises and a blessing.

Some feel a sexual relationship between two people of the same gender is sinful because scripture only permits sexual activity between a man and a woman in marriage. To begin with, that is a misunderstanding of scripture. This was shown in the preceding chapter. Scripture does not condemn all sexual activity outside the marriage of a male and a female. Some examples are polygamy, males with concubines and wives' slave women, and premarriage (Esther and likely Ruth). In scripture, a more consistent norm than marriage for allowing sexual activity between two people is the promise (unwritten) by the male to be committed to the economic wellbeing of the female and family.

Even then, there are exceptions like Abraham and Sarah who banished from the family Hagar and her son Ishmael, and like the command of Ezra to Hebrew men who possessed foreign wives to send them and their children home. The opportunity for relationships to be strengthened by promises and commitment need to be incorporated into a win/win paradigm. At present the church does not offer a validated promise for two people of the same gender who want support in their committed relationship but is quick to condemn them for being intimate. This is like pouring salt into their wounds.

Chris Glaser in his book, *Uncommon Calling: A Gay's Struggle to Serve the Church,* calls this hypocritical posture *spiritual abuse.* He feels that their (gay and lesbian) relationships are reduced to sexual practices and their desire to serve as God's called people is maligned as a "gay agenda."[6] While the church has no hesitation to support heterosexual relationships with promises, it withholds such support from those of the same gender who want their relationship bound by an ethical structure.

At the same time, the church declares these same-gender relationships sinful and promiscuous. How can they be promiscuous if the church will not bless the promises they want to make? A spiritual win/win paradigm is greatly strengthened when people are supported by promises that give support and hope for the future; it will likewise free church and society from being insensitive and hypocritical.

Time to Travel a More Excellent Way

In his letter to the Christians in Corinth, Paul apparently realized their lack of unity would not be resolved by reason or one group overpowering the other groups or by favoring one group over another. In the end, unity and motivation for mission must come from God, who is the spirit of love, who then inspires acceptance of each other, validation of each other's gifts, and realization that diversity has a greater strength for reaching others with the good news of Christ. When the church travels a more excellent way, it will be guided by the grace of God and the universal need for fulfilling relationships.

On the one hand, as people of grace, the church will be proactive and positive rather than reactive and negative. Efforts will be made to try to see relational needs from the perspective of singles as well as those who seek marriage. In the mid-sixteenth century, the Council of Trent ruled in behalf of the Roman Catholic Church that the priesthood must practice celibacy. In contrast, the Reformed church considered celibacy a special gift from God for those who are led by the spirit to practice celibacy from their heart for life.

Not only is it unnatural (Calvin's word), but it is a contradiction of our confessional belief to impose celibacy upon singles whether they be heterosexual or homosexual persons. At the same time the grace of sexual abstinence could be expected because it is provisional until a lifelong commitment is made with a partner; it can also be applied to all people. To create statements in confessional standards that categorize people can leave them with a deep sense of not belonging, not being welcomed, or being more sinful than others, although that may not be the intention of those who favor such statements.

For example, before G-1.0106b in the Book of Order of the Presbyterian Church (USA) was replaced in 2010, the second sentence read: "Among these standards is the requirement to live either in fidelity within the covenant of marriage between a man and a woman, or chastity in singleness."[7] Two categories of people are mentioned in this sentence: those married and those single. The phrase *chastity in singleness* is directed toward two groups of people: heterosexual persons who are single and all homosexual persons unless married to someone of the opposite gender.

For the homosexual person who is living in a committed monogamous partnership with a person of the same gender, *chastity in singleness* is hurting. The two have actually made their promises public. These people are not actually single but assumed single because the only acceptable category for couples living together intimately is the marriage of a man and a woman. They are not allowed to fit into that category. Likewise, no other form of partnership is considered acceptable and valid. They have been categorically declared morally unfit to serve Christ's church as an elder. Categorically, both are considered less moral than someone married who engages in sex with his/her spouse outside the spirit of love and tenderness with no intention of enriching the relationship.

Now look at this situation from the perspective of both persons. You have been categorically declared morally unfit to serve as an elder. Even though the minister and some members say you are welcome to be a member of the congregation, deep down you do not feel that you belong. Your sin is so horrible that it has been categorically written in the constitution. At the same time you begin to wonder. *Why are some other categories people fit into not mentioned? In fact, these are the only two mentioned. Why are those who bear false witness not mentioned or those who cheat or steal? In fact, some of the elders on the session are divorced and have remarried. Jesus says they are committing adultery. Why are they insiders while we are outsiders? The one that applies to us is not even a violation of the Ten Commandments.*

The rest of that paragraph in the *Book of Order* read, "Persons refusing to repent of any self-acknowledged practice which the confessions call sin shall not be ordained and/or installed as elders, deacons, or ministers of the Word and Sacrament."[8] The confessions of the church on numerous occasions declare violation of the Sabbath sinful. Violation, according to the Larger and Shorter Catechisms, not only includes worldly employment and forms of recreation but also causing others to work who are "under our charge" and all needless works (7.057-7.062; 7.225-231). How many of us ministers, elders, and deacons leave Sabbath worship to dine at a restaurant or purchase an item from the grocery store or attend a concert or a major league baseball game on Sunday?

Can we declare these works of necessity or forms of recreation that require the work of someone else? When we violate the Sabbath we are breaking the fourth commandment. To emphasize its importance among the ten, twice as much is said about this commandment in the confessions than the other nine commandments. More is said in scripture about this commandment than all others except the first two. If this paragraph in the Book of Order had been supported with honesty and integrity, the Presbyterian Church (USA) would have had difficulty finding many morally fit persons to be an ordained officer or minister. I consider this deleted paragraph still a relevant concern because at the 2012 meeting of the General Assembly there were overtures to reinstate it in the Book of Order.

Return to those who have been categorically banished from office in the church because they live in a committed relationship but it is not validated. If you were those persons, would you feel you belong to this particular church or denomination? There is something lacking in its level of acceptance, in its practice of hospitality, and in its level of integrity. The minister or some members of a congregation in this denomination may say, "*We love you and accept you in our congregation, but you are not allowed to be a church officer, and we feel uneasy about letting you teach our children in church school or serve as a youth leader; nevertheless, please believe us when we say we accept you and want you to be a member of our church family.* If you were one of these persons, how would you feel?

Now that this paragraph in the constitution (G-6.0106b) has been eliminated, the responsibility to determine the qualifications of its officers has returned to congregations and the qualifications of ministers would return to governing bodies. At the same time, the denomination has not taken the step to allow validation of the partnerships of two people of the same gender. So the time has come to be more proactive, to practice the grace of God, and be hospitable and accepting rather creating rules that marginalize gifted and loving people. That is still the more excellent way.

The time has come to recognize the created need of all human beings to live in relationships of love and justice undergirded by the fruits of the spirit. If we put ourselves in the shoes of gays and lesbians, we will begin to think relationally rather than sexually. To establish 20/20 vision, I think it is best to hear from gay and lesbian persons on the value of relationships.

Mary Hunt writes: "Lesbian feminists have not defined ourselves according to sexuality. Rather, we have defined ourselves according to certain relational commitments to other women, or what I am calling female friendship . . . we are reclaiming the word *lesbian* for what it has always meant, namely women loving women without fixating on the presence or the absence of genital activity to define it."[9] Hunt feels that both Hollywood and Madison Avenue have distorted what is most valued in women loving women. Both portray such relationships as neurotic, superficial, one-dimensional, stereotypical, and sexually focused. In contrast, Hunt lists these basic qualities of lesbian relationships: *mutuality, friendship in community, and honesty in dealing with sexuality, nonexclusivity, flexibility, and other-directedness.* She also says not all lesbian relationships lead to the expression of sexuality.[10]

Concerning gay relationships, Michael Clark writes: "A truly liberated sexuality is one that affirms the wholeness of our beings as persons-in-relationship . . . The process of re-envisioning our sexuality begins with the adamant reaffirmation that our sexuality permeates all of who we are as persons and gay men: our sexuality should *in no case* be reduced to merely genital functions . . . To be human is to be in relationship—with ourselves, with other persons . . ."[11] Perhaps heterosexual persons can learn from homosexual persons to think relationally rather than sexually and travel a more excellent way.

The medieval foundational structure for relationships still used in the twenty-first century needs radical renovation with a new breath of life. Some religious groups have recognized this need. The English Friends in 1963 expressed a new view of that time in *Towards a Quaker View of Sex.* They said, "One should no more deplore homosexuality than left-handedness . . . Homosexual affection can be as selfless as heterosexual affection, and therefore we cannot see that it is in some way morally worse."[12] The United Church of Christ has gone on record in ordaining its first pastor who has a same-gender partner.

In 2001 the Presbyterian Church (USA) voted down an overture that would prohibit the blessing of holy unions among those of the same gender as long as they are not identified as a marriage. In 1986, the Reformed church in the Netherlands declared full acceptance of gays and lesbians. In the year 2000, the State of Vermont voted to recognize the civil union of two people of the same gender. In 1999, the Supreme Court of Canada gave approval for purposes of family law for same-gender partners to be considered spouses.

Basis to Validate Committed Partnerships
Church Tradition

In the early church or first 700 years of its life and growth, the Christian church did not validate or bless any relationship formally with a ceremony. Marriage was a civil institution in the Roman Empire, requiring consent of both persons. That was the legal basis for marriage. Roman citizens also practiced monogamy, which was a change in the cultural patterns of the Jewish nation from which Christianity sprang. St. Augustine, in the fourth century, said a wife is one who lived in faithfulness to a man. That was the essence of a validated committed relationship.

Of course there were no validated committed partnerships among friends or among those of the same gender. As the Christian church became more influential in the fourth century, Christian leaders spoke against same-gender sexual behavior, primarily because it had absolutely no procreative potential. At this time in church history, marriage also began to lose spiritual status to celibacy. This alternative to marriage has no Jewish roots; it was seldom practiced in the Roman culture, but some Christians believed the gift of celibacy was spiritually superior to marriage. According to St. Augustine, sexual activity in marriage was only for procreating children; even then, it was a sin if pleasure were derived from the sexual experience. John Boswell writes: "Augustine urged wives to direct their husbands to prostitutes if they wished to indulge in any sexual activity that was not procreative."[13]

From the sixth century to the mid-twelfth century, the church once again did not openly oppose homosexual relationships. Celibate religious life grew in popularity, offering women freedom from the consequences of marriage where birthing children was dangerous and marital relationships were seldom enjoyed. In religious communities (abbeys), women experienced more personal power, their relational needs were better fulfilled, and they had opportunity to study and become literate. Men, likewise, were drawn to the celibate priesthood. They too could devote their lives to study, avoid obligations of warfare, and enjoy a community among equals. Religious communities had special appeal for lesbian and gay people who were considered *outsiders* in secular culture. It also gave them opportunity to live in relationship with others who were gay and lesbian persons.[14]

During this time two significant developments occurred in meeting relational needs. First, ceremonies of *same-gender friendships* or *passionate friendships* were blessed similar to *holy or civil unions* today.[15] Both clergy and laypeople engaged in these special same-gender unions as early as the fifth century. Second, later in this same period the church participated in wedding rites for heterosexual marriages. James Nelson writes: "Our conventional wisdom has assumed that Christian history has been all of one piece, uniform in its clear disapproval of homosexuality. In fact, a closer look at the tradition tells us that there were periods of remarkable acceptance.[16] Following the mid-twelfth century, church and culture opposed homosexual practice as sinful and a crime, so from that time to the mid-twentieth century, homosexuals retreated into the closet.

Church tradition does not provide a consistent pattern for either marriage of man and woman or partnerships for those of the same gender. Over half of church history, marriage was solely for procreation with little emphasis on the quality of the relationship. Even to this time, marriage has been dominated by a patriarchal perspective that places the female in a secondary role. Singles, for the most part, depended on family or convents and monasteries to fulfill their relational needs. Mobility and urbanization have virtually eliminated communal opportunities (family and religious orders) for singles whether they are homosexual or heterosexual persons.

Throughout history, changing patterns of cultural life rather than theology have shaped practices and patterns of marriage as well as addressing the needs of singles. I think the time has come to address from a biblical and theological perspective the needs of singles and those who marry. Perhaps the time has also come to construct a new ethical foundation that will best address the needs of both groups. I believe the present-day image of *partnership* more fully describes fulfilling relationship for singles, whether the relationship is for a male and female or for two people of the same gender.

Scripture

If we are looking for a verse or verses of scripture to quote that support or oppose the validation of committed partnerships for singles whether heterosexual or homosexual, they are not there. In chapters two and three we examined the seven passages in scripture that refer to same-gender sexual activity. It was concluded these passages do not address the desire of two people of the same gender to have their loving and committed *partnership* validated by their church community. Likewise, Jesus does not address this issue in his ministry. It was concluded that direction may be given by examining not only scripture as a whole but also the major themes of scripture as influenced by the ministry of Jesus Christ. That was done in chapters five and six.

Respond to the Created Need to Live in Fulfilling Relationships

Since much space in this book has already been devoted to the rationale to oppose validation of committed partnerships for singles, I will examine biblical theology that supports the validation of committed partnerships. First, the validation of committed partnerships for singles is a response to the universal and created need to live in fulfilling relationships. Although the degree of relational needs varies among human beings, part of being human involves living in fulfilling relationships as emphasized in chapter six.

This need is expressed in the second chapter of Genesis: "The Lord God said, 'It is not good that the man should be alone. I will make him a helper as his partner'" (Genesis 2:18). The text does not say the man needs a wife. According to God, the man needs a *partner*. God first creates all kinds of animals and creatures; they did not fulfill the role of *partner*. Then God created someone of same substance, the man's rib, as a *partner*, and that was satisfying. To respond to the loneliness of Adam, God creates a *partnership* with the advent of Eve. More will be said about *partnerships* in the next chapter.

Today we satisfy our relational needs in different ways as we connect with fellow human beings of the same substance. Those relational needs are first met in the nuclear family but eventually spread to include extended family and friends. Development continues until movement from the family occurs. Upon leaving home, most people begin looking for an intimate relationship that replaces the needs fulfilled by a relationship with the family. For some the pattern is recreated with a *marital partnership* and the beginning of a new family, so this cycle continues.

Others, for different reasons, remain single. Some want to achieve educational goals and become stable in a career before they enter into a *marital partnership* that often leads to procreation. At the same time, upon leaving home they need fulfilling relationships. Some at this point in life are coming to terms with their sexual orientation, realizing they are attracted to those of the same gender rather than to heterosexual persons. Others want a significant heterosexual partner, but the way does not seem clear to them. Still others are insecure about making a marital commitment at this point in life or simply prefer being single with their relational needs being satisfied in multiple ways. All these situations have one thing in common: the need to live in fulfilling relationships. This need becomes apparent when young adults leave their birthing home.

Our biblical faith ranks our relational need so high that it is a given part of being human. Sometimes, in efforts to fulfill that need we are our own worst enemy. Self-centeredness stands in the way. For this reason both scripture and Jesus Christ teach that the most important relationship in our life is with God. We are children of God. Through Christ, our relationship with God becomes personal and substantive. That relationship enables us to become more godlike, which is really the capacity to be human or to be the human being God wants us to be (a future manuscript). We are then better equipped to live in fulfilling relationships with others and they with us.

So the stories of faith in scripture are essentially stories about relationships: relationship with God and relationships with others. Most of the stories have highs and lows because of humanity's relationship with God and struggle with self-centeredness. Some of the stories contain hope, some contain despair. Some reflect good news, some are tragic. Some encourage us, some warn us. Some are marked by deep faith, while others reveal the peril of selfishness. But most of the stories of faith in scripture are about relationships and their importance and the central place of God.

The story of Christ is the story of God's love for the world like open arms embracing us in God's self or family. The story of Christ is the story of God's desire that we live in relationships with one another in the spirit of love, joy, peace, patience, kindness, generosity, faithfulness, gentleness, self-control, honesty, mercy, compassion, and justice to mention some of God's spiritual gifts that make relationships fulfilling. This desire is communicated clearly in twenty-five of the twenty-seven books of the New Testament. Nearly all Christians recognize that "to love God and to love our neighbor as we love ourselves" is the central theme of biblical revelation.

The church has an important role in supporting people to love themselves as children of God, which involves coming to know and accept themselves as unique creatures who live in relationship with God. The church has the privilege to help nurture their relationship with God so they can live in relationships of love with one another.

When people know and accept themselves, realizing they are unconditionally accepted by their faith community, they are prepared and will be supported in responding to their singleness. They, better than anyone else, will know the nature of a fulfilling relationship. As long as that relationship is marked by the fruit of God's spirit, whether it be a *marital* or a *same-gender partnership* or a cluster of relationships centered around friends, church, family, community, or vocation, it will reflect the will of God in meeting that person's relational needs.

Endnotes: Chapter Eleven

[1] John Boswell, "Homosexuality and Religious Life: A Historical Approach," in *Sexuality and the Sacred* edited by James B. Nelson and Sandra P. Longfellow (Louisville: Westminster/John Know Press, 1994), p. 361.

2   Peter Gomes, *The Good Book* (New York: William Morrow and Company, Inc., 1996), p. 165.

3   Walter Wink, "Biblical Perspectives on Homosexuality," *The Christian Century*,(December 7, 1979), p. 1085.

4   James B Nelson, "Sources for Body Theology: Homosexuality as a Test Case," *Sexuality and the Sacred*, (Louisville: John Knox/Westminster Press,`1994), p. 377.

5   Robin Scroggs, *The New Testament and Homosexuality* (Philadelphia: Fortress Press, 1983), p. 123.

6   Chris Glaser, *Uncommon Calling: A Gay Christian's Struggle to Serve the Church* (Louisville: Westminster/John Knox Press, 1996), pp. 180-84.

7   *The Church and Its Officers: G-6.0106b* in Book of Order: Constitution of the Presbyterian Church (USA), Part II (Louisville: The Office of the General Assembly, 2001), G-6.0106b

8   Ibid.

9   Mary E. Hunt, "Lovingly Lesbian," in *Sexuality and the Sacred*, edited by: James B. Nelson and Sandra P. Longfellow (Louisville: John Knox/Westminster Press, 1994), p. 172

10 Ibid., pp. 174-79

11 J. Michael Clark, "Men's Studies, Feminist Theology, Gay Male Sexuality" in *Sexuality and the Sacred*, edited by: James B. Nelson and Sandra P. Longfellow (Louisville: John Knox/Westminster Press,1994), p. 220

12 Quoted by James B. Nelson, "Homosexuality and the Church," in *Christianity and Crisis*, Vol.37, No.5: April 4, 1997, p. 67

13 John Boswell, "Homosexuality and Religious Life: A Historical Approach," p. 364

14 Ibid., p. 364-366.

15 John Boswell, Christianity, Social Tolerance, and Homosexuality (Chicago: University of Chicago Press, 1980), pp. 188-195.

16 James B. Nelson, "Sources for Body Theology: Homosexuality as a Test Case," p. 380.

CHAPTER TWELVE

Validated Committed Partnerships: Their Nature and Value

So God grant us for tomorrow ways to order human life
That surround each person's sorrow with a calm that conquers strife.
Make us partners in our living, our compassion to increase,
Messengers of faith, thus giving hope and confidence and peace.
Jane Parker Huber

The Nature of Committed Partnerships
Introduction

Marriage in one form or another has been part of the cultural scene long before Abraham and the beginning of the Hebrew family that evolved into the Jewish nation; it has been part of the cultural scene with little influence imposed upon it by the early Christian church. Marriage is one of the oldest cross-cultural institutions associated with the human race. We believe it was instituted by God long before God created the Jewish nation, and its nature has changed to adapt to the changing patterns of culture, not the theological perspective of Judaism or Christianity. Nowhere is it written in biblical law that marriage is the only institution to be supportive to the significant relationship of two people. The symbol of marriage is organic.

It is presumptuous of me to assume there could be a possible change made to the symbol of marriage. But as James B. Nelson writes: "New rites can be created to meet legitimate needs unmet by existing symbols. There are, indeed, gay and lesbian Christian couples living in long-term, permanently-intended covenantal relationships who earnestly desire the affirmation of their religious communion."[1]

I believe it would be a mistake to alter marriage radically to attempt to meet the many different kinds of relational needs in this age; however, during the past two centuries the primary purpose of marriage has been expanded to emphasize mutual support and love between husband and wife in order to experience a fulfilling relationship. Marriage continues to embrace its unique sexual symbol: *the two shall become one.*

At the same time, marriage can also be seen as a *mutual partnership* in much the same way of same-gender partners. As referred to in the previous chapter, the second story of creation (Genesis 2:18-23) uses the term *partner* when seeking a solution for the aloneness of Adam: "*I will make him a helper as his partner.*" Upon the creation of a woman, Adam and Eve lived in a newly created *partnership.* This new relational paradigm entitled *partnerships* should be shared by the marriage of a man and a woman and union of same-gender couples whose committed relationship is validated.

At the same time the *marital partnership* retains its uniqueness while the same-gender partnership likewise retains its uniqueness. Both would continue to be civil unions with the blessing of their religious community if they so choose. Both share the same sacred relational value safeguarded by the same or similar legal standards. What then would be one example of the nature of committed *same-gender partnerships?*

Partners, Not a Marriage

A committed *same-gender partnership* is parallel to a *marital partnership* but not identical or an appendage to marriage. It has a life of its own. As shown in chapter nine, the biblical symbol for marriage is the image of the two (male and female) becoming one. When that symbol is placed alongside the command of the first chapter of Genesis: "Be fruitful and multiply," the symbol of marriage becomes organic as seen in the physical oneness of the male and female in an effort to conceive and be faithful to the command of the creator God. That symbol is inappropriate for two people of the same gender in partnership.

Chapters nine and ten summarized the history of marriage in the Middle Eastern and Western cultures. Throughout history its symbol, *a sexual union (two shall become one),* has maintained consistency. In Old Testament Israel sexual union was primarily for the procreation of children, and in some cases enriched the union of those in relationship. Sexual intercourse was not considered sinful although the couple was ritually unclean for a short period of time. After the third century, the church came under Greek and Roman influence. Prominent Greek philosophy considered the material and physical sinful and opposed to the spiritual potential of humanity. Many early church fathers influenced by this way of thinking accepted the symbol of marriage as a sexual union but only for the purpose of procreation.

John Calvin and Martin Luther attempted to expand the symbol of marriage, saying the sexual union is not only for procreating children but to help maintain unity in the relationship. Whether they were successful or not I cannot answer with documentation, but my feeling is that the relational dimension of marriage continued to lack strength until the twentieth century when the patriarchal/hierarchical view of the marriage relationship began to be challenged by mutuality, which is more consistent with the teaching and ministry of Christ. During this time genuine partnership was given birth and is slowly growing to join with procreation as a major purpose in the marriage of a man and woman.

A committed partnership creates a relational union. Its biblical origin actually precedes the symbol for marriage in both accounts of creation. In the first chapter of Genesis the text reads: "Let us make humankind in our image, according to our likeness, and let them have dominion over . . . So God created humankind in his image . . . male and female he created them" (1:26-27). At the time of creation male and female are clearly God's steward partners in caring for the rest of creation. There are no hierarchical implications in the text.

The term *partner* in the second story of creation means *one who shares* (from partaker). This *partnership* is three-dimensional. The male and female live in relationship with one another as they live in a servant relationship with the creator God and with God's creation. They share their lives with each other in relationship with their creator and in relationship to their steward calling to partnership with God in caring for the earth and all upon it. *Sharing* belongs to both persons in the partnership; therefore, by definition partnership is an experience of mutuality.

If the relationship evolves to a state of domination/subjection, then sinfulness has become the dominant force and the two people have missed the target or God's intention for their relationship as described in the third chapter of Genesis. In the second chapter of Genesis the text reads: "And the Lord God formed man from the dust of the ground and breathed into his nostrils the breath of air . . . then the Lord God said, 'It is not good that the man (dust creature) should be alone. I will make him a helper as his *partner*' . . . and the rib that the Lord God had taken from the man he made into a woman and brought her to the man. Then the man said, 'This at last is bone of my bones and flesh of my flesh" (2:7, 18, 22-23). In the second story of creation, the word partner is actually used. The manner of creation emphasizes mutuality in the relationship as each is created from the same substance.

It can be assumed that following the creation of the woman, the original man was not the same, for part of him was used in the creation of the woman, so in a sense the final creation of man and woman occurred simultaneously as in the first story of creation. However, the important message in this story is *partnership,* and it is clearly expressed. It too has a stewardship perspective as expressed by action of God: "The Lord God took the man and put him in the garden of Eden to till it and keep it" (2:15). When the *partner* is created they become steward-partners with God.

In both accounts of creation the symbols of marriage follow the symbols of partnership. It seems to me that marriage has an additional dimension, which through history has become a distinct and dominant symbol: the two shall become one and be fruitful and multiply. This symbol was virtually imposed upon all members of the community of Israel for the purpose of procreation. Jesus and Paul changed its application from all people to only those who choose to marry, so in the life of the church procreation becomes the dominant symbol for marriage using the symbol, "the two shall become one." The symbol for a *partnership* between two people of the *same gender* will be different from the symbol of marriage.

The term *partner* has become popular in our culture. It creates a personal and positive image in the minds of most. It is a transgender term that means it does not communicate gender bias. Note the many different ways the term *partner* is used to describe how we share life together with no gender bias: business partner, spiritual partner, swing partner, tennis partner, law partner, workout partner, lab partner, dorm partner, travel partner, married partner, and etc. The term *partnership* creates the same image of mutuality: limited partnership, business partnership, community partnership, investment partnership, and spiritual partnership.

In the American culture husbands and wives sometimes refer to each other as partners: *he/she is my partner for life; we are partners in reaching this goal; parenting requires partnerhood.* At a symposium I attended on same-gender relationships the lesbian panel member always referred to her housemate as *my partner.* In my presence, nearly without exception I hear two people in a same-gender relationship refer to each other as *partners*. In our local newspaper, *The Athens Banner-Herald*, the headline on September 5, 2012, read, "UGA (University of Georgia) faculty seek domestic partner benefits." A few days later the same newspaper printed an article that this request was granted.[2] In our culture, *partner/partnerships* have become common terms to describe special and significant relationships, including marital and same-gender relationships.

The term *partner* is also used in the New Testament. The first disciples of Jesus were fishing partners: "For he (Peter) and all who were with him were amazed at the catch of fish that they had taken; and so also were James and John, sons of Zebedee, who were *partners* with Simon" (Luke 5:10). Paul, emphasizing the unity of the church, writes to the Corinthian Church: "For we are *partners* working together for God" (1 Corinthians 3:9 GNB). Writing to Philemon, Paul says, "So if you consider me your *partner,* welcome him as you would welcome me" (1:17). Then in Hebrews, "For we have become *partners* of Christ" (3:13).

In every instance the term *partner* is relational and positive, communicating a mutual or shared calling, mutual or shared commitment, mutual or shared purpose and mission, and mutual or shared life together with mutual or shared responsibility and freedom. The term *partner* is also used in scripture to mean the same as the term *friend.* Jesus tells his disciples: "No one has greater love than this, to lay down one's life for one's friends. You are my friends if you do what I command you" (John 15:13-14). What then does Christ expect of us? "This is my commandment, that you love one another as I have loved you" (John 15:12, 17). Partnership is relational in a positive way.

Homosexual persons usually define themselves relationally rather than focusing upon sexuality. For example, Mary Hunt writes: "We (lesbian persons) define ourselves according to certain relational commitments to other women, or what I am calling female friendships."[3] J. Michael Clark says much the same concerning commitments among gay men: "A truly liberated sexuality is one that affirms the wholeness of our being as persons-in-relationship . . . to be human is to be in relationship with ourselves, with other persons, with the earth and the cosmos, and with God."[4] Since homosexual persons place priority upon both relationship and mutuality before sexual expression and behavior, the term *partnership* best describes their committed relationship. Now that mutuality is becoming a characteristic of many marriages, *partnership* can be descriptive of the committed marital relationship.

Ethical Structure for Committed Partnerships (Marital or Same-Gender)

At this point the ethical structure will be shaped from a biblical and Christological perspective. Paul's description of the body of Christ in his letters to the Ephesians, Romans, Corinthians, and Colossians serves as the symbol or image for *committed partnerships*. Christ, head of the body, provides spiritual substance and guidance for the partnership. The various members of the body must be committed to the head and to each other in order to be true to themselves and helpful to one another. The role each member plays is not for pure self satisfaction but for the common good or for the good of the relationship as a whole. In this way both persons in the partnership are supported and cared for; the relationship thrives and remains healthy.

The image of the body provides important principles in the ethical structure. First, in the *partnership* every facet of life, such as roles and decision-making, are to be shared mutually. One partner does not have expectations for giving or receiving that is not mutually shared by the other partner. This is one reason the term *partner* is so strong. Second, there is no gender bias to the partnership. Unlike marriage, it can include two people of the same gender. It can also be comprised of male and female. Third, the partnership is composed of two people, so it is monogamous rather than polygamous. In the business world, partnerships often include many people, so clarity at this point is necessary. Fourth, the partnership will be sealed with the promises shared with each other. Fifth, promises are made public to indicate a celebration of the committed relationship, to invoke God's blessing upon them, and also to seek the support and validation of family, friends, and church.

It is believed God calls all human beings to live in relationships of love and justice; however, some human beings are called to enjoy wholeness by living in a committed marriage between male and female. Some are called to a life of celibacy (singleness) as a particular mode for serving Christ. As the Helvetic Confession states: "Let them not lift up themselves above others, but let them serve the Lord continuously in simplicity and humility."[5] For those for whom marriage or singleness is not appropriate or wise, it is believed God calls them to live in committed partnerships.

The committed partnership is a covenant by which two people are bound together by God's spirit of love and grace, and are called to support one another in their life journey of Christian discipleship. With Christ as their head, their relationship will be embraced by the fruits of the spirit, which are love, joy, peace, patience, kindness, generosity, faithfulness, gentleness, and self control (Galatians 5:22-23).

The charge given to those in this special relationship is expressed by Paul to the Colossians: "Clothe yourselves with compassion, kindness, humility, meekness, and patience. Bear with one another, and if anyone has a complaint against another, forgive each other; just as the Lord has forgiven you, so you also must forgive. Above all, clothe yourselves with love, which binds everything together in perfect harmony. And let the peace of Christ rule in your hearts, to which indeed you were called in the one body. And be thankful" (Colossians 3:12-15). Note: all these spiritual qualities are *relational*. The closing note of thanksgiving is important because it is the affirmation of mutual dependence upon God, the giver of the fruit of the spirit, who sustains the partnership and enriches the life of each partner.

In preparation for the service of a *committed same-gender partnership or marital partnership,* the two people consult with their minister to prepare for their life together. Some examples for discussion are:

1) Sharing their families of origin, noting strengths and weaknesses, the extent of the family influence, and what will be difficult to leave in order to form a healthy partnership.

2) The nature of their commitment to Christ with ongoing examples of spiritual discipline and resources that will spiritually empower the growth of the relationship.

3) The ethical framework of a *committed partnership* and *the body of Christ as symbol* of the partnership; male and female also retain the sexual symbol: *the two shall become one.*

4) The meaning of the covenant promises made to each other.

5) The way the committed partnership is similar to and different from marriage.

6) How the presence of God's unconditional love helps the two people accept the different personality characteristics of each, thus enabling the personality of the *partnership* to expand and to become more dynamic.

7) Relational topics like communication, conflict, sexuality, and children.

8) Ways to be open to the support of the church, family, and friends, and at the same time ways to support them.

9) The nature and form of the worship service of commitment.

10) The importance of identifying roles mutually with annual assessment of those roles; as life experiences change, roles should change.

11) The legal requirements of the state (if applicable).

Following the service of the *validation of the committed partnership,* opportunity for additional sessions are offered to deal with dynamics of the relationship, with particular attention to communication, roles, methods for conflict management, financial management, sexuality, relationship with extended family and friends, support from the faith community, and other topics of specific concern. For young adults who have the vision of marriage, this structured time together with a third party should greatly prepare the couple for a *partnership* that lasts *"till death do us part"* marked by love and happiness.

The Service of Commitment

The commitment service is a gathering for the worship of God, where in the presence of God and witnesses two people speak their promises of love and faithfulness to each other and seek the help of God and the prayers of the people so their relationship may be strengthened. It is hoped that the couples will prepare portions of the service themselves to impress upon them the value of what is said in the commitment. The liturgy for worship will contain some or all of the following elements:

Call to worship with scriptural sentences
Purpose and meaning of committed partnerships
Expression of relational commitment
Promises based on recognition of sinfulness and dependence upon
    Jesus Christ and the fruits of the spirit
Old and New Testament readings
Promises of the two people
Validation and support from the congregation and family
Hymns, special music, and prayers
Charge and God's blessing on the committed (same-gender or
    marital) partners

The Sexual Relationship

As emphasized in chapter four, sexuality is more than erotic desire, which precipitates sexual behavior or *coitus* among two people. Sexuality not only involves what males and females do or say or look like, it also involves who they are as humans. The whole being of sexuality is so mysterious that who we are as sexual beings and what we do as sexual beings interact with each other, shaping us spiritually, physically, psychologically, and mentally.

Perhaps most important, sexuality is the capacity to relate with fellow humans with kindness, love, joy, peace, patience, goodness, faithfulness, self-control, compassion, justice, honesty, and a listening ear. Our sexuality also gives us the capacity to relate to God, who is spirit. In conclusion, our sexuality is that attraction toward others that communicates both the need and value of living in relationships. It is a good gift from God.

It is assumed that a *committed partnership (same-gender or marital)* includes total commitment with one another that not only includes concern for the spiritual, emotional, and mental wellbeing of each other but also the economic wellbeing of each. Since the relationship is built on mutuality, together the two people are encouraged to reach a mutual decision concerning the nature of their material support for each other. The sexual activity between the two persons, likewise, needs to be dealt with privately and mutually among the two. A *committed partnership (same-gender or marital)* enables the two people to give primary attention to their relationship.

The Value of Committed Partnerships

For thousands of years marriage has served human beings as the major institution to bring male and female together in relationships to conceive children through sexual activity, to provide for the maintenance of the family, and to enjoy refuge from loneliness through community. While some aspects of marriage have changed along with the changes in culture, its basic purpose and boundaries are deeply rooted in culture and religion. Since the growth of mutuality has enriched many marital relationships, I think the term *partnership* best describes both marital and same-gender relationships. What then is the value of committed partnerships for the partners, for the religious community, and for society?

Value for the Partners (Same-Gender or Marital)

First, the partnership is bound by spiritual/relational values as the priority. When the spiritual values of love, joy, kindness, mercy, gentleness, humility, compassion, faithfulness, and self-control are mentioned, they only have meaning within the context of relationships. In the ancient community of Israel, the marriage of a man and a woman sometimes did not have an ethical structure that is spiritual in nature, which is first directed toward the purpose of enriching the relationship. Marriage was bound by rules perpetuated to protect the family. This was important at that time.

The Catholic Theological Society of America prepared a paper on human sexuality in 1977 representing an alternative to traditional Catholic moral theology. They concluded that relationships are moral when they are mutual, when they support the spiritual growth of both persons in marriage, and when both persons are committed and faithful. They realized that many marriages were corrupted with immoral behavior because the church has been more concerned about sex than spiritual values.

The CTSA studied and interviewed gay and lesbian persons in this area to learn they already focus on the nurture of the relationship with the support of spiritual values. They concluded that homosexual attraction is the natural sexual orientation of this minority group. This means same-gender sexual attraction is not a deviation from nature. Coming from this Catholic society whose roots are deep into *natural theology* (Thomas Aquinas), this statement expresses much authority. They feel homosexuality is like left-handedness, which is present in about 12 percent of the population. Some societies discriminated against left-handed children, forcing them to use their right hand. Some, guided by natural law, actually declared being left-handed is sinful because it was unnatural. In fact, the term *left* has a negative connotation: left out, left behind. Of course, we now know that being left—or right-handed is a natural consequence of brain wiring.[6]

Second, in a *validated committed partnership* the two people are able to make public a personal commitment. It gives the relationship honesty and integrity. Currently, among most couples of the same gender who share a home, personal and intimate commitments have been kept private with very little said in public. The two people know they could be ridiculed and declared to be "living in sin" by the religious sector and many in society. Honesty and integrity contribute another spiritual dimension to the relationship, enabling each person to be more true to self, which then enhances their spiritual development and the quality of the relationship.

Third, a *validated committed partnership* provides community support. Two individuals who are committed to one another and live in the same home have now become a family or community. They cease being only individuals; they now share their life with another individual. Their small community of two needs larger communities who will support them, who will serve as mirrors so they see their real selves as partners who enable each other to enjoy relationships with others and together in relationship with others. They need the same support from others that all families need.

Without the validated support of family, church, friends, and community, the two in their privacy can turn inward into themselves and become isolated from others. This is seldom a healthy way to develop a lasting, quality relationship. A validated committed partnership frees the partners to look beyond themselves to others while at the same time looking inward and focusing upon each other. Most people in a committed relationship still need to have relationships with others that help them continue their development toward being a whole person.

Fourth, a *validated committed partnership* broadens opportunities for spiritual development when both in the committed partnership are fully accepted by their faith community. They are full members of their church with the opportunity to use all the gifts God has given them. The congregation, led by God's spirit, can now elect them as officers or ministers.[7] With *validated committed partnerships*, the issue surrounding ordination ceases to be a problem.

Fifth, a *validated committed partnership* fully incorporates the two people of the same gender into the mainstream of society. Hopefully, they will be able to enjoy the civil rights all citizens are expected to enjoy. At the same time, they can be contributors to the quality of life in the community. The opportunity to give as well as receive, to accept others as well as being accepted, and to serve as well as being served will strengthen not only each partner but the partnership as a whole. In reality, what benefits the partners will likewise have value for both the religious community and civil community.

Sixth, a *validated committed partnership* has personal value for each person. As it has emphasized in this book, the partnership responds to the relational needs of singles; it responds to the statement in Genesis: *it is not good for the human to be alone.* In that context, it provides for each person economic, emotional, medical, household, safety, health, transportation, social, and parenting (where applicable) support. As is written in Ecclesiastes: *Two are better off than one, because together they can work more effectively. If one of them falls down, the other can help him up. But if someone is alone and falls, it's just too bad, because there is no one to help him. If it is cold, two can sleep together and stay warm, but how can you stay warm by yourself? Two men can resist an attack that would defeat one man alone. A rope made up of three cords is hard to break* (Ecclesiastes 4:9-12, *Good News Bible*).

Many in a present-day marital partnership already experience these values. In validating committed same-gender partnerships, these personal values will also enrich their relationship and strengthen their family, community, and faith community ties. As a result, I believe our culture and family life in general will be greatly enriched.

Value for the Religious Community and Society

Not only does the paradigm *validated committed partnerships* have value for partners but also for the religious community and society. I will mention five significant contributions. You may add others as well.

First, since the relationships have a strong ethical structure built upon Jesus Christ and the spiritual values that are the fruit of the new creation in Christ, it gives both the religious and secular community confidence that standards of morality will rise rather than decline. Both religious and secular communities have been dependent upon laws as the means to maintain a high standard of morality. Laws and their enforcement are, at best, an external effort to maintain standards of morality. Paul reminds Timothy, *"Law is good if it is used as it should be used. It must be remembered, of course, that laws are made, not for good people, but for lawbreakers and criminals, for the godless and sinful* (1 Timothy 1:8-9). Paul has an important point. Law seldom changes the hearts of those it regulates, controls, and imprisons; in fact, it often generates hostility on the one extreme and self-righteousness on the other.

Ironically, both extremes use the law for self-serving purposes. Those who are hostile often attempt to find ways to skirt laws in order to accomplish what is gained by breaking the law, bringing no punitive consequences. Self-righteous persons focus upon the letter of the law that is clearly discernible and can be measured, but ignore the spirit of the law or the purpose for which the law was created. In a real sense, the self-righteous abuse the law, but feel they gain superior spiritual status over those who cannot possibly obey every facet of the written law. That was a major issue Jesus addressed in his ministry.

In contrast, those who live in committed partnerships are nurtured to live by grace, which is an ethical structure built upon Christ as emphasized in chapter two. The spiritual values of Christ, the head of the partnership, will then be reflected in the relationship. This paradigm treats all persons as children of God and considers all relationships to be sacred. The motivation to live by spiritual values originates within the heart. As Paul writes: "There is no law against such things" (Galatians 5:23). And to the Romans Paul says, "Love does no wrong to a neighbor; therefore, love is the fulfilling of the law" (13:10).

Second, *same-gender validated committed partnerships* become public. What was once hidden becomes seen for what it really is: committed relationships between people who are no different from those who have made promises in *marital partnership* between a male and female. Those in committed partnerships embrace high ethical values; they want to live in a community of high ethical values, where people respect faithfulness in relationships, where people share in making the church reflect the servant qualities of Christ, and where the community becomes a positive and strong influence upon the lives of all its members. When those living in *same-gender validated committed partnerships* are free to be seen for who they really are, it produces an openness and a high level of honesty that reduces fear and anxiety, which are eventually replaced by trust.

Third, those in *same-gender validated committed partnerships* will contribute to the religious and secular community a treasure of gifts and services. The church now has an additional community of people who are gifted and who can be instrumental as servant people involved in Christian ministry. During a time when people are reducing time for volunteering, this additional resource can provide a stimulus to expand ministry rather than reducing ministry. The same is true in the life of the community. Since those in validated committed partnerships are now public and trusted, community and church will invite and challenge them to use their gifts for the common good.

Fourth, *same-gender validated committed partnerships* set everyone free from the negative and personally destructive activity of judging others. Those in the partnerships are no longer victims of another's personal inclination to judge them harshly as immoral people. More so, those who are really set free are those who feel compelled to do the judging. Hardly anything is more counterproductive than judging others. This role is like playing God; it gradually destroys our hearts, the capacity within to grow spiritually. Those who judge others are always the losers, so in this case public validation frees people from thinking they need to judge. Of course, Jesus has already freed us from this burdensome role we often impose upon ourselves, but validation serves as icing on the cake. Church and society can now enjoy a true sense of community.

Fifth, *same-gender validated committed partnerships* will actually serve to strengthen both marriage and family. Partnerships of the same gender, for example, set people free to be who they are and to be public about it. I have read about many situations and have had firsthand experience with situations where homosexual persons were afraid to accept who they were for fear they would be rejected by their family, their friends, and their church. They did what culture expects of everyone. They married living under illusion things would work out; some even thought marriage would change their homosexual orientation. Well, that did not happen even though they produced children.

As a result, the marriages are now broken and dissolved. Spouses have been emotionally and spiritually damaged; children have not only been victims of these marital failures, they have had to deal with the reality of having a homosexual parent at a time when homosexuals are generally regarded as abnormal and/or sick. They also have to deal with the *big secret,* which is now no secret. Many marriages broken, innocent children caught in the middle and hurt. As a minister I have personally witnessed these tragedies in life.

How can we prevent these tragedies from happening? It seems to me that validating committed *same-gender partnerships* will give homosexual persons an authentic option to meet their relational needs without feeling compelled to marry someone of the opposite gender.

As you think about *validating committed partnerships*, you may see other contributions this paradigm would make to enhance the quality of life among the partners and within community and religious life. I believe this paradigm will raise the ethical values or morality of our society. Everyone wins. More so, combat in church and society on the topic of human sexuality with specific attention given to homosexuality will be over.

No more fighting. Together all groups, including homosexual persons, can focus constructively on building healthier communities where attention is given to those spiritual values that build positive and strong relationships. The relational paradigm, *validating committed partnerships*, demonstrates what it means to *live by grace* with the help of the fruits of the spirit in building fulfilling relationships.

Now is the time for the church to come to terms with these struggles in our culture. If we do not, someone else will, and the church will then have to adapt in much the same way it has adapted to cultural changes over the years concerning marriage. For example, names are already being attached to the blessing of same-gender committed relationships. Some titles I have seen in the newspaper are *same sex unions, same sex marriages, holy unions, domestic partners, civil unions, same-sex partners, and marriage.* Some states have legalized marriage for two people of the same gender. It is often advertised as *same-sex marriage,* which causes many to become preoccupied with the sexual side of the relationship, which distorts the relational purpose same-gender couples are seeking.

Often politics takes the easy way without providing a great deal of substance. Laws and practices for marriage have already been established, so no further work needs to be done. Debate, vote, and sanction marriage for same-gender couples and then close the book. Move to the next task on the agenda. The quick and easy way. If the government wants to legalize the marriage for same-gender partners, it should not dictate sameness for Christian denominations. By continuing to focus upon *same-gender partnerships,* Christian denominations maintain a title of this institution, which reflects the primary purpose of the union.

If marriage is the only way government handles this issue, Christian denominations are left to give substance and purpose behind this new and acceptable public bonding of two people who are of the same gender. Unlike the history of marriage, the focus needs to be on the partnership. The failure of so many marriages (about 47 percent) annually reveals that the church and culture need to be more supportive in preparing couples for marriage, which for many is still moving from a hierarchical to a far more complex mutual relationship.

Marriages need more preparation and nurture if they are going to reflect genuine mutuality among husband and wife. Perhaps when *same-gender partnerships* become public and acceptable they will help strengthen marriages by their example of mutuality. Perhaps our culture will begin to see that marriage between a male and female needs to be understood also as a *partnership*.

The church has a unique opportunity to give moral substance to a change, which is inevitably going to occur in our culture. One significant way to help all people live in lasting and fulfilling relationships involves providing positive leadership in establishing a new relational paradigm: *validating committed partnerships* and then educating the public on the reasons for choosing this new umbrella title for both marriages of male and female and unions of same-gender couples.

Those who choose marriage will enjoy a *marital partnership;* for some it will be a *same-gender partnership.* Each partnership will retain its uniqueness, but both will share meaning and integrity because they will focus upon nurturing quality relationships. As we live in a time of great change, the church is given a unique opportunity to be like salt, which enriches the quality of life. What the future has in store for us, I do not know, but I do know the church has something unique to offer so that what is shaped will reflect both quality and integrity. In the epilogue we will explore the future and the changing face of the family.

Endnotes: Chapter Twelve

[1] James B. Nelson, "Homosexuality and the Church," in *Christianity and Crisis,* p. 68.

[2] Lee Shearer, UGA Faculty Seek Domestic Partner Benefits, in the *Athens Banner-Herald,* (Athens Newspapers Inc., Athens, Georgia, September 5, 2012), p. 1.

3   Mary E. Hunt, "Lovingly Lesbian," in *Sexuality and the Sacred*, p. 172.

4   J. Michael Clark, "Men's Studies, Feminist Theology, Gay Male Sexuality" in *Sexuality and the Sacred*, pp. 219,220

5   *The Helvetic Confession* in "The Book of Confessions" (Louisville: Materials Distribution, 1996), p. 116: 5.245.

6   Rosemary Redford Ruether, "Homophobia, Heterosexism, Pastoral Practice," in *Sexuality and the Sacred*, edited by: James B. Nelson and Sandra P. Longfellow (Louisville: John Knox/Westminster Press, 1994), p. 391.

7   Herbert Anderson and Robert Cotton Fite, *Becoming Married* (Louisville: Westminster/John Knox Press, 1993), p. 15.

Families of the Future:
Using All God's Gifts to Enrich
God's World

Christ's example, Christ's inspiring, Christ clear call to work and worth,
Let us follow, never faltering, reconciling folk on earth.
Men and women, richer, poorer all God's people, young and old,
Blending human skills together, gracious gifts from God.
Jane Parker Huber

Introduction

The content of this book has focused primarily on human sexuality, marriage, same-gender partnerships, and the belief that God created human beings to live in fulfilling relationships. There is no evidence that God was selective by applying this truth only for those who are Jewish and Christian, or only for heterosexual men and women, or only for those who commit themselves to marriage. No, it appears from biblical study and from interview research that all humans are created to live in fulfilling relationships. This includes gay, lesbian, and transgender persons, as well as heterosexual singles both young and old. Since this is clearly communicated in Holy Scripture and was a need before every aspect of created life was affected by the fall of humanity, we can conclude God is responsible for this relational need, and it is good. Likewise, we are not responsible for our sexual orientation any more than we are responsible for the color of our eyes and skin or whether we are left-or right-handed. I have asked hundreds of heterosexual and homosexual persons whether they can recall when they chose their sexual orientation. All the answers were the same: "I did not choose my sexual orientation. That's who I am and I had nothing to do with it."

Being homosexual does not reduce the need to live in fulfilling relationships, and marrying a heterosexual seldom works for either person. That has been tried countless number of times to the chagrin and pain of both, as well as their children and extended family. As children of the creator God who is love, what are we going to do to be supportive to the needs of 5-10 percent of our population? I have suggested unconditional acceptance and hospitality. That is God's response to us who are sinful.

Surely we can do the same for this minority of people who are not even responsible for their orientation and are trying to fulfill a relational need for which they are not responsible. I am sure if I were in their shoes I would feel that God is responsible to some extent for this dilemma. Beyond that, I would have to live in a society that generally prefers I not be here. Because of this, it is necessary for us to represent God in living by God's grace, and thus open our arms fully in a spirit of hospitality.

If nothing else, it gets God off the hook, but in the end it gives us an opportunity to be godlike. Perhaps that's one reason God created us in God's image or likeness. Maybe the problems that stem from God's good creation are for us to solve. Perhaps that is what it means to be God's steward-partner.

Much has been said publicly and definitively about the sinfulness of homosexuality. From pulpits, in political halls, across airwaves on radio and television, and in books and magazines, we have been told that inclusion of homosexuals and validation of their committed partnerships will destroy the family as we have known it since God instituted it in the days of Adam and Eve. Giving an inch on the full inclusion of gays and lesbians into the church will cause family values to be a thing of the past. These statements are nearly verbatim pronouncements I have heard and read for the past twenty years.

In this epilogue, I hope to show two things. First, the condition of the family without dealing with hospitality for homosexuals through committed partnerships has its own set of challenges, stresses, and opportunities as it experiences phenomenal change; second, validating committed *same-gender partnerships* may help put heart back into family life. To begin with, if we are fearful about losing God's intention of family and values as modeled in scripture, it is necessary to examine that model and those values so that we know what we could lose.

The Face of Biblical Families: Caught in Stress and Conflict

Old Testament

In a sermon on Father's Day, June 18, 2000, I said, "I want you to take a moment and identify a family in the Old Testament you would recommend as a model for families today." I gave them a minute to contemplate. For many, in this age of surround sound a minute is a long time of silence; however, it needed to have been longer than that, because no one could identify a model family among God's biblical families. Yes, they were familiar with biblical families.

In our congregation scripture is the basic resource not only for church school, but for developing liturgy and sermons for worship, for our Wednesday afternoon Logos program, and for week-day adult studies. They could not identify one family in the Old Testament as a

model to emulate. I knew that would be their response before giving
them the task because I systematically went through the Old Testament
endeavoring to find this model for family life and family values that so
many ministers are fearful of losing.

Families in the Old Testament seem to have the same struggles that
families of the twenty-first century have. Abraham and Sarah actually
banished Abraham's son Ishmael and his mother from the family, not
to mention how Abraham sexually used Sarah when his life was in
danger in Egypt. Then we see Isaac doing the same thing with his wife,
Rebecca, who chooses her twin son Jacob as her favorite over Esau.
Through trickery and intrigue she and Jacob devise a plan to rob Esau
of his father's blessing.

As life continues in Israel, family problems escalate rather than
being resolved by a high standard of family values. We know all too
well about Joseph and his brothers. By the way, Joseph was his father's
favorite, but how could Jacob develop family values when he fathered
so many sons by four different women?

Then comes Moses. What do we know about his family? Can you
recall the name of his wife or wives and sons? What about daughters?
What about Moses' second wife? Moses was a man with a mission, a
very effective agent of God in establishing the Hebrew nation. But if he
spent any time with his family, we do not know about it. That's probably
the reason he died alone on Mt. Nebo and Pisgah and was buried by the
Lord with no one knowing the place of burial (Deuteronomy 34:1-9).

Even King David, the man after God's heart and the king the
Hebrew nation dearly loved, experienced family problems that brought
indescribable grief and anguish. Ruth and Naomi come the closest in
reflecting ethical values and ideals, but they were not a typical family,
and they were of the same gender. Actually, we know very little about
the family life of people of faith in the Old Testament. The glimpses that
we are given are filled with sinful experiences. They have a contemporary
ring to them.

New Testament

We are exposed to families in the New Testament even less than in the Old Testament. The brothers of Jesus played no role in his ministry. What were the names of his sisters? What about his childhood and those turbulent teen years? What he does say about families is usually metaphorical and puzzling. Peter had a wife, but we do not even know her name. Did he simply leave her for three years while involved as Jesus' disciple? No one knows. Paul's marital/family situation is even more mysterious. When writing to the Corinthian Christians about marriage, he suggests to those who are single to remain single, the same as he.

We learn very little about the families of faith in scripture, certainly not enough for them to serve as models for family life and family values in this age. I am not being facetious or cynical; I am trying to be honest with the scripture and what it says and does not say. That was the commitment I demonstrated in chapter one concerning homosexuality and scripture. There are a few instructive passages in scripture that refer to relationships in families. In Deuteronomy we are told to teach our children that *the Lord God is one and we are to love God with all our heart, soul, and strength.* Proverbs contains some advice to young men about seeking the wise counsel of their parents and to refrain from sexual immorality. The fifth commandment tells children to obey their parents if they want to live long lives.

In the New Testament Paul repeats the same injunction to the Ephesians; he then warns fathers not to provoke their children to anger and nurture them in the ways of God (Ephesians 6:1-4). In conclusion, scripture was obviously not written as a manual for parenting and family life any more than it is a manual of sexual ethics. Where then did this ideal family model and family values originate if they can't be discerned from scripture? What is it that many people are fearful of losing if the community of faith opens its arms to homosexual persons and validates committed partnerships?

Beyond Patriarchy

I think I have been looking in the wrong place for the answer; very likely that is true for most of us in the church. I believe some in the church are frantically trying to preserve a secular or cultural norm called *patriarchy* and *hierarchy*. What is feared of being lost is a clear sense of power, authority, and discipline imposed by force from above with immediate and quiet subjection, obedience, and service from below. Those cultural norms were present in Hebrew culture as well as all the other countries in the Middle East and even the West, where a taste of democracy was experienced from time to time. While patriarchy is fading from Jewish culture today, it remains strong in countries like Iran and Iraq, with Afghanistan being the prime example. Following September 11, 2001, we were given the clearest vision of ancient patriarchy as seen in Afghanistan while under Taliban rule.

It is strange that the church is striving to preserve the secular norm of patriarchy in this age in America, which has sought to be democratic since its conception. The norm for patriarchy or hierarchy emerged from a worldview of a three-tier universe: the earth is flat with heaven or God above (superior) and darkness or devil below (inferior).

From this ancient worldview Aristotle developed the great chain of being identifying that which is superior in ascending order, with the gods on the top of the ladder, who were likewise divided in order of superiority, then angels, then humans, who were likewise divided in order of superiority with adult men on the top of the human ladder. Males became the norm by which the rest of life is judged. Of course, authority and power were likewise claimed by those at the top of the ladder, while those below were forced to be obedient and subservient. This included women as well as children and slaves. They were property of the father and husband.

Patriarchy was the substructure of family life that produced the values of authority and obedience supported by force. It begins with marriage, where the wife was the property of the husband and then moved upward to live in subjection to the husband. Could these be the primary values many of today's families are losing? The same is true of society, in particular our schools. Many in the church are frantically trying to hold on to this ancient norm of patriarchy that is based on an ancient worldview many no longer embrace. I suppose some strongly defend preserving patriarchy because they hope it will help church and secular society maintain discipline and order.

The church needs to come to terms with this reality that is creating much confusion and is leading us down dead-end streets, causing despair and division. The flame of freedom burns brightly in our time and people are not going to be oppressed or pushed to the margins of life simply to make life easier for those in control. It's time to move beyond patriarchy to seek other avenues for maintaining discipline and order. We need to begin by examining marriage and redefining it.

A strong theological and biblical option is seen in Christology. Paul says it well to the Galatians: "There is no longer male and female, for all of you are one in Christ Jesus" (3:28). John Patton and Brian Childs write: "Some kind of authority conveying hierarchy is essential for family living. The decision to have children is a decision to exercise authority. Children do not come into the world as equal partners with their parents."[1]

Rather than using the term *hierarchy*, I prefer the image of mutual parenting by exercising authority through servanthood. To give up hierarchy is in no way giving up authority and responsibility. Authority imposed upon people is seldom constructive. Authority is much more powerful when it is given in response to being a serving, loving, and leading parent or teacher. It is not necessary to claim authority through a mechanical hierarchal system. In the Christology model, Jesus himself, living in a strong patriarchal/hierarchal society, suggests the servant leadership model for all of life when he said to his disciples: "Whoever wishes to become great among you must be your servant . . . for the Son of Man came not to be served but to serve and give his life a ransom for many" (Mark 10:43, 45).

The servant leader paradigm emphasizes mutuality in the husband/
wife relationship, thus expanding the marital personality, giving it more
diversity and strength for family life where there are children. Roles
for the husband/wife and mother/father are not gender biased since in
Christ there is neither male nor female. This frees the husband and wife
to change and adapt their roles as the family situation changes in the
context of their God-given gifts.

This biblical and Christological model, whose symbol is the *body of
Christ,* involves every member of the family in sharing responsibility for
the wellbeing of the entire family (body). The foundation of the body
symbol is God's grace, which assures all members of the family/body
of unconditional acceptance, with the expectation to use their gifts for
the common good.

Both church and society seem ready for a model that was suggested
implicitly by Jesus Christ and the apostle Paul. This model is flexible
and strong; it is inclusive with boundaries. It encourages individuality
within community; it provides freedom and expects responsibility. The
body model best responds to the changing face of the family in our
time. The condition of the family has its own set of challenges, stresses,
and opportunities as it experiences phenomenal change.

The Face of Families in the Twenty-first Century
The Diversity of Family Structure

The face of families has changed considerably in the past fifty
years. The family days of Ozzie and Harriet Nelson and June and Ward
Cleaver of the 1950s-1960s linger like a flickering candle flame caught
in a rush of wind. It was a great time for birthing children, so that by
1970 married couples with children under age eighteen accounted for
40 percent of all households in the United States, while only 6 percent of
homes were headed by single parents. Today, single-parent households
have increased to approximately 15 percent, while households with
a father, mother, and children have declined to 25 percent. As baby

boomers age, our country is experiencing a significant population shift, and the face of families is changing. This is not necessarily negative, but it will influence changes in many other areas of community life, especially where economics is involved.

The rise to 53 percent of young women conceiving their first child out of wedlock will significantly alter the structure of family life in the future. Some women do not marry after getting pregnant out of fear of a failed marriage. I think this fact emphasizes that youth need much more than rules to help them uphold standards of sexual morality. It also illustrates that sexual activity occurs long before young people are considering marriage. These women and their sex mate(s) are most likely heterosexual persons. Homosexuals have had virtually no influence on this moral problem.

Another change facing family life is the pressure for two incomes, revealing that parents are spending less and less time with their children. They call on institutions and nannies to help rear their children. Women comprise more than half of the workforce. The workplace presents a real challenge for families of the future as demands on the time of employees continue to rise. Two-income families are causing changes throughout culture and the religious sector.

Daycare centers, after-school programs, restaurants, housekeeping businesses are thriving services for the family. Banks and retail stores have longer hours; convenience foods dominate space in grocery stores. The one-car garage is a thing of the past. Our secular society experiences many other changes because of two-income families. Churches and charitable organizations are devising different and flexible strategies to encourage volunteerism. Many churches have added a staff person simply to coordinate volunteers. The changes that have occurred are not negative; they are the result of choices we make.

A single parent employed full-time has challenges with time limitations and managing the family. Some are seeking same-gender singles to live in and help. This also provides an adult companion for conversation and relationship. This is another example where validated committed partnerships can strengthen family life.

Another large group of single persons is electing not to marry or have not found a satisfying mate. This has increased the number of single people who live alone. Some of these singles are married to their job, and they are seeking relationships without marriage. One study shows that couples in a child-free marriage experience greater marital bliss, less marital conflict, and more shared leisure time than couples with children.

Another economic factor mentioned earlier in this book is that women are older when they marry and have children, deferring family formation until after they finish their education and get their first job. The median age of mothers of firstborn children is now twenty-seven, the oldest at any time in American history. Men are even older when they marry and father children.

A high divorce rate (approx. 47 percent) continues to be a major cause of diversity in the structure of family life. It creates two households for children, with a single nurturing parent for a period of time; remarriage then causes another shift for children. At this point, a single friend of the parent may be much easier for the children than a lover who competes for the parent's time. Some children of divorced parents are reared by their grandparents. Remarriage following a divorce or death of a spouse often creates blended families. Visiting the parent who does not have custody also effects the child's weekend commitments.

A relatively new change in the structure of family life is the rise of nontraditional families. More and more couples living together outside of marriage are producing or adopting children. What is called "boomerang" families are on the increase. These are families where post-high school or post-college students or divorcees who were or would be on their own are returning home to live with their parents. Gay and lesbian families are becoming more public and open since church and society are more responsive to their situation. More families adopt children from outside the United States with different racial and ethnic backgrounds.

Interracial families are becoming commonplace. Intermarriage among people of different religious faiths, ethnic backgrounds, and educational backgrounds occurs more often.

One of the significant changes in the structure of family life is occurring with older adults. Life expectancy has increased but men still die before women, leaving another large group of singles whose income is generally lower than that of men. As baby boomers approach the age of retirement, the numbers will swell, causing a significant change in the face of culture. Many will be moving to live with a son or daughter, thus changing the structure of both families.

Many other patterns of living are also affecting the structure of family life. In the past fifty years there has been a significant change in mobility, with families owning more than one automobile. The availability and affordability of automobiles have greatly influenced lifestyle. For youth it has contributed to liberation from family influence to peer influence at an age in life when many are not mature enough to handle the availability of sex, alcohol, and drugs. The automobile has also contributed to a shift to an urban and suburban lifestyle.

Those living in rural areas often work in a town or city and also drive to these places to satisfy their social life. To feel that rural living frees families from the perils of urban influence is an illusion. Mobility has also contributed to the fragmentation of the extended family, which was often the arena of inclusion for those having difficulty meeting their relational needs such as singles, divorcees, homosexuals, and those mentally and physically challenged.

Neighborhoods are likewise reflecting this diversity, with the possible exception of economic diversity. When our family moved into our suburban neighborhood in 1971, it was middle-class and Caucasian, with households consisting primarily of husband, wife, and children. Now, that same neighborhood has Caucasians, African-Americans, Hispanics, couples with children, couples without children, single parents with children, singles without children, retirees, divorcees, widows and widowers, college students, unmarried heterosexual couples, and same-gender partners. Schools, likewise, reflect this diversity. These changing trends have a significant impact on the future of families.

Impact of Changing Trends

I agree with Herbert Anderson and Robert Fite, who write: "It is unclear what form marriages and families will take in the decades ahead. One thing seems certain, however. The networks that people will identify as family are likely to be formed as much by choice as by bloodline."[2] What I identify as the impact these changing trends will have on family life are my personal observations after serving as a pastor for over forty years. I was part of the Ozzie and Harriet era as a teen; I have experienced the changes of the past fifty years. By the way, I am optimistic.

Stress on Functioning as a Family

Whenever I am faced with a great deal of diversity, it creates stress to function in a healthy way. For example, when I am with one of my granddaughters, she is continually asking me questions. Before I answer one question, she is asking another. This barrage of different questions eventually creates stress for me. Stress is not always negative. It can be a wake-up call. I think that is where we are with the family. It is not healthy if the stress is paralyzing, but as a catalyst for openness to constructive change, stress serves a useful purpose.

As emphasized in this book, the family has at least three major functions: to give all family members an opportunity to enjoy fulfilling relationships beginning with God and each other and then with other human beings; to enable all family members to mature and come to know who they are as gifted human beings created in the likeness of God; and to nurture and to socialize children in an environment of grace, unconditional love, justice, mercy, and other fruits of God's spirit.

When these family life functions are priority, then families will recognize stress for what it is and make the necessary changes. For example, I observe some families who overextend themselves economically, so both spouses commit themselves to full-time jobs that make extra time demands on them. When the husband and wife realize the stress is preventing them from having a fulfilling relationship, they stand back and acknowledge their standard of living is unnecessarily high. They can simplify their lives by changing jobs, reduce their standard of living and become a one-or a one-and-a-half-income household.

Stress is a warning signal like pain. It serves as a catalyst for change. In most cases, families have so many options for a good life, it can be overwhelming. Back in the 1950s my family did not have many choices. Life came simple. Today, we can choose to simplify. For example, I grew up in a family of six; our middle-class home had one bathroom. We managed with little difficulty. My wife and I have four sons, a family of six. Our middle-class home has two-and-a-half baths. In our family it seems the number of bathrooms continues to increase with each generation. This simple situation serves as an example that many people have space for choices that can help maintain the primary function of family life.

When families run out of choices, stress then becomes devastating. Once again in my experience as a pastor, single-parent families have a narrow range of choices. In most cases, the stress is caused in a threefold way: money, time, and lack of adult companionship. A single partner-friend could make a big difference in this situation if the single parent is open to that option and a partner-friend is available. Once again, among the three choices, the single partner-friend is seldom considered, and not much can be done about the money option, so it is usually the time option that gets attention. Stress on single parents and the economically poor come with the fewest choices to maintain healthy family functioning.

Isolation and Individualism

Because of diversity of family structure in our culture, I have noticed two responses. First, some parents and families believe that the traditional family (the Ozzie-Harriet model) is the only healthy model. So out of fear of contamination they withdraw and isolate themselves. They may move to a rural area, or they may keep to themselves, seeking community contact only where traditional families are present. Some may home school their children out of fear of contact with those who are different, racial, ethnic, religious, or economic. As families, they become withdrawn and individualistic.

A whole subgroup culture is emerging because of these fears. Those who can afford it are sending their children to private schools, many located in churches. Public schools are losing the richness that diversity can provide because of the growth of private schools. Megachurches are developing in response to this same fear and concern. They attempt to provide programs to meet every family need from Christian education and worship to recreation, school, sports programs, aerobics, and social events. These responses have become a subculture, insulating people from exposure to diversity.

These choices are also creating isolation for other people who have not chosen to be isolated. It is a reverse form of racial segregation. For years it was called "white flight," describing white families vacating a neighborhood when a family of another race moves into it. Now, the concept has spread to many arenas of cultural life as some families seek refuge from a much broader diversity than simply racial.

The reasons given for this choice of isolation are a better education where discipline is practiced, the fear of violence, drugs, sexual immorality, and the loss family of values, which means no one is looked up to as source of authority who will determine for children and youth right from wrong. The terms "right from wrong" usually refer to absolute standards found in the law with the Ten Commandments as an example. Those who are stereotypically associated with these social problems and isolated categorically are African-Americans, Hispanics, gays and lesbians, feminists, liberal intellectuals, social activists, counter-culture whites, and some low-income whites.

Isolationism has polarized our society and created division in our mainstream church communities. In our society it has created a wave of fear and a return to the creation of more laws, with more tax dollars allocated for law enforcement. It has also been the source for hate groups who bomb abortion clinics and beat and kill homosexuals in the name of God and morality. Efforts to stem crime and violence with more laws have been fruitless. For the most part, homosexuality has not been a significant part of the many changes that impact family life. Yet many ecclesiastical bodies have created laws (rules) to prohibit full membership to those who out of a God-given relational need have a committed *partnership* with someone of the same gender.

History has shown that little can be achieved by trying to control external behavior. Laws are necessary but they usually focus on the problem rather than the solution. Jesus teaches that lasting change occurs from within, within the heart. The time has come to examine another paradigm that may have lasting value because it puts primary emphasis upon humanity's spiritual potential rather than humanity's depravity. It focuses on the solution rather than being preoccupied with the problem. This paradigm begins with grace, God's unconditional favor and hospitality that reaches out to all and says, "Come, let us as members of the body of Christ live in fulfilling relationships of love, for we believe this is still a more excellent way."

Healthy Hearts Sustain Families Amidst a Changing Face
Return to the Nelsons and Cleavers?

Would I return to the 1950s and 1960s if the opportunity were given, to those days before we were beset with so many changes creating future shock? My answer is a no. I lived those days as a teen and young adult, and they were wonderful for me. I remember what those days were really like. In many respects they were good days for some, but they were still dark days of social oppression for many. For example, the personality models of the fifties/sixties (Nelsons and Cleavers) are white Anglo-Saxons. In many areas our social values today are much higher than they were fifty years ago. I would not choose to take the ethics and values of the 1950s and impose them on society today.

It would mean segregation and unequal opportunity for African-Americans and not simply in the South, but all over the United States. It would mean a return to patriarchy, where women existed to serve and satisfy their man, who was head of the household and breadwinner. It would mean an innocence based on blindness and self-righteousness, only to be exposed by a captured American spy whose name is Gary Powers. It would mean, as a male, adopting a role clearly designed for men and imposing a stereotypical role on women. It would mean having zero knowledge about same-gender attraction. I was not even familiar with the term *homosexual* back in the fifties, but other demeaning terms were used out of total ignorance, creating fear, causing the closet door not only to be shut but also locked.

Returning to the fifties would mean saying what I think others want to hear, rather than speaking the truth. In many ways, the fifties were a time of loneliness and superficiality, because the *in crowd* was clearly defined, the gates were firmly secured, while genuineness was skin deep. I think fascination with the new media called television validated the Nelson/ Cleaver role model that represented a minority of the population.

Church and society have come a long way in raising our social conscience, in compelling us to be more genuine and honest, and to consider values like peace, justice, love, and acceptance. Those spiritual values were seldom spoken in the fifties. Some attribute the decline of personal morality to these changes. I do not. I think the phenomenal changes that have occurred in the past fifty years could be the catalyst compelling us to go beyond written rules and laws that too often serve those who created them. They push some people to the margins of life. They prevent others from being part of the mainstream.

The Other Side of Diversity

Diversity is part of the fabric of being an American. It's not a new thing. The walls that have kept us apart are crumbling. That's the new thing. We are no longer separated by law or ethnic pressure, even though remnants remain. We who are Gentile Christians should have no problem with this. Referring to alienation between Jews and Gentiles in the first century, Paul writes to the Ephesians: "For he (Christ) is our peace; in his flesh he has made both groups into one and has broken down the dividing wall; that is, the hostility between us. He has abolished the law with its commandments and ordinances, that he might create in himself one new humanity in the place of two, thus making peace . . ." (2:14-15).

With Christianity, diversity is a given. Paul, an orthodox Jew, came to terms with the good news that Christ came to reveal, "God so loves the world." Paul realized that this new religious movement was not a sect of Judaism, but would embrace people of all races, nationalities, and stations of life. In Christ, differences no longer separate us, but "all are members of the household of God" (Ephesians 2:19). Paul means full members of God's household.

So from the celebration of diversity, Paul creates an image or a symbol for these groups of new Christians who are extremely different from one another. It is the image of the human body. The body communicates both diversity and unity. In some way, the hands, arms, eyes, toes, stomach, etc. are wired to the head (brain), which sends them messages. When they respond in obedience, the different parts of the body function and accomplish their purpose for the wellbeing of the entire body. That's unity in diversity.

The biblical image of the body with Christ serving as the head is the symbol or image for the paradigm *validating committed partnerships* (VCPs). This paradigm is designed to address the diversity that has been set free in our society when the walls of a segregated society came tumbling down. The time has come for all to have the opportunity to move out of the ghettos into suburbia, out of the closet into the light of a new day of peace and unity, of love and justice, and fulfilling relationships.

Christianity is our hope in strengthening families of the future. Diversity should be no more a threat to families than for two people planning to marry. Herbert Anderson and Robert Fite write, "Becoming married means learning to live with difference. Every human system must learn how to live with difference and diversity in order to grow and flourish. They feel that diversity is a sign of God's extravagance, and without diversity human beings are not fully free to be creative because they do not have sufficient options from which to choose . . . To impose premature or unnecessary limits (laws) to difference is a rejection of God's generosity."[3]

In my experience of marriage preparation, differences between the bride and groom have become a given; for them to have a fulfilling marriage, they have to learn to affirm and celebrate their differences. That is where the experience of God and the spirit of unconditional love enable two people to affirm the differences within each other. I tell them, when acceptance of differences occurs, the marital personality expands and the relationship becomes dynamic. So together they spend time talking about their families of origin and they take a temperament inventory, both of which reveal their differences. I remind them the consequence of selfishness is often competition, fighting over who is in charge (hierarchy-control).

When the spirit of God (love, joy, kindness, gentleness, etc.) is present in the relationship, the couple can enjoy both their unity and their uniqueness. This leads to *mutuality*, another word that emerges from the image or symbol of the body of Christ. Of course there are limits to how much diversity a marriage or a family or a church or a community can manage. Only those involved in blending can determine how much diversity they can handle.

It seems to me that we are placing too many expectations on marriage and family as both are perceived by many in our culture.

Once again, in biblical times through the early church, the nature and purpose of marriage changed in order to accommodate the pressures and changes in culture. In the community of Israel, marriage was for the procreation of children and the maintenance of the family so there would be descendants to carry on the family name and inherit property. Both marriage and family had an economic purpose, which means *care of the household*. If the wife were barren, then adaptation occurred to accommodate the goal of having children. Hagar, the servant girl, is given to Abraham so a child can be conceived. Romance and loving relationships were not an expectation placed on marriage. Marriages were arranged by families and consummated in the early teens.

Then comes the medieval period; marriage became secondary to singleness (celibacy), which was a higher or superior spiritual state. By the sixth century celibacy was required for Catholic clergy. Only the act of procreation within marriage legitimatized sexual activity. Then, in the sixteenth century came the Protestant Reformation. Both John Calvin and Martin Luther reacted strongly to required celibacy for clergy, claiming it was against natural law. They introduced another dimension of marriage in the human sexuality debate.

They believed God also instituted marriage for the welfare and happiness of husband and wife; that is to say, marriage should be a loving and fulfilling relationship. The sexual side of the relationship should support their happiness. As the two become one physically to conceive children, the two become one spiritually as an expression of their love for one another. Since the sixteenth century, the relational expectation was placed on marriage, as well as reproduction and maintenance of the family.

It was not until the twentieth century that the relational dimension of marriage began to take hold in the practice of *mutuality*. In the present age, *mutuality* has become the primary focus of marriage for many; everything else has remained the same. Procreation and responsibility for the socialization and maintenance of the family remained responsibilities in marriage. Now, in the twenty-first century,

marriage and family have been surrounded by numerous changes; many
are due to the growth of science and technology that should make family
life easier, but these products cost money. Perhaps the most important
cultural change for marriage has been liberation. A male-dominated
society is diminishing. Patriarchy and hierarchy are being replaced by
mutuality, which makes life more complex and less efficient, but at the
same time more fair and exciting.

The automobile has given youth significant freedom. More than
half the workforce is now made up of women, and money, which means
power, can be translated into the declaration: "I don't have to remain
in this crummy abusive marriage. I don't need your money anyway, so
I am out of here. Goodbye!" So the divorce rate began climbing and
reached 50 percent of those married, dropping to about 47 percent at
the present time. Many other forms of diversity related to lifestyle and
moral standards are likewise seen as a threat to the wellbeing of marriage
and family. Virtually none have any connection with homosexuality.
It has become commonplace for couples to live together before their
marriage vows are spoken. I have been surprised that the church has
said little about this. A *validated partnership* may be the answer. That
would be another book.

Honesty has reached its height. Rather than simply living together
anonymously like invisible ghosts, some people of the same gender
who have been housemates and active in their church communities
are telling it like it is: "*We are loving, committed partners living in a
monogamous relationship. More so, it would mean a great deal to us to have
our relationship validated by our families, friends, and yes, our church.*"
Some are actually using the term *marriage.* Some in the church want to
be supportive; others in the church feel that a validation is advocacy for
the practice of sin. At this point, church denominations dealing with
this issue are seriously divided.

One purpose for writing this book is to share with its readers what
I believe the scripture says and does not say concerning marriage and
singles involved in committed intimate relationships, whether they be

homosexual or heterosexual. While the scripture declares same-gender sexual activity sinful in specific situations like temple prostitution, rape, and pederasty, scripture says nothing about those in a committed relationship. So the scripture does not shut the door on validating and blessing same-gender or heterosexual committed relationships.

The second purpose behind writing this book is to remind all of us of the good news that we are saved by God's grace through faith in Jesus Christ; then, out of gratitude, we are called to live by the grace of God by practicing hospitality to all people. It is this gracious spirit of God that compels us to find a way to be fully inclusive to those of the same gender living in a committed relationship. This grace, by the way, is not cheap. It comes only in the context of a deep commitment to the authority of scripture and the willingness to seek the truth concerning what the Bible actually says and does not about homosexuality and marriage.

Third, since God created all people with the need to live in significant or fulfilling relationships, such relationships should not be denied to those attracted to others of the same gender, especially since they are not responsible for their sexual orientation. Fourth, I wrote this book hoping to help us find a resolution to the division we are experiencing concerning the *validation of same-gender partnerships*.

Fifth, since marriage itself has experienced many significant changes through its history and especially the past sixty years, I believe time has come to redefine marriage. With priority focusing on the relationship and mutuality, marriage has become a *partnership* for many.

Sixth, through biblical study I suggest that it is not best for a same-gender committed relationship to be an appendage of marriage. It is clearly a *partnership*. I suggest that both marriage and same-gender unions share the umbrella title of *partnership*. Each will also retain its uniqueness. Male and female unions will be called *marital partnerships*, and same-gender unions will have the name *same-gender partnerships*. Both remain civil unions supported by legal standards. In the civil union, both may bear the term *marriage*. That should not prohibit the church from blessing the civil union with its unique distinctions:

marital partnership and *same-gender partnership.* Both will also share the relational symbol of the *body of Christ,* which creates the image of unity within diversity. Marital partnerships will retain an additional biblical symbol, *the two shall become one,* the symbol of procreation.

Finally, in response to those who feel this paradigm would destroy the family and family values we cherish, I believe marriage and family are already under phenomenal stress and same-gender relationships have contributed very little to add to that stress. Many other factors of change in the past fifty years that are positive have also placed stress on marriage and family. The demise of the ancient patriarchal model (cultural) based on a worldview few now accept has left us without an anchor to keep marriage stable, but we now have an opportunity to seek the biblical model of the *body of Christ* as a new point of stability and guidance. The body model encourages us to live in mutuality within marriage, with the family under the guidance of servant leaders. I believe the paradigm *validating committed partnerships* (VCPs) may be the key in supporting both marriage and family.

So rather than being fearful that *validated committed partnerships* among two people of the same gender will destroy the family and family values, the world may be surprised. These special relationships bound by God's spirit could be the key in helping put heart back into marriage and family life with all its diversity. They may be the model to encourage the church to use all God's gifts to enrich God's world. Perhaps in *validating committed partnerships,* we have found *a still more excellent way.*

> *So God grant us for tomorrow ways to order human life*
> *That surrounds each person's sorrow with a calm that conquers strife.*
> *Make us partners in our living, our compassion to increase,*
> *Messengers of faith, thus giving hope and confidence and peace.*
> Jane Parker Huber

Endnotes for Epilogue

1   John Patton and Brian Childs, *Christian Marriage and Family: Caring For Our Generations* (Nashville: Abingdon Press, 1988), p. 132.

2   Herbert Anderson and Robert Fite, *Becoming Married* (Louisville: Westminster/John Knox Press, 1993), p. 27.

3   Anderson and Fite, pp. 90-91.

BIBLIOGRAPHY

Books, magazines, newspapers, and periodicals

Achtemeier, Paul. "Romans." *Interpretation: A Bible Commentary for Teaching and Preaching*, Louisville, 1985.

Albom, Mitch. *Tuesdays with Morrie*. New York, 1997.

Anderson, Jr. H. R. "How Does It Feel to Be Excluded?" *The Presbyterian Outlook*, September 27, 1999, Richmond, 1999.

Anderson, Herbert and Robert Cotton Fite. *Becoming Married*. Louisville, 1993.

Arndt, William F. and F. Wilbur Gingrich. *A Greek-English Lexicon of the New Testament and Other Early Christian Literature*. Chicago, 1952.

Barclay, William. *Introducing the Bible*. Nashville, 1997.

Barclay, William. *The Acts of the Apostles*. Edinburgh, 1961.

Barclay, William. *The Letter to the Corinthians*. Philadelphia, 1975.

Barclay, William. *The Gospel of St. John Vol.1*. Philadelphia, 1975.

Barclay, William. *The Gospel of St. Matthew Vol. 2*. Philadelphia, 1975.

Barclay, William. *The Letter to the Romans*. Edinburgh, 1960.

Barth, Karl. *The Doctrine of Creation: Church Dogmatics III, Part 2*. Edinburgh, 1960.

Barth, Markus. *The Sermon on the Mount—Smythe Lectures*. Decatur, GA, 1962.

Boswell, John. "Homosexuality and Religious Life: A Historical Approach," in *Sexuality and the Sacred* edited by James B. Nelson and Sandra P. Longfellow. Louisville, 1994

Boswell, John. *Christianity, Social Tolerance, and Homosexuality*. Chicago, 1980.

Brocke, Christopher. *Marriage in the Medieval Ages*. Oxford, 1989.

Bruce Bawer. *Stealing Jesus*. New York, 1995.

Buchanan, John M. *Being Church, Becoming Community*. Louisville, 1996.

Burgess John P. "Rethinking Sexuality," in *The Presbyterian Outlook*, February 25, 2002 Richmond, 2002.

Clark, J. Michael. "Men's Studies, Feminist Theology, Gay Male Sexuality" in *Sexuality and the Sacred,* edited by: James B. Nelson and Sandra P. Longfellow. Louisville, 1994.

Cragg, Gerald R. "Exposition." *The Interpreter's Bible Vol. 9*, Nashville, 1951.

Easum, William M. *Sacred Cows Make Gourmet Burgers*. Nashville, 1995.

Ellis, Ralph. "Silent No More" in *The Atlanta Journal-Constitution*. Atlanta: April 13, 2002.

Enslin, Morton S. "The New Testament Times: Palestine," *The Interpreter's Bible Vol. 7,* Nashville, 1951.

Espinoza, Galinal. "There Goes the Bride," in *Modern Maturity-AARP*. Washington, July/August 2002.

Etzler, Carole A. *Someone You Know: Stories of Gay Men in the Presbyterian Church, U.S.* Atlanta, 1979.

Farley, Margaret A. "Sexual Ethics," *Sexuality and the Sacred,* ed. James B. Nelson and Sandra P Longfellow. Louisville, 1994.

Ferris, Theodore P. "Exposition." *The Interpreter's Bible Vol. 9*, Nashville, 1951

Fuchs, Eric. *Sexual Desire and Love: Origin and History of the Christian Ethic of Sexuality and Marriage,* New York, 1983.

Gagnon, Robert. *The Bible and Homosexual Practice*, Nashville, 2001.

Geis, Sally B and Donald E. Messer, *Caught in the Crossfire*. Nashville, 1994.

Glaser, Chris. *Uncommon Calling: A Gay Christian's Struggle to Serve the Church*. Louisville, 1996.

Gomes, Peter J. *The Good Book: Reading the Bible with Mind and Heart*, New York, 1996.

Hall, Douglas John. *God and Human Suffering*. Minneapolis, 1986.

Helminiak, Daniel A *What the Bible Really Says About Homosexuality*, San Francisco, 1995

Hunt, Mary E. "Lovingly Lesbian," in *Sexuality and the Sacred*, edited by James B. Nelson and Sandra P. Longfellow. Louisville, 1994.

Kendrick, Paul. *The Roman Mind at Work*. Princeton, 1958.

Knox, John. "The Introduction." *The Interpreter's Bible Vol.* 9, Nashville, 1951.

Koenig, Tricia Dykers. Letter to Editor of *The Presbyterian Outlook*, Richmond, August 2-9, 1999.

Lovelace, Richard. *Homosexuality and the Church*. Old Tappan, N.J., 1978

Meacham, Jon. "A Case for Change: Celibacy and Marriage," *Newsweek*: May 6, 2002 New York, 2002.

Mish, Frederick C, Editor *Merriam Webster Collegiate Dictionary*, Springfield, 2001.

Nelson, James B. "Homosexuality and the Church," *Christianity and Crisis* Vol.37, No. 5, April 4, 1977.

Nelson, James B. *Sexuality and the Sacred: Sources for Theological Reflection*, Louisville, 1994

Nelson, James B. "Sources for Body Theology: Homosexuality as a Test Case," *Sexuality and the Sacred*, Louisville, 1994.

Nicolosi, Joseph. "What Does Science Teach about Human Sexuality?" in *Caught in the Crossfire*, edited by Sally B. Geis and Donald E. Messer. Nashville, 1994.

Nouwen, Henry. *Reaching Out: The Three Movements of the Spiritual Life.* New York, 1975.

Patton, John and Brian Childs. *Christian Marriage and Family: Caring For Our Generations.* Nashville, 1988.

Presbyterian Hymnal. The Presbyterian Church, (USA), Louisville, 1990.

Rohr, Richard. "Where the Gospel Leads Us," in *Homosexuality and the Christian Faith,* edited by Walter Wink. Minneapolis, 1999.

Rogers, Jack. "Ecclesiastical McCarthyism?" *The Presbyterian Outlook,* March 18-25, 1996.

Rose, Ben Lacy. "Mary was Not an Unwed Mother" in *The Presbyterian Outlook.* Richmond, December 6, 1999.

Ruether, Rosemary Redford. "Homophobia, Heterosexism, Pastoral Practice", in *Sexuality and the Sacred,* edited by: James B. Nelson and Sandra P. Longfellow. Louisville, 1999.

Schonauer, Betty, Brick Bradford, William Showalter, Leonard LeSourd, Catherine Jackson, Robert Whitaker, *Healing for the Homosexual.* Oklahoma City, 1978

Scroggs, Robin. *The New Testament and Homosexuality.* Philadelphia, 1983.

Swordlow, Joel L. "New York's Chinatown." *National Geographic Vol. 194, No. 2,* Washington, 1998.

Thorson-Smith, Sylvia. *Reconciling the Broken Silence.* Louisville, 1993.

Vrissimtzis, Nikos A. *Love, Sex, Marriage in Ancient Greece.* Greece, 1997.

Westerman, Claus. *Genesis1-1.* Minneapolis, 1974.

Willimon, William. "Acts." *Interpretation: A Bible Commentary for Teaching and Preaching.* Atlanta, 1988.

Wink, Walter. *Homosexuality and Christian Faith.* Minneapolis, 1999

Wink, Walter. "Biblical Perspectives on Homosexuality," *The Christian Century,* Chicago, December 7, 1979.

Witte, John Jr. *From Sacrament to Contract.* Louisville, KY, 1997.

Presbyterian Church (USA) Study Papers and Constitution

Book of Confessions: Constitution of the Presbyterian Church (USA), Louisville, 1999.

Book of Order: Constitution of the Presbyterian Church (USA), Louisville, 2001

Continuing the Conversation: A guide for congregational study on issues of human sexuality. Louisville, 1992.

Divorce and Remarriage with Special Reference to Ordained Minister. A paper for study issued by 118th General Assembly of the Presbyterian Church in the United States, Atlanta, 1978.

The Helvetic Confession in "The Book of Confessions." Louisville, 1996.

Is Christ Divided? (PCUSA), *Louisville,* 1988.

Keeping Body and Soul Together: Sexuality, Spirituality, and Social Justice. A document prepared by a special committee on human sexuality for 203rd General Assembly of the Presbyterian Church (USA), Louisville, 1991.

Marriage: A Theological Statement. A paper adopted by the 120th General Assembly of the Presbyterian Church in the United States, Atlanta, 1980.

Presbyterian Understanding and Use of the Holy Scripture, *A Study Adopted by the 123rd General Assembly of the Presbyterian Church (USA),* Louisville, 1992.

The Church and Homosexuality. A paper adopted by the 190th General Assembly of the Presbyterian Church in the United States of America, New York, 1978.

The Church and Homosexuality: A Preliminary Study. Atlanta, 1977.

The Nature and Purpose of Human Sexuality. A paper adopted by the 120th General Assembly of the Presbyterian Church in the United States, Atlanta.